Threat Assessment Workbook

A product of truth and empowerment by

JONATHAN T. GILLIAM

IF FOUND PLEASE RETURN TO:

_____

NAME

_____

PHONE NUMBER

A POST HILL PRESS BOOK

Sheep No More Workbook #1
Threat Assessment
© 2019 by Jonathan T. Gilliam
All Rights Reserved

ISBN: 978-1-64293-233-1

Cover Photo by Barry Morgenstein Photography, barrymorgenstein.com
Interior Design and Composition by Spiro Graphics, Inc.

Post Hill Press
New York • Nashville
posthillpress.com
Published in the United States of America

Dedicated to the one true God who created the universe, and to His son Jesus, through whom God created all things. My devotion to Your will burns in me like a fire.

In remembrance of the warriors that served selflessly, and in so many cases, gave their lives for freedom. The lessons encapsulated in this book were bought with your blood. Thank you, may it never be in vain.

For the American Citizenry. May this book empower you and increase your awareness. Ultimately, your safety and the strength of this great Nation lies in your hands.

THE AWARENESS BIBLE

This workbook will forever change the way you see your surroundings.
First, read *Sheep No More: The Art of Awareness and Attack Survival*. Next, apply
the attack techniques you learn there into the real world and onto the pages of this
Threat Assessment Workbook. Finally, when you are finished with this assessment,
the stage will be set for your completion of the third book in the *Sheep No More*
trilogy, Workbook #2, Defense Assessment.

Whether you are an experienced police officer, a special forces operator, or an
individual that has never even thought about securing your surroundings, the Attack
and Defend system you are about to employ will simplify the threat assessment
process and open your mind to true awareness and a secured life.
Are you ready to get empowered?

Let's Roll!

**To join in the conversation, go to Twitter@attackanddefend or
www.jonathanTgilliam.com/attackanddefend**

Key Terms

Attack—Aggressive action against a place or enemy forces with weapons or armed force, typically in a battle or war.

Attacker—A person or animal that attacks someone or something.

Attack and Defend—The back and forth technique of defending a person, place, or thing through the development of an attacker's mindset and utilizing it to gain target information that is compiled into an attacker's target package, which leads to awareness and attack avoidance.

Attack Probability—Statistical calculations that rate the most likely place for an attack by assigning a number percentage.

Attack Possibility—Statistical calculations that reduce the likelihood of an attack to either yes or no.

Attacker's Avenues of Approach—An air or ground route of an attacking force leading to its objective.

Awareness—Knowledge or perception of a situation or fact.

Criticalities—The five specific parts of a target (including Critical Assets, Critical Areas, Critical Times, Vulnerabilities, and Attacker's Avenues of Approach) comprised of the exploitable information sought after and utilized by attackers to build a target package and used by defenders to ensure proper defenses.

Critical Asset—Facilities, systems, and equipment which, if destroyed, degraded, or otherwise rendered unavailable, would affect the reliability or operability of operations.

Critical Area—Soft target areas considered to have a heightened threat and easy access for an attacker.

Critical Time—Specific times when a critical area is under the highest threat.

Criminal—A person who has committed a crime not in the furtherance of political aim.

Defense—The action of defending from or resisting attack.

Defender—A person or animal attempting to ward off attack from an attacker.

Deranged—Mad; insane.

Hard Target—A building, facility, or area (critical area) that has been secured, making it less likely to be attacked.

Plan of Attack—Ideas or actions intended to deal with a problem or situation.

Private Sector—The part of the economy involved with enterprise not controlled by the state.

Procedures—Established and approved order of actions.

Public Sector—The part of the economy concerned with providing various government services.

Shared Threats—Possible or probable attacks shared by multiple locations or people or threats that, if carried out as an attack, could affect other nontargeted locations or people.

Soft Target—A building, facility, or area (critical area) that is difficult to protect.

Strategy—The thinking process required to plan a change, course of action, or organization. Strategy defines, or outlines, desired goals and why you should go about achieving them.

Surveillance—Observation for the purpose of information collection. Can be carried out electronically, in vehicle, or on foot.

Standard Operating Procedures—The standardization of tactics, techniques, and procedures into a step-by-step process for streamlined operations.

Task Organization—The process of assigning operations, tasks, work in an organized fashion.

Terrorism—The use of fear, intimidation, and violence in the pursuit of a political aim.

Terrorist—A person who carries out or facilitates when, where, how, and why a terror attack is carried out.

Tactics, Techniques, and Procedures (TTP)—Particular standard operating procedures utilized by attacking forces.

Tactics—The specific actions you take in implementing your strategy.

Techniques—The specific style or form used or applied to tactics.

Target Package—Information collected in order to develop an accurate picture of a given target for the purpose of attacking or defending.

VBIED—Acronym for vehicle-borne improvised explosive device.

Vulnerability—Identifiable areas of a location, facility, or person being exposed to the possibility of being attacked.

Threat Assessment Workbook
INFORMATION COLLECTION

Building a Threat Assessment Package

ANY PERSON OR GROUP attempting to set up defenses should realize that aggressive, accurate attackers work diligently to develop the same knowledge and understanding of a facility the defenders are trying to secure. Concentrating on a target's critical areas, critical times, vulnerabilities, and attacker's avenues of approach, the attackers will attempt to reverse engineer defensive standard operating procedures to build an all-encompassing target package. The defender should be able to reverse their own knowledge in the same way and apply it from an attacker's point of view by simply changing their mindset back and forth from attacker to defender mode. The only difference between these two planners is in the semantics of the assessment product they produce. Attackers create a target package and the defender will create a Threat Assessment Workbook. Both are the same in that they are searching for the most likely and effective attack that would possibly happen.

Focusing on the Target Equation, you can simplify your information collection that will make up your Attack and Defend Threat Assessment Workbook. Based on the understanding you have developed from *Sheep No More: The Art of Awareness and Attack Survival*, you can see that defining an attack by who carries it out or the weapon/ method being employed is secondary to the development of a target package in the overall attackers assessment. At it's most simplistic level, a target package and/ or threat assessment can be defined as the specific discoveries included in an assessment package of a chosen target. This includes the specific categories of a target's critical assets (CA), critical areas (CAR), critical times (CT), vulnerabilities (V), and its attackers avenues of approach (AVP), combined with effective tactics (TAC), techniques (TQS), procedures (P), and motivation (M) of the specific attackers themselves. Remember this equation is not meant to completely mimic military target packages, but it will encompass all the information you will need to complete a threat assessment on yourself and your surroundings:

(CA+CAR+CT+V+AVP) + (TAC+TQS+P+M) = Target Equation

Remote
Information Collection

(Tools for Remote Surveillance)
- Internet
- Mapping programs
- Library
- Newspapers

General Online
Information Collection

GENERAL INFORMATION IS THE easiest of all information to collect. When you go onto a computer to collect basic information about a target, it is possible to find out hours of operation, event times and dates, addresses, demographics, past incidents, and even shared threats. Most of us do this type of general information collection on a daily basis without even realizing it when we are seeking a place to eat, a movie to watch, or entering travel information into a GPS device. All of this is exactly the general information that attackers collect remotely when building an attack package.

Collecting information usually starts far away from the target and slowly works you inward without any fancy gadgets or training. Remember, most attackers would rather never set foot near a target location before an attack if possible, as this is the most vulnerable area and time for their attack to be thwarted. If an attacker is recognized or questioned when performing surveillance (this includes petty criminals and terrorists alike), they are less likely to actually carry out an attack at that location. Basically, if a target is too hardened or if the awareness is too great, the attacker will go elsewhere and pick a softer target, and so you should begin to understand why discovering as much as possible remotely is so important for carrying out a threat assessment.

On-Site Information Verification and Collection

In order to chart the assessment information as well as historical threat information, you need a better understanding of where to begin with on-site information verification and collection. Even though you may be there every day, try and walk around each sector as if you were doing surveillance on it.

If your home is the sector, you could get in your car and approach from the freeway to see how you might do surveillance in your neighborhood. When it is dark one night, go for a walk through around your house and see what an attacker would see. Peer into your children's windows and see what an attacker would see. On a random night ask your family to sit inside and listen to see if they can hear or spot you sneaking around and looking in through a window. Are there creeks on the porch? Will the dog bark? Make it a game with the children and let the teenager know how serious of an exercise it actually is. When the kids are asleep, see how much noise outside it takes to wake them up. All of this, performed with the attacker's mindset, not the defender's, will help you verify what you have discovered about the sectors you are assessing. **Although the same techniques can and should be applied to other sectors of your life (work/ business, vacation locations, recreation areas, places of worship etc.) you should refrain from sneaking into places and peering in through windows unless permission has been granted and it is known that you are doing a threat assessment.**

Threat Assessment Workbook
CHARTING INFORMATION
(example)

This fillable workbook begins with an overview of how the empty pages will be filled.

Overall there are basically three types of fillable pages that will repeat in each Sector (1-10).

1. The Information Outline Sheet

All information that is to be charted, put in bullet statement or outline format, or sketch will be done on this type of page.

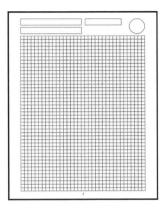

2. Threat Assessment Sector Overview

This will include information concerning first responders and other important responder information an attacker may take into account when building a target package (same as your threat assessment package).

3. Target Equation Worksheet

This is where you will enter all the information you have collected into a brief overview of the different types of attacks that could occur in each sector.

SECTOR

OVERVIEW

(example)

Threat Assessment Sector Overview
Example

Attackers often include in-depth descriptions of the area and /or activity that occurs in their plans. It's important that you look at your sectors the same way as the attackers when assessing.

Most of the fillable areas on this page are self-explanatory.

THREAT ASSESSMENT SECTOR OVERVIEW

Sector: *HOME*

Date: *01/01/2019*

Prepared by: *Jonathan T. Gilliam*

Situation: *Five member family (including father, mother, two children and one teenager) living in a three bedroom, ranch style home, in a rural low crime area. House is occupied during the week from 5pm until 8am the following day except weekends when the family is usually around the house doing various individual things. Home is in the vicinity of a freeway exit and dry creek bed that runs behind the house.*

Sector Overview: *Little to no security precautions are set up and standard operating procedures are nonexistent and / or ignored by most family members. Neighborhood is considered low crime, middle income with one sexual offender registered three blocks away. Petty burglary of cars and dogs has been reported in the immediate area.*

Note: Make sure you print out map and directions to pertenant police precincts.

Police Departments:	PD Contact Information:	PD Response Times:
Little Rock Police Department	*xxx-xxx-xxxx*	*LRPD 2-10 min*
Pulaski County Sheriff's Office	*xxx-xxx-xxxx*	*PCSO 20-40 min*

Crime Level: *LOW*	Possible Threat Level: *MEDIUM*

Known Terror Threats: *No known terror threats*

Known Criminal Threats: *Dog theft / Petty burglary of cars*

Note: Make sure you print out map and directions to all trauma centers. Always make the effort to proceed to a level i trauma center if the injury is life threatening.

Trauma Centers:	Trauma Center Level (I, II, III):	Response Times:
University of Arkansas for Medical Sciences (UAMS)	*University of Arkansas for Medical Sciences (UAMS)*	*15 min*
Baptist Health Medical Center		

Weather Conditions:

Spring	Summer	Fall	Winter
Avg temp 80deg F	*Avg temp 92deg F*	*Avg temp 70-85deg F*	*Avg temp 40deg F*
Often rainy	*Often Dry*	*Often rainy with thunder storms*	*Some snow*

All of this information is available online.

Remember, different sectors could have different police departments and precincts as well as closer hospitals

SECTOR
CRITICAL ASSETS (CA)
(example)

Critical Assets (CA) Assessment
Example

In order to keep your lists organized and readable, graph paper has been provided so that you can use the boxes to formulate a cascading outline for your information. For example, FAMILY is a critical asset header. Under the header FAMILY, members are listed and described, forming sub headers.

Whenever you see the round page number circle, you know it is important for keeping pages in their proper order.

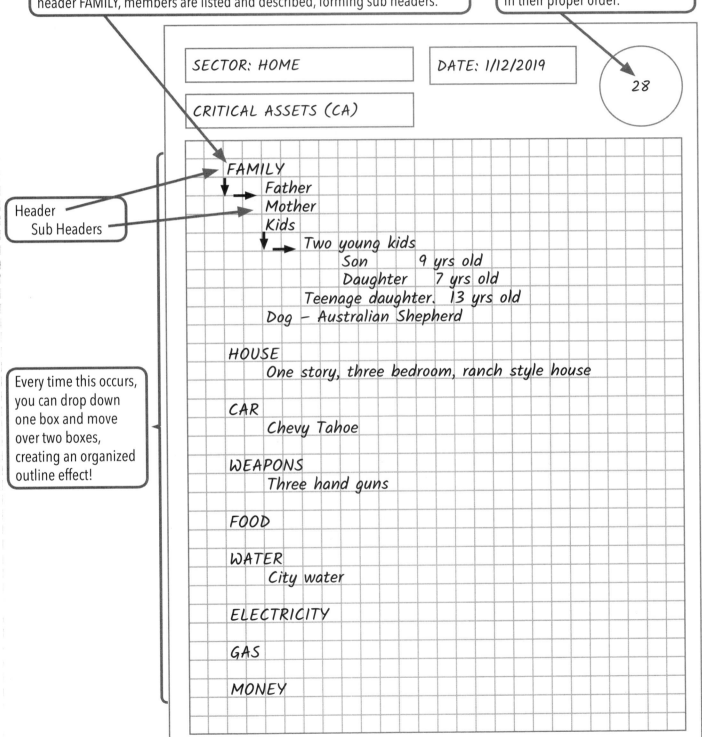

SECTOR: HOME

DATE: 1/12/2019

28

CRITICAL ASSETS (CA)

FAMILY
    Father
    Mother
    Kids
        Two young kids
            Son   9 yrs old
            Daughter   7 yrs old
        Teenage daughter. 13 yrs old
    Dog — Australian Shepherd

HOUSE
    One story, three bedroom, ranch style house

CAR
    Chevy Tahoe

WEAPONS
    Three hand guns

FOOD

WATER
    City water

ELECTRICITY

GAS

MONEY

Header
    Sub Headers

Every time this occurs, you can drop down one box and move over two boxes, creating an organized outline effect!

SECTOR
CRITICAL AREAS (CAR)
(example)

Critical Area (CAR) Assessment
Example

Remember, when you look at your sectors and evaluate everything that is critical (including the areas) you must look at them as an attacker, not a defender. Not yet at least

SECTOR: HOME   DATE: 1/12/2019   29

CRITICAL AREAS (CAR)

YARD
    Back yard fenced in with 6' privacy fence

CHILDREN'S BEDROOM

ADULT'S BEDROOM

DOORS

WINDOWS

A/C UNIT

GARAGE

SECTOR
CRITICAL TIMES (CT)
(example)

Critical Time (CT) Assessment
Example

> Remember, lists do not need to be extensive, but they do need to be exhaustive. Attackers go to great lengths to identify details and so should you!

SECTOR: HOME

DATE: 1/12/2019

30

CRITICAL TIMES (CT) :

8 a.m. to 4 p.m.

9 p.m. to 5 a.m.

SECTOR

VULNERABILITIES (V)

(example)

Vulnerabilities (V) Assessment
Example

This is where the rubber meets the road!!! Put on your attacker glasses and identify EVERY possible vulnerability that can be exploited in order to carry out an attack. If the bad guys can identify these specifics about your life, then you can too. Take your time, details are of the utmost importance here!

NOTE: The lists on this page are abbreviated for space, but **should include vulnerabilities (V) for ALL headers and sub headers from the sector categories CA, CAR, CT, and assessment outlines you actually do in each sector package.**

Refer back to *Sheep No More*, page 36 for a complete outline information input example.

SECTOR: HOME

DATE: 1/12/2019

31

VULNERABILITIES (V)

CRITICAL ASSETS
FAMILY
    Father
    Mother
        Without the parents, family would suffer and possibly be split up from one another
    Kids
        Two young kids
            Son 9 yrs old
            Daughter 7 yrs old
                Both young kids are very helpless
                Prone to finding trouble and wandering off
                Can be easy prey for child predators
        Teenage daughter. 13 yrs old
            Extremely forgetful
            Main person responsible for leaving doors, windows and garage unlocked or open
            Can be easy prey for sexual predators
    Dog – Australian Shepherd
        Very Expensive
        Dog stays in the house during the day but has an X-large doggy door to the back yard
        Neighbor's dog was stolen and used as bait dog in a dog fighting ring in nearby city
HOUSE
    All family belongings are in the house
        Three handguns, jewelry and emergency cash (in the safe inside the garage)

CRITICAL AREAS
YARD
    Front yard is not fenced in and allows access to children's bedroom windows
        as well as central A/C and Heat unit
    Back yard is fenced in with high wooden privacy fence (good for hiding
        attack actions from neighbors)
CHILDREN'S BEDROOM
    Located towards front of house unprotected by the privacy fence
DOORS
    Wooden front door
        Often left unlocked by children and teenager

CRITICAL TIMES
8 a.m. to 4 p.m.
    Statistically the most likely time for burglary because no one is home
        and house is unprotected
9 p.m. to 5 a.m.
    Statistically the most likely time for robbery and child abduction because
        everyone in the house and around the neighborhood are asleep

SECTOR
AVENUES OF APPROACH (AVP)
(example)

Avenues of Approach (AVP) Assessment
Example

SECTOR: HOME

DATE: 1/12/2019

32

AVENUES OF APPROACH (AVP)

FREEWAY
  Easy access to the neighborhood
  Quick getaway

CREEK LOCATED OUTSIDE REAR PRIVACY FENCE
  Easy place for criminals to covertly access neighborhood

SEVERAL WINDOWS AND DOORS AROUND THE HOUSE
  When left open these windows and doors create an easy
  access for nefarious individuals into the house.

Critical Areas
Sketch Example #1

Draw a sketch of the area or include a map here. In many cases you can use the sketch and/or map to point out criticalities, including areas, times, vulnerabilities and avenues of approach. Use a red highlighter to point out critical areas and attack avenues of approach that you discovered while doing information collection from the attackers point of view.

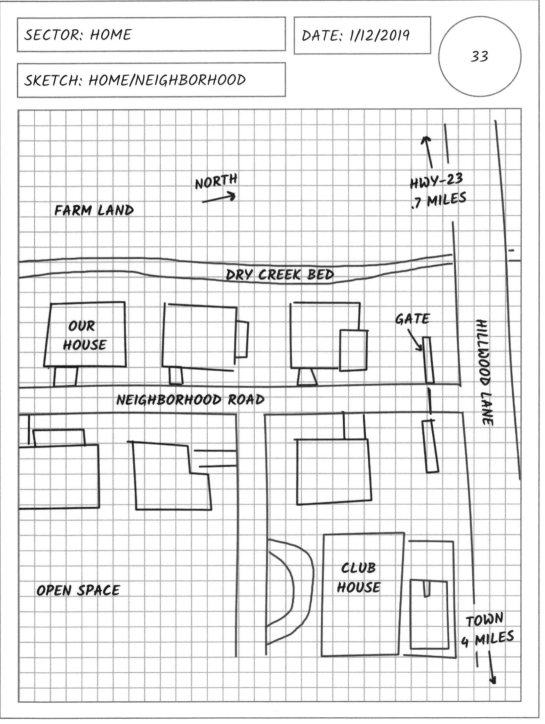

SECTOR: HOME

DATE: 1/12/2019

33

SKETCH: HOME/NEIGHBORHOOD

NORTH

FARM LAND

HWY-23
.7 MILES

DRY CREEK BED

OUR
HOUSE

GATE

HILLWOOD LANE

NEIGHBORHOOD ROAD

CLUB
HOUSE

OPEN SPACE

TOWN
4 MILES

Critical Areas
Sketch Example #2

Draw a sketch of the area or include a map here. In many cases you can use the sketch and/or map to point out criticalities, including areas, times, vulnerabilities and avenues of approach. Use a red highlighter to point out critical areas and attack avenues of approach that you discovered while doing information collection from the attackers point of view.

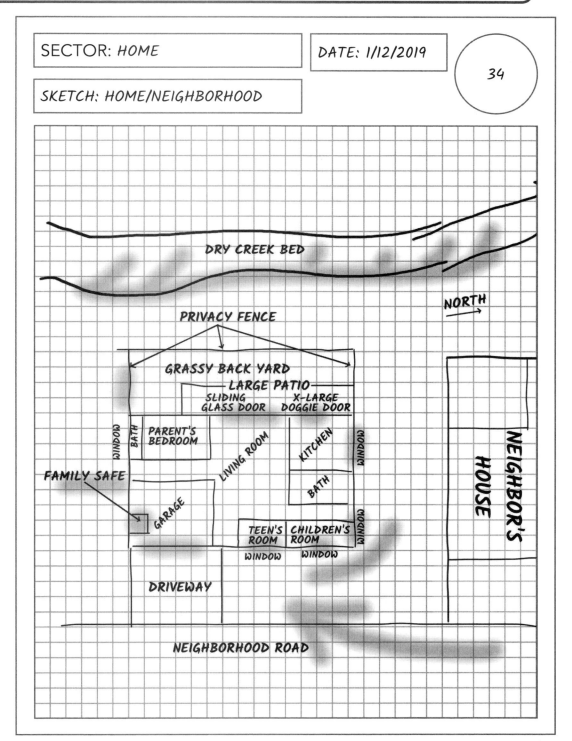

SECTOR: *HOME*

DATE: *1/12/2019*

34

SKETCH: *HOME/NEIGHBORHOOD*

DRY CREEK BED

NORTH

PRIVACY FENCE

GRASSY BACK YARD

LARGE PATIO

SLIDING GLASS DOOR

X-LARGE DOGGIE DOOR

WINDOW

BATH

PARENT'S BEDROOM

LIVING ROOM

KITCHEN

WINDOW

FAMILY SAFE

BATH

GARAGE

NEIGHBOR'S HOUSE

TEEN'S ROOM

CHILDREN'S ROOM

WINDOW

WINDOW

WINDOW

DRIVEWAY

NEIGHBORHOOD ROAD

Threat Assessment Workbook

TARGET EQUATION

(example)

Target Equation Worksheet
Example

This is the culmination of all the information you have collected and analyzed utilizing the attacker's mindset. Everything you write in here should become a part of your memory and understanding of the life you live and the world in which you live it.

In many cases, information may be repeated in several target equation answers. I have repeated the avenues of approach in this example because you may have repeating avenues of approach for different attacks. Do not just write "refer to above."

Details are important here!

Target Equation Worksheet

Sector: *HOME*

Date: *1/1/19*

35

Type of attack: *Robbery*

Time of attack: *9 p.m. to 5*

Avenues of Approach: *Nearby freeway allows for quick in and out of neighborhood, while the deep dry creek bed behind the house allows for stealthy access to the neighborhood and home.*

Vulnerabilities: *Family sleeping, doors, windows, garage unlocked, easy access for criminals into the neighborhood from nearby freeway and dry creek bed.*

Type of attack: *Burglary*

Time of attack: *8 a.m. to 5*

Avenues of Approach: *Nearby freeway allows for quick in and out of neighborhood, while the deep dry creek bed behind the house allows for stealthy access to the neighborhood and home.*

Vulnerabilities: *No one is home, easy access for criminals into the neighborhood from freeway and dry creek bed.*

Type of attack: *Child*

Time of attack: *5 p.m. to 8 a.m.*

Avenues of Approach: *Nearby freeway allows for quick in and out of neighborhood, while the deep dry creek bed behind the house allows for stealthy access to the neighborhood and home.*

Vulnerabilities: *Helpless children, outside a lot, windows are located outside the privacy fence, windows unlocked, children's room on the opposite side house from parents' room.*

What you see above is the sum of this target equation.
(CA+CAR+CT+V+AVP) + (TAC+TQS+P+M)

LET'S

GET

STARTED

"There is no greater tool to defeat an enemy than an aware human!"
— Jonathan T. Gilliam

Threat

Assessment

Workbook

S1

SECTOR 1

SECTOR 1

OVERVIEW

THREAT ASSESSMENT SECTOR OVERVIEW

Sector:	Date:

Prepared by:

Situation:

Sector Overview:

Note: Make sure you print out map and directions to pertinent police precincts.

Police Departments:	PD Contact Information:	PD Response Times:

Crime Level:	Possible Threat Level:

Known Terror Threats:

Known Criminal Threats:

Note: Make sure you print out map and directions to all trauma centers. Always make the effort to proceed to a level 1 trauma center if the injury is life threatening.

Trauma Centers:	Trauma Center Level (I, II, III):	Response Times:

Weather Conditions:

Spring	Summer	Fall	Winter

SECTOR 1

CRITICAL ASSETS (CA)

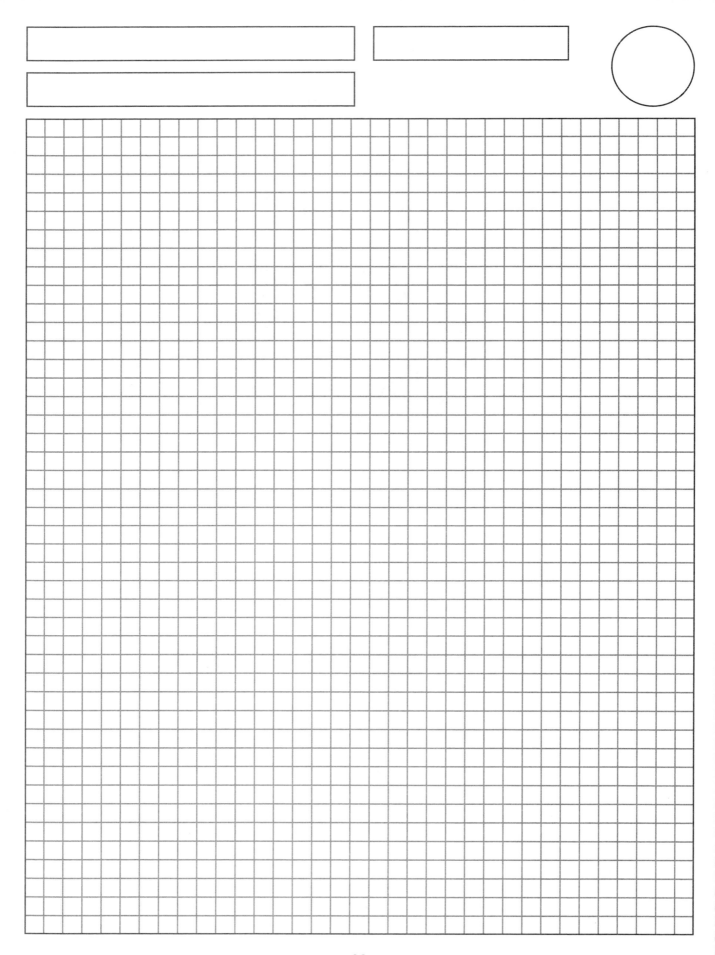

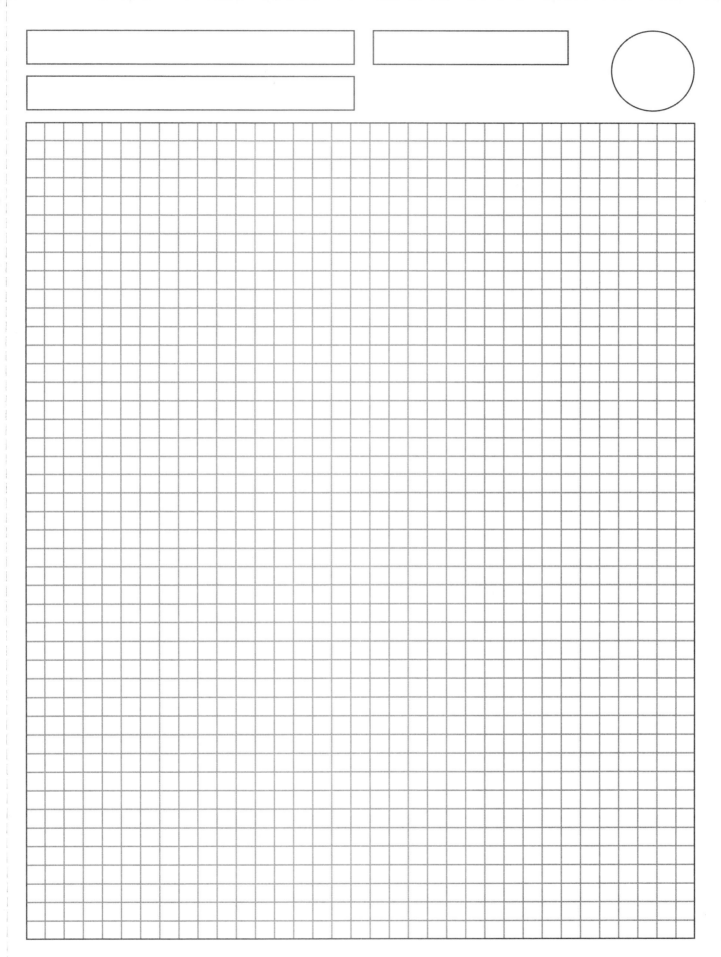

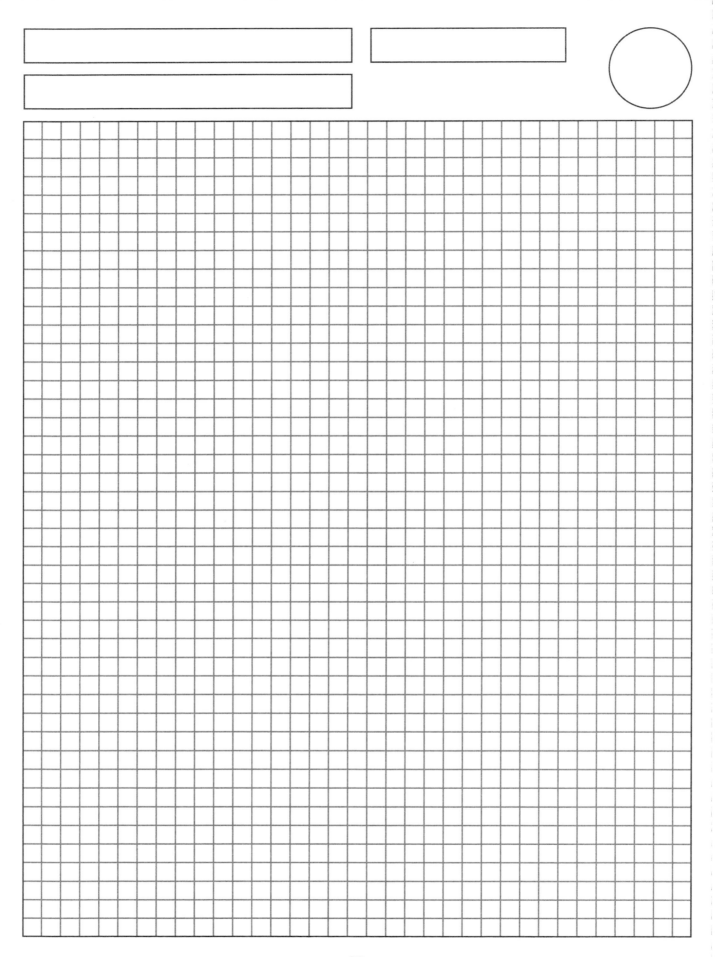

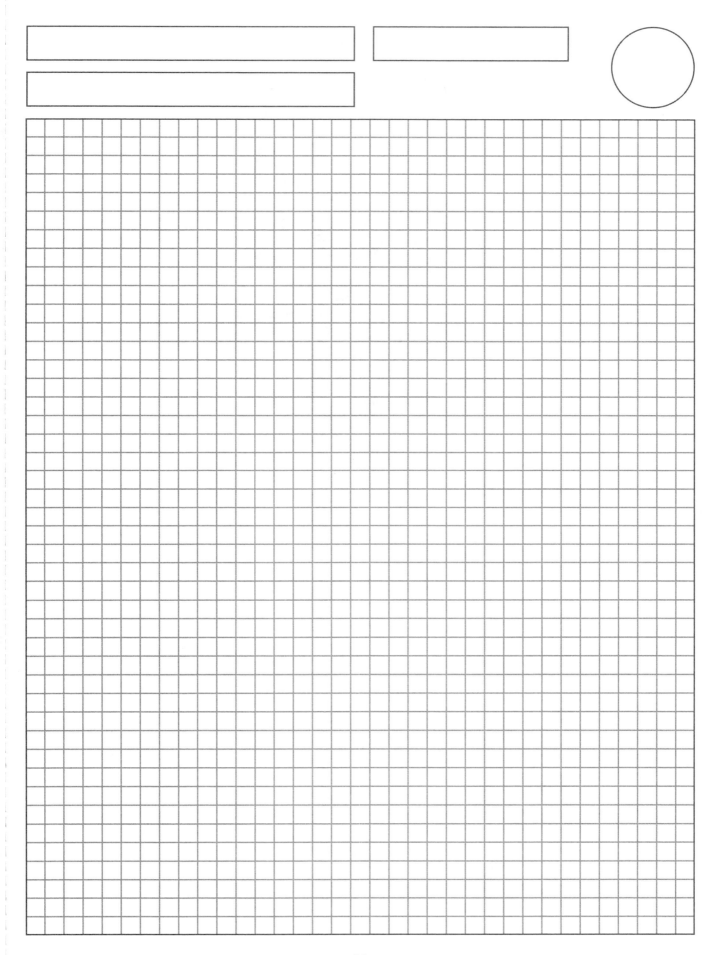

SECTOR 1

CRITICAL AREAS (CAR)

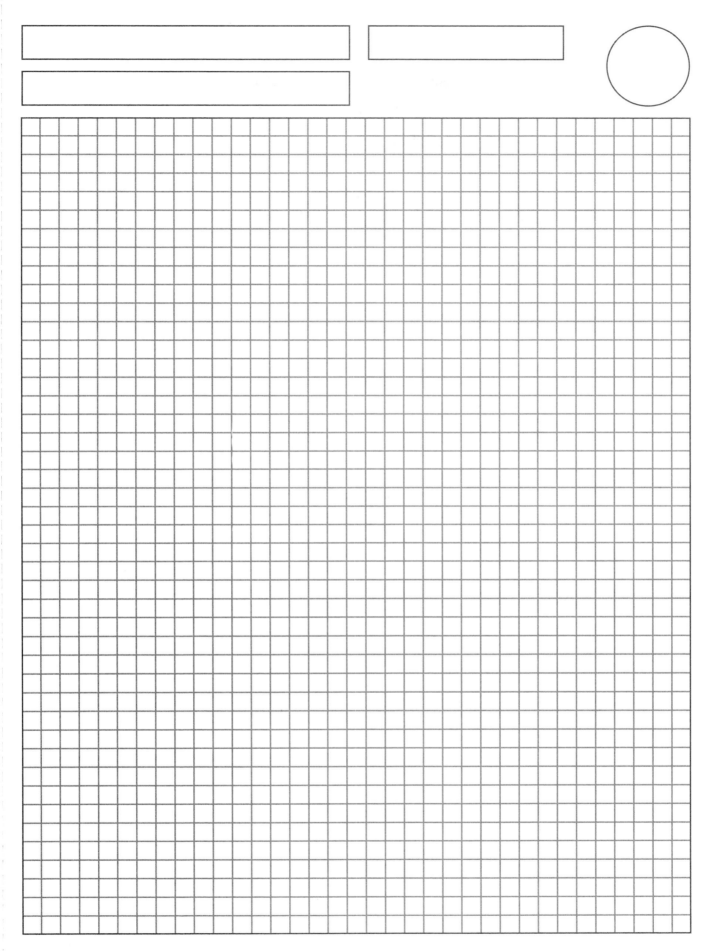

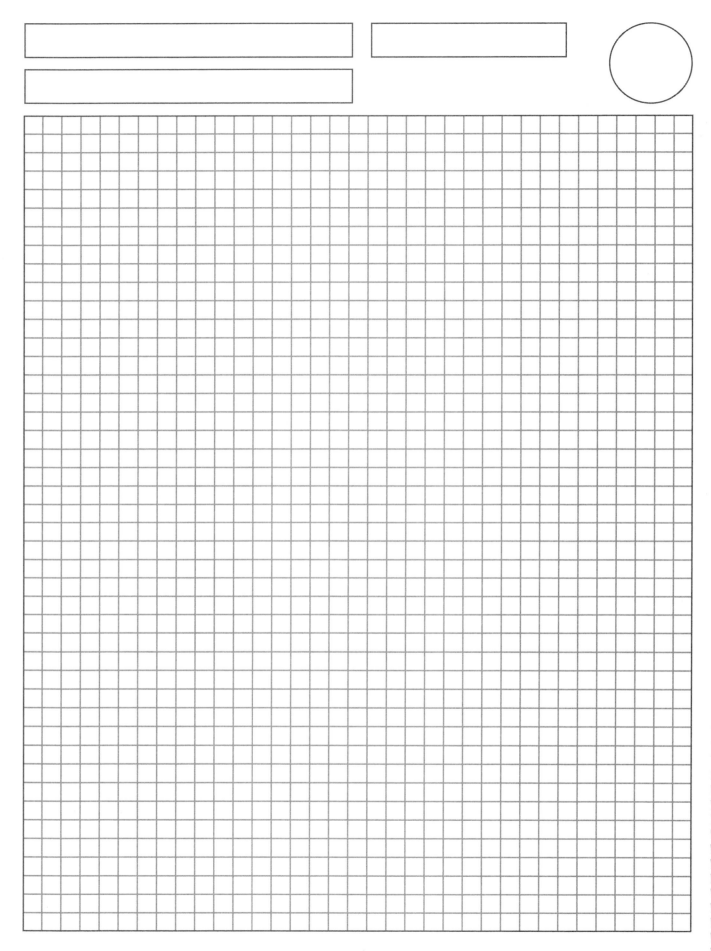

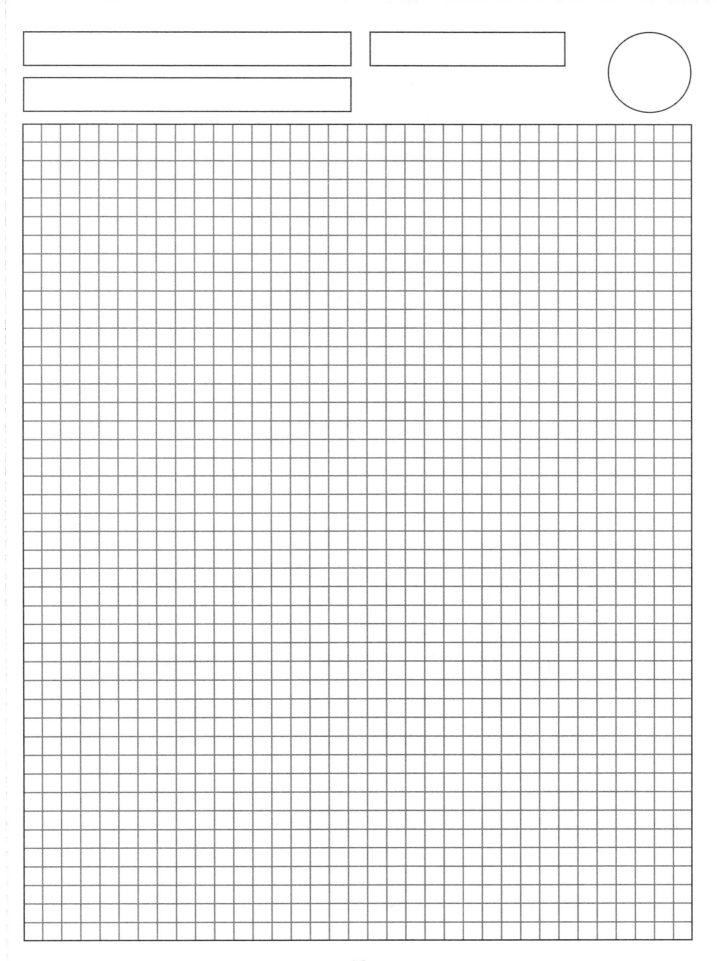

SECTOR 1

CRITICAL TIMES (CT)

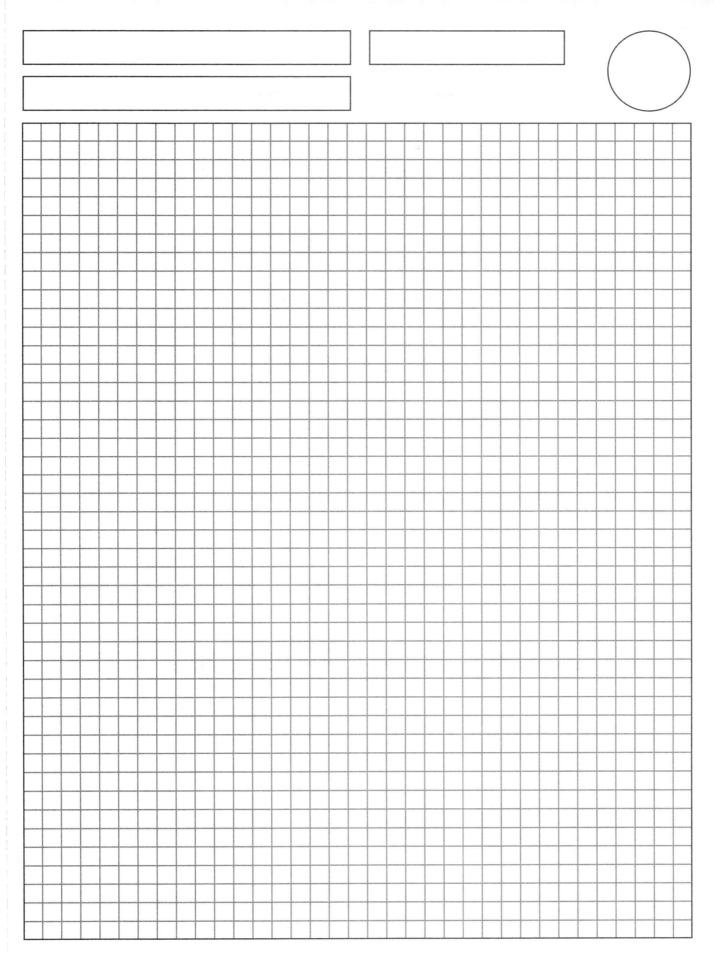

SECTOR 1

VULNERABILITIES

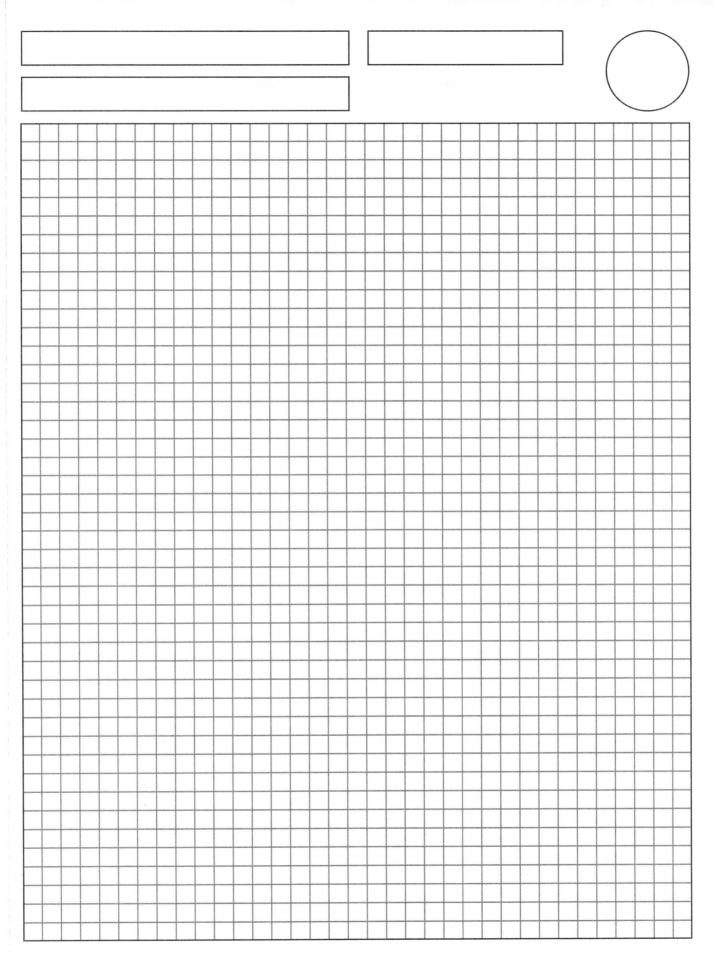

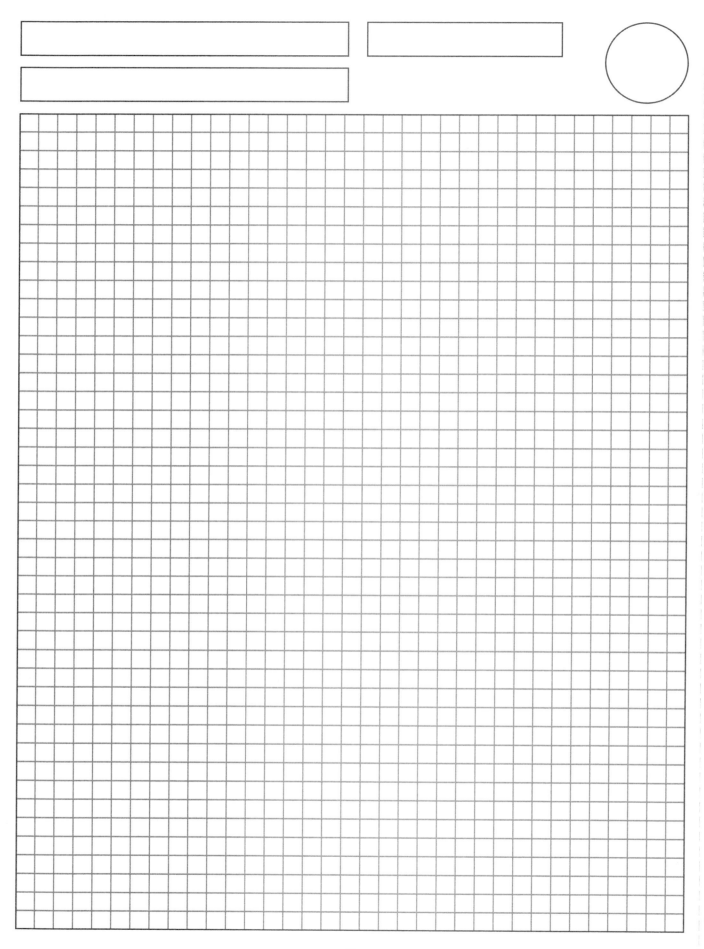

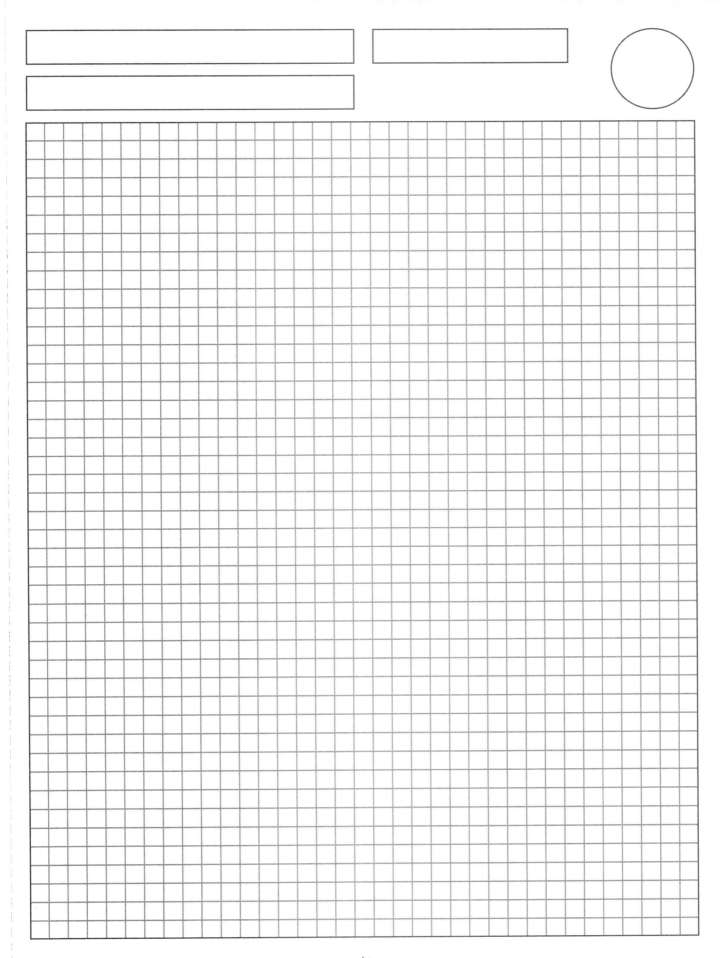

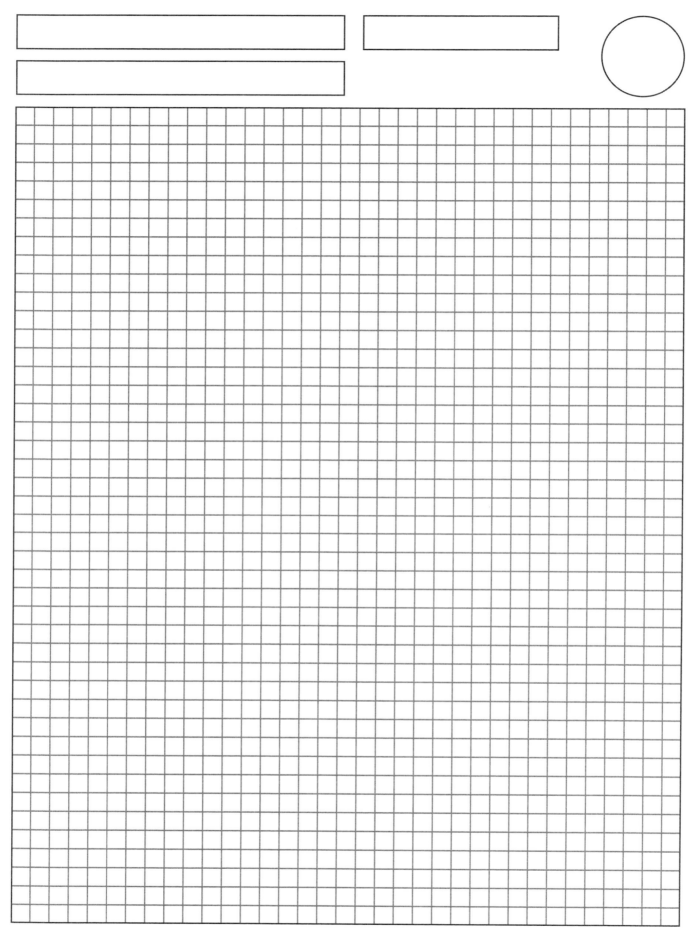

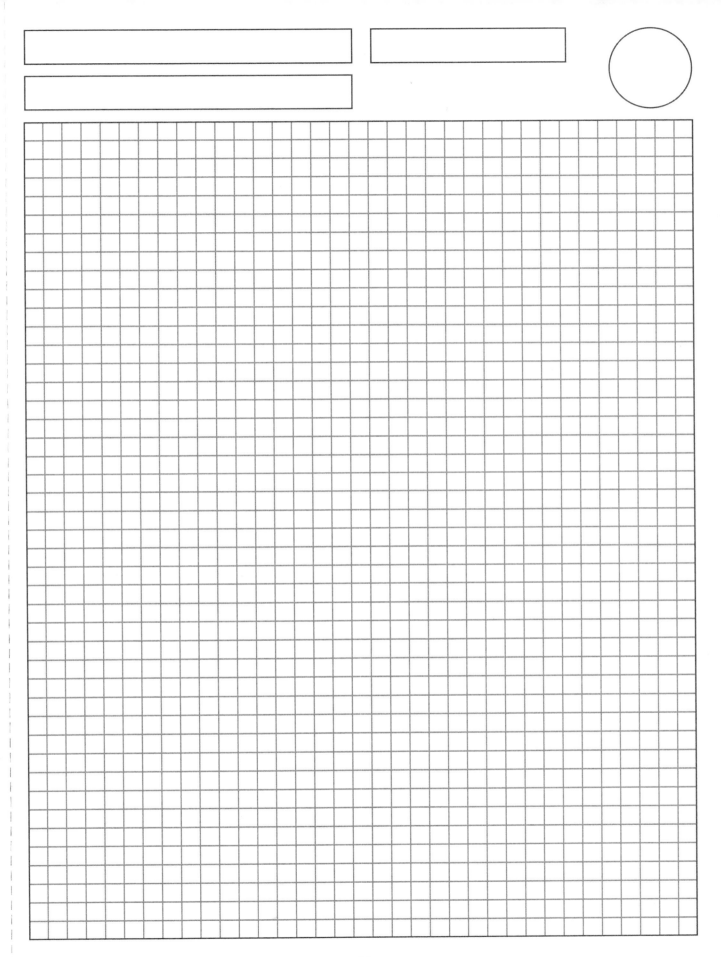

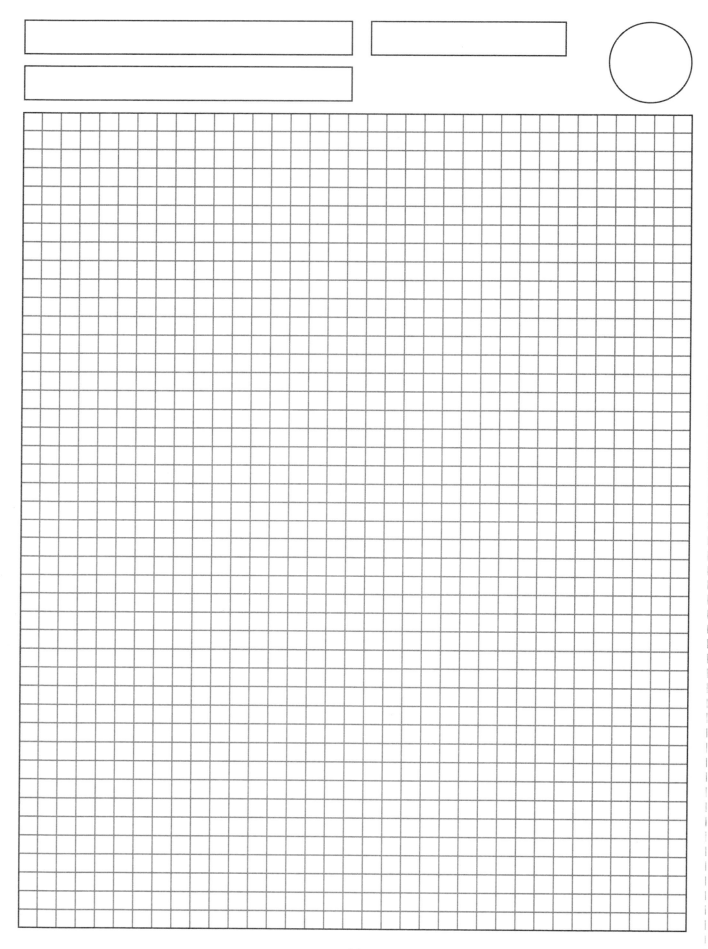

SECTOR 1

AVENUES OF APPROACH (AVP)

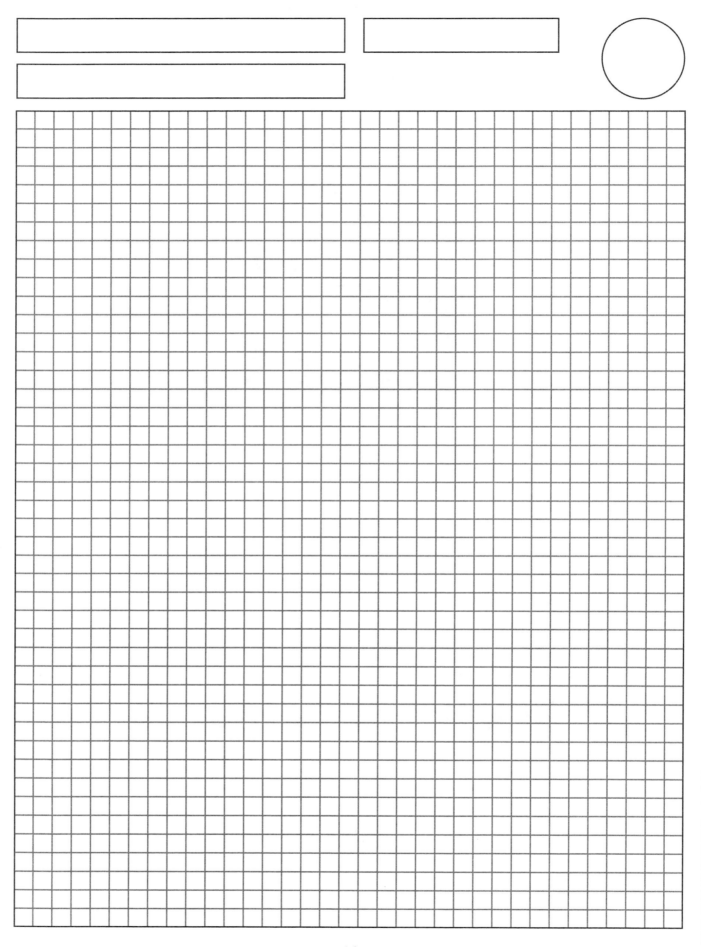

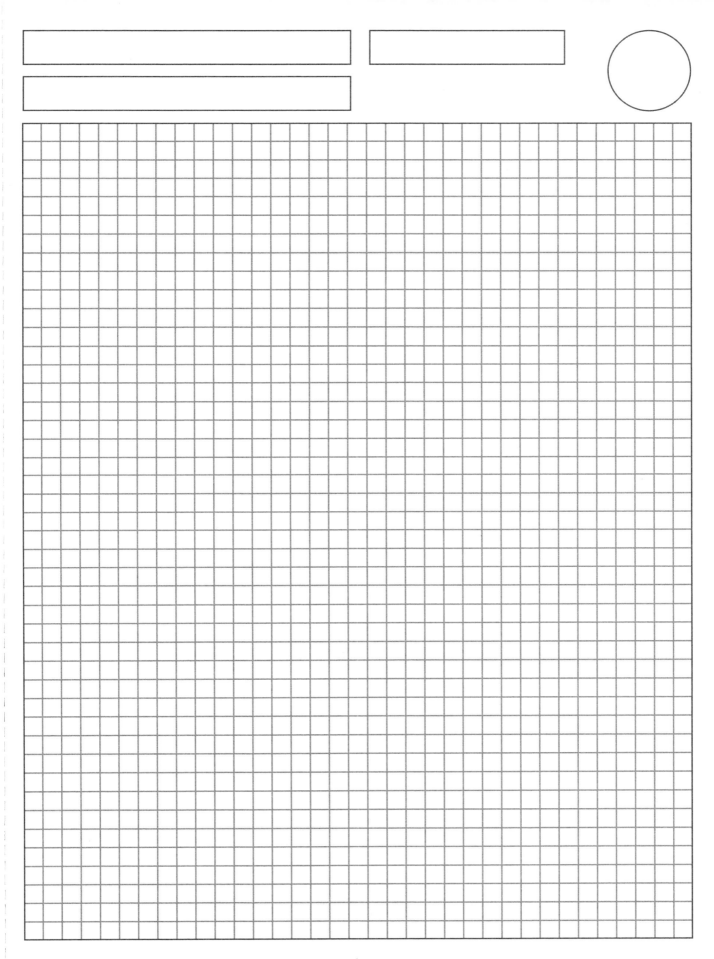

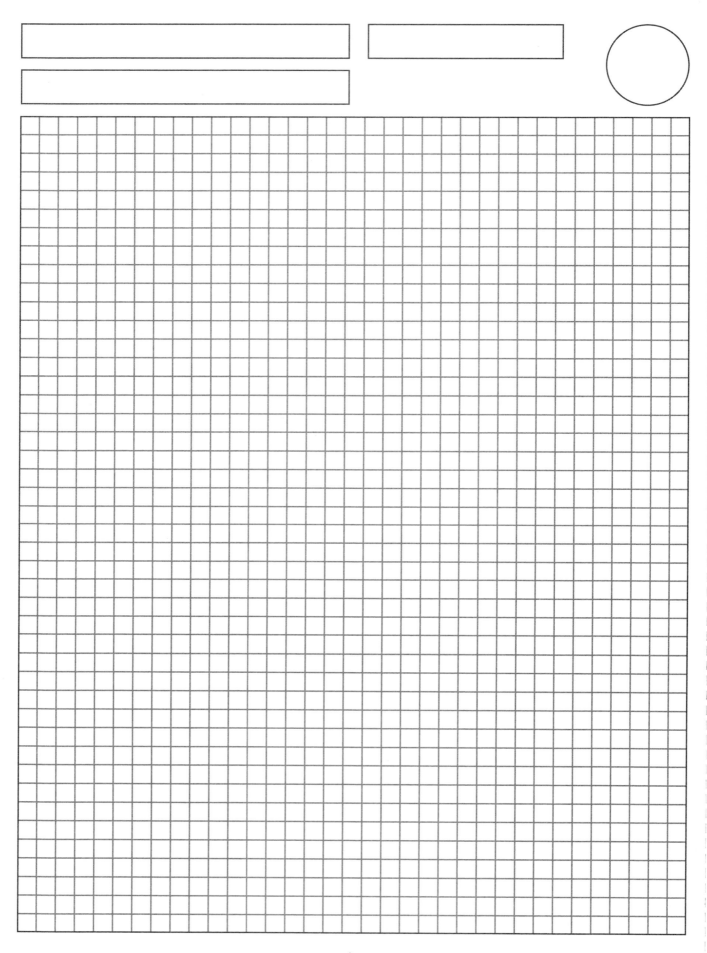

SECTOR 1

TARGET EQUATION

TARGET EQUATION WORKSHEET

Sector:

Date:

Type of attack:

Time of attack:

Avenues of Approach:

Vulnerabilities:

Type of attack:

Time of attack:

Avenues of Approach:

Vulnerabilities:

Type of attack:

Time of attack:

Avenues of Approach:

Vulnerabilities:

TARGET EQUATION WORKSHEET

Sector:	Date:

Type of attack:	Time of attack:

Avenues of Approach:

Vulnerabilities:

Type of attack:	Time of attack:

Avenues of Approach:

Vulnerabilities:

Type of attack:	Time of attack:

Avenues of Approach:

Vulnerabilities:

TARGET EQUATION WORKSHEET

Sector:

Date:

Type of attack:

Time of attack:

Avenues of Approach:

Vulnerabilities:

Type of attack:

Time of attack:

Avenues of Approach:

Vulnerabilities:

Type of attack:

Time of attack:

Avenues of Approach:

Vulnerabilities:

TARGET EQUATION WORKSHEET

Sector:

Date:

Type of attack:

Time of attack:

Avenues of Approach:

Vulnerabilities:

Type of attack:

Time of attack:

Avenues of Approach:

Vulnerabilities:

Type of attack:

Time of attack:

Avenues of Approach:

Vulnerabilities:

TARGET EQUATION WORKSHEET

Sector:

Date:

Type of attack:

Time of attack:

Avenues of Approach:

Vulnerabilities:

Type of attack:

Time of attack:

Avenues of Approach:

Vulnerabilities:

Type of attack:

Time of attack:

Avenues of Approach:

Vulnerabilities:

S2

SECTOR 2

SECTOR 2

OVERVIEW

THREAT ASSESSMENT SECTOR OVERVIEW

Sector:	Date:

Prepared by:

Situation:

Sector Overview:

Note: Make sure you print out map and directions to pertinent police precincts.

Police Departments:	PD Contact Information:	PD Response Times:

Crime Level:	Possible Threat Level:

Known Terror Threats:

Known Criminal Threats:

Note: Make sure you print out map and directions to all trauma centers. Always make the effort to proceed to a level 1 trauma center if the injury is life threatening.

Trauma Centers:	Trauma Center Level (I, II, III):	Response Times:

Weather Conditions:

Spring   Summer   Fall   Winter

SECTOR 2

CRITICAL ASSETS (CA)

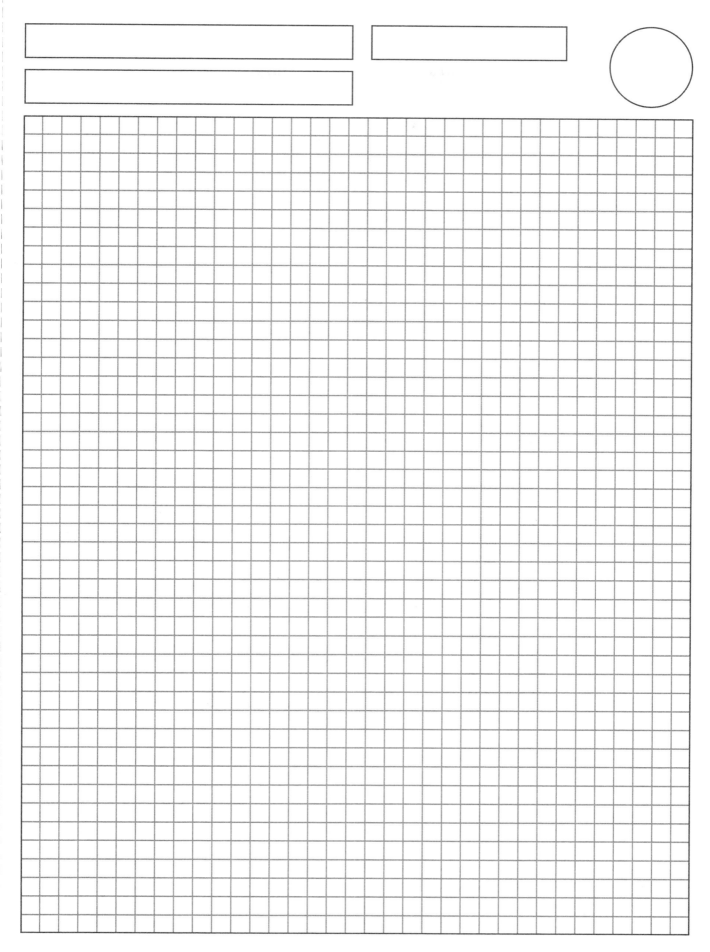

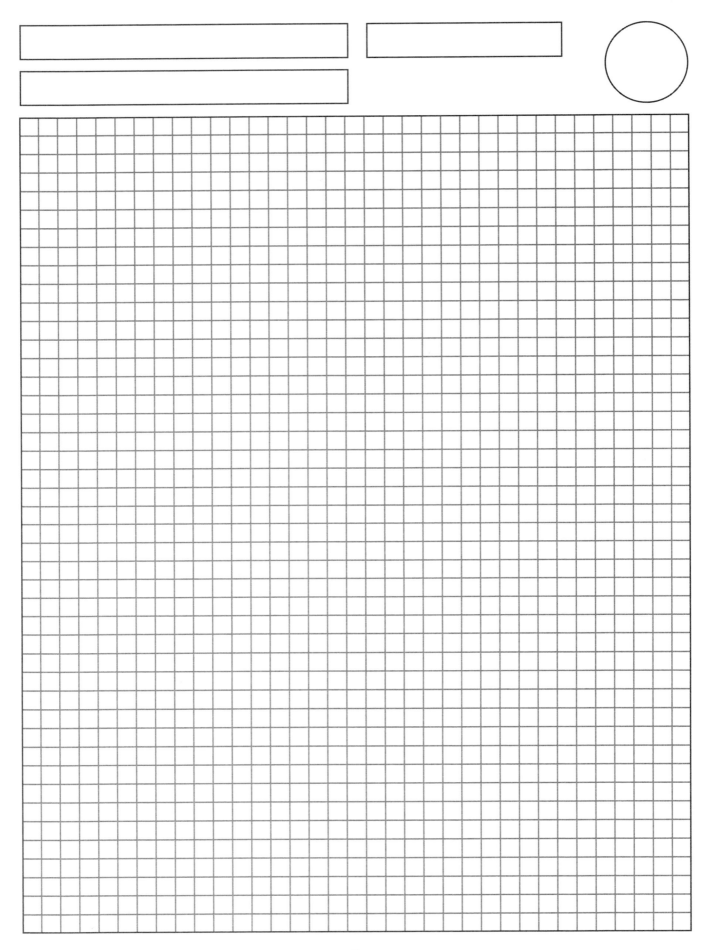

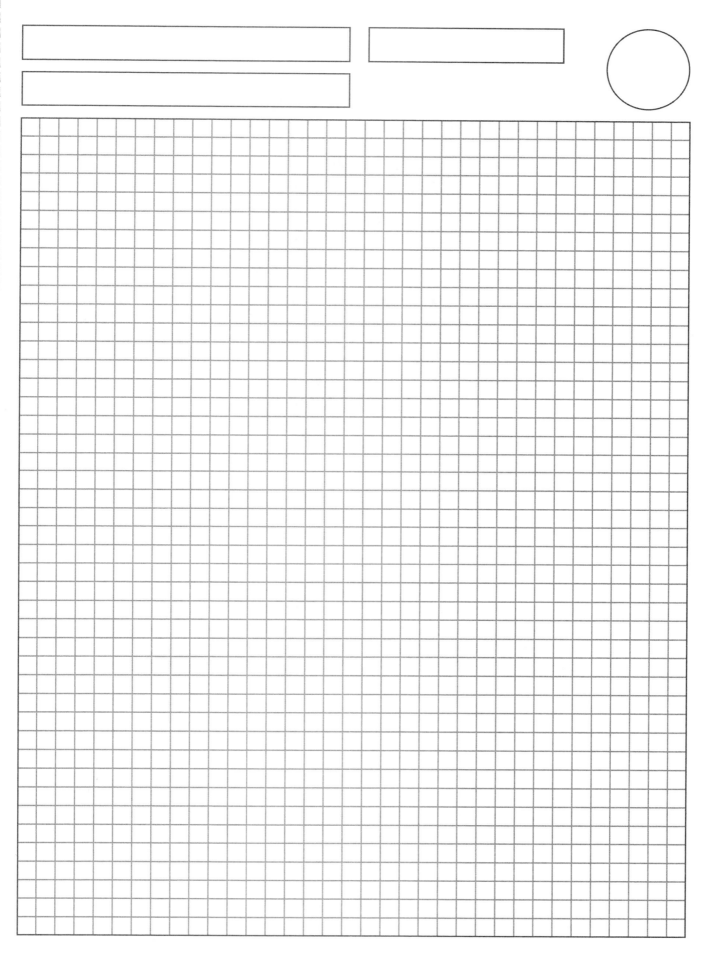

SECTOR 2

CRITICAL AREAS (CAR)

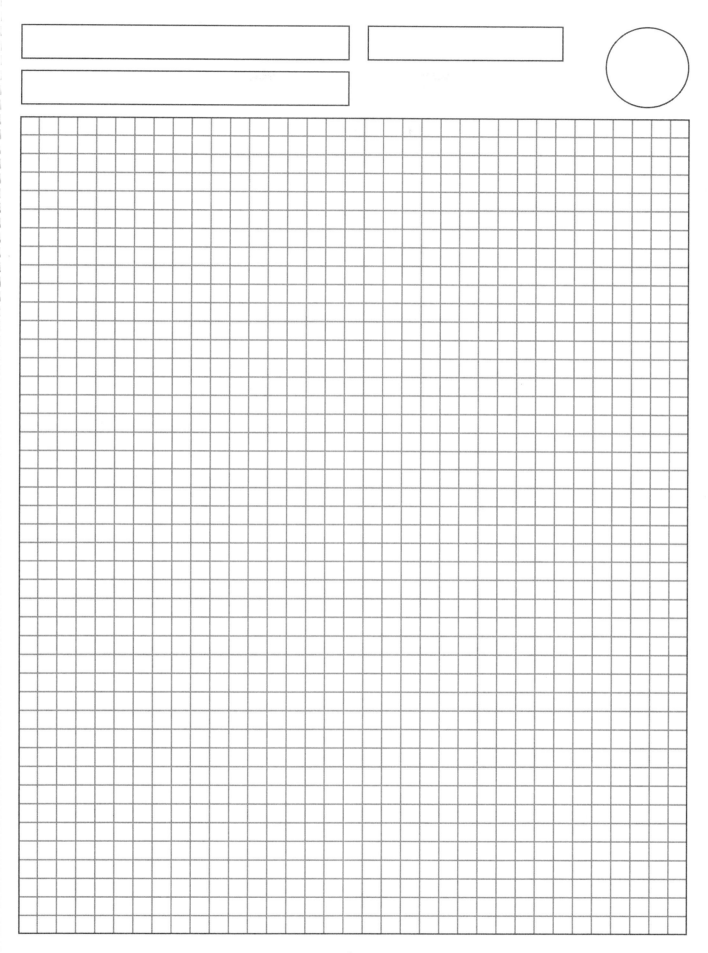

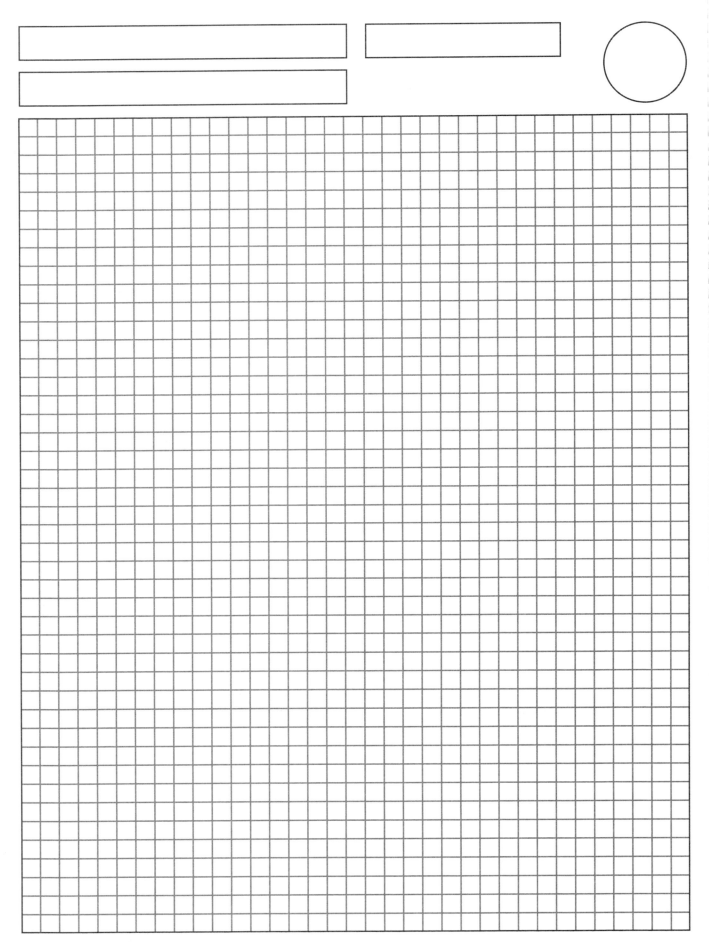

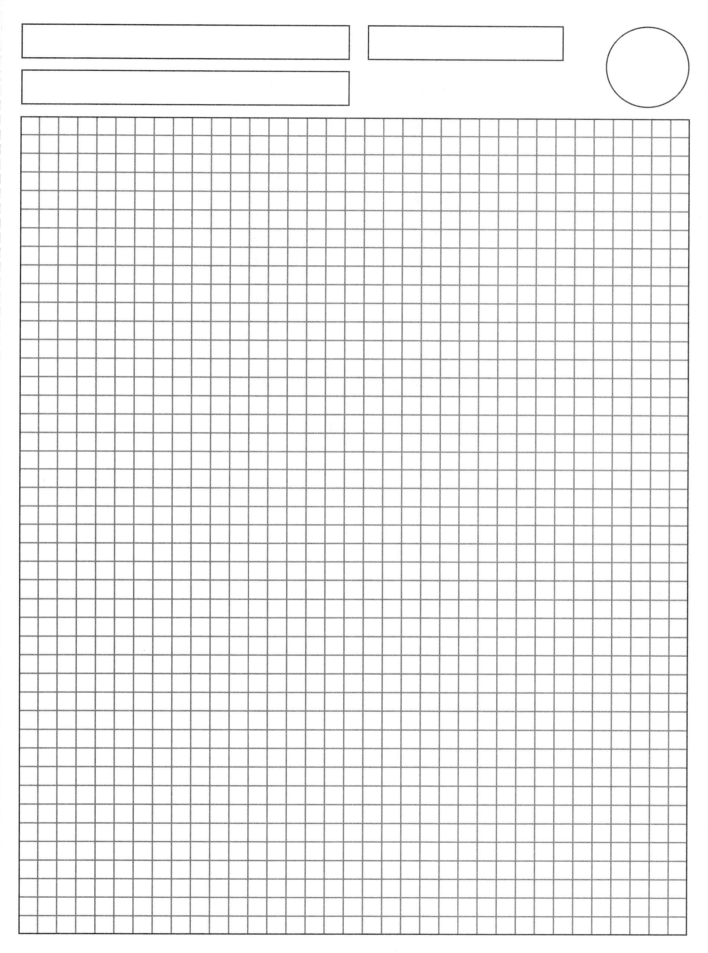

SECTOR 2

CRITICAL TIMES (CT)

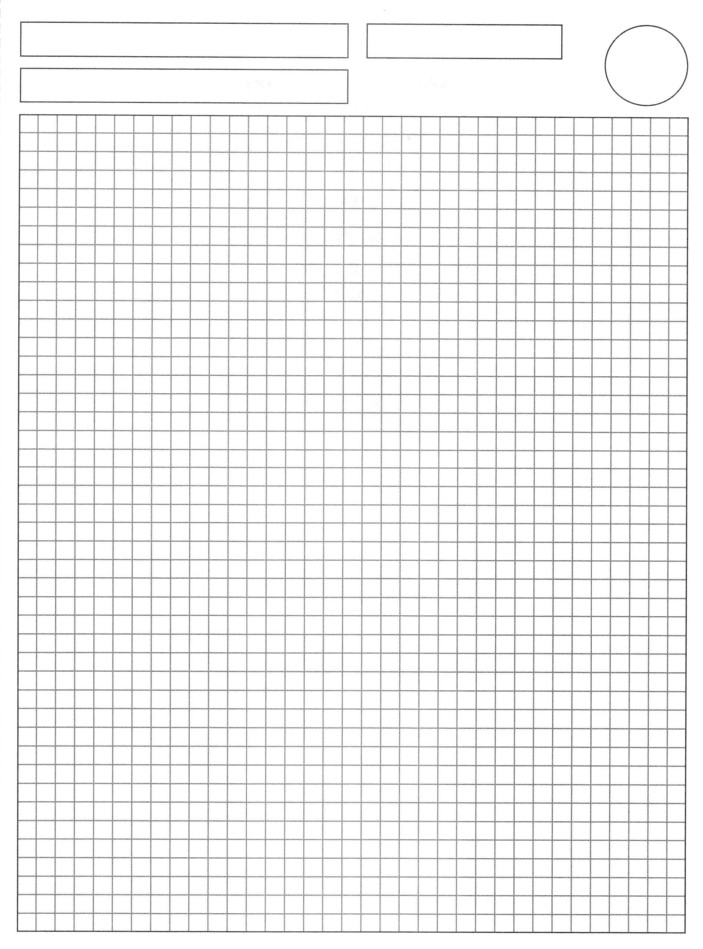

SECTOR 2

VULNERABILITIES

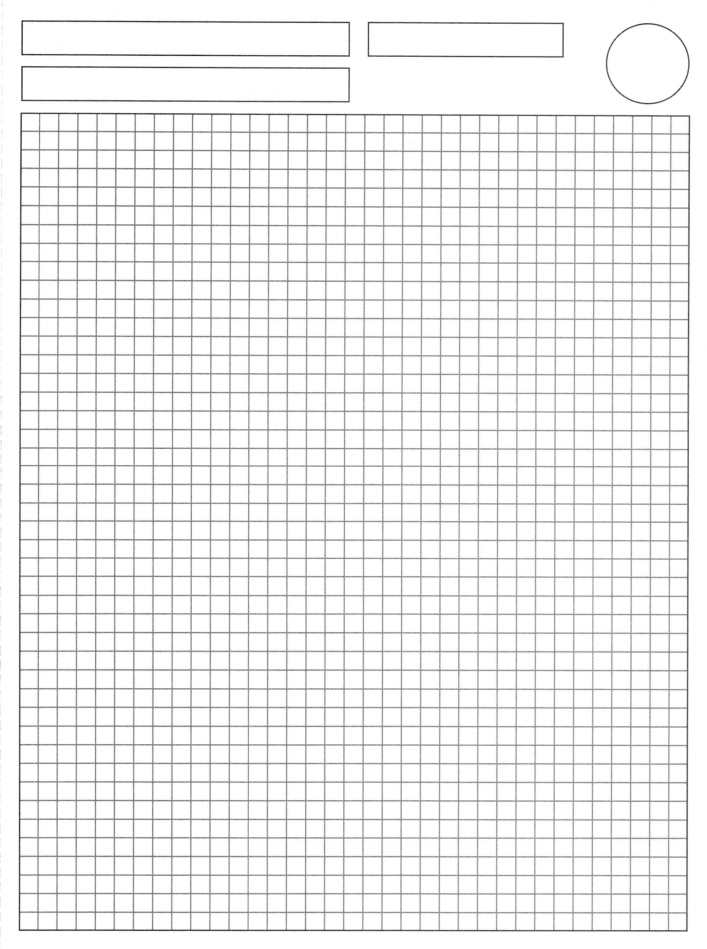

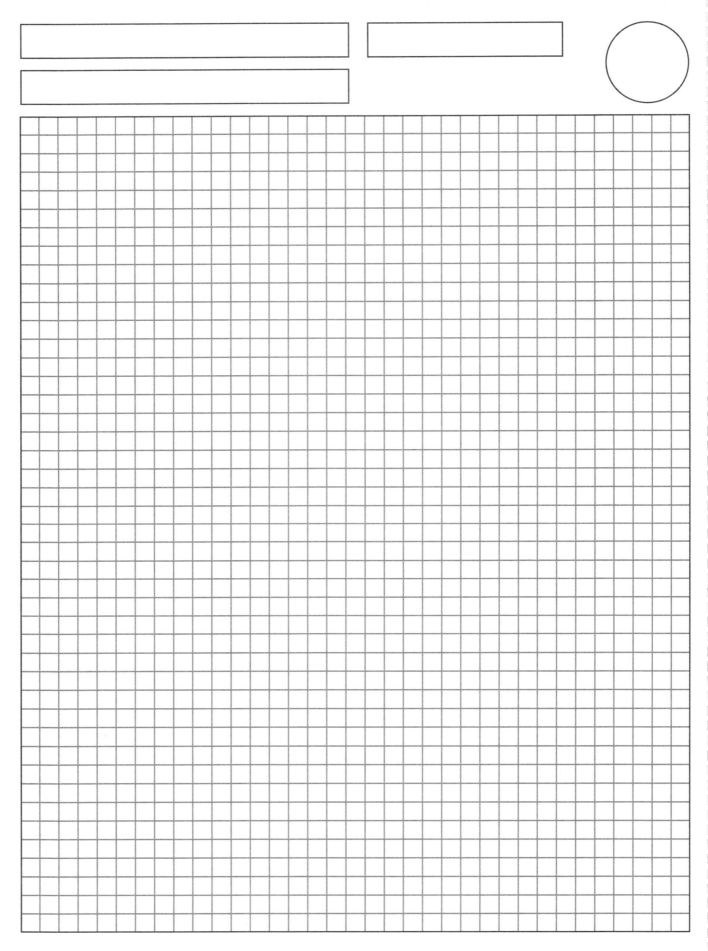

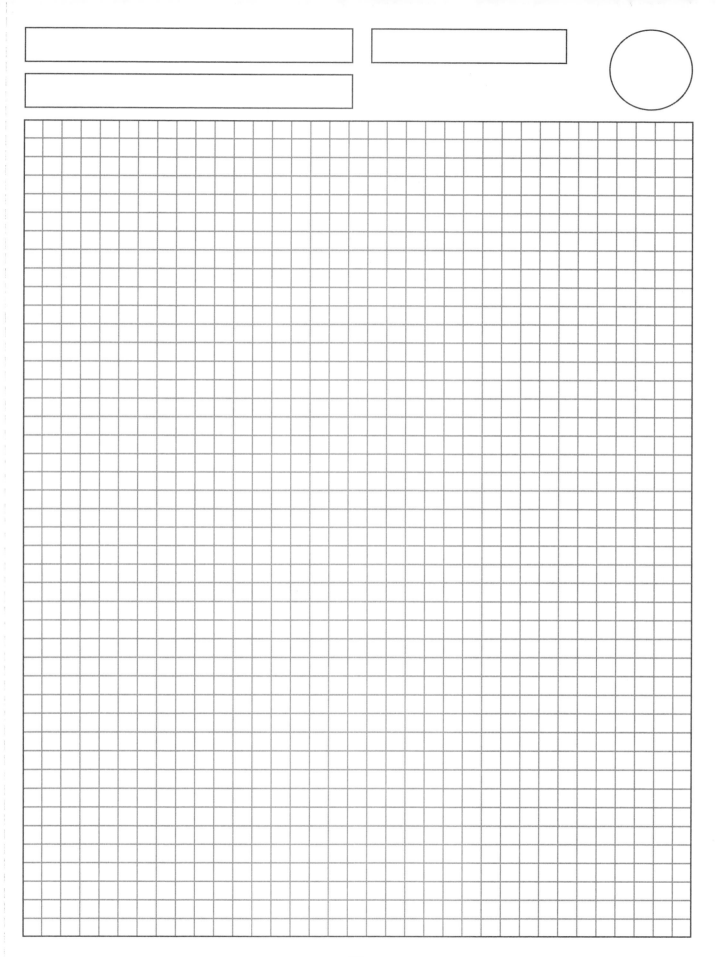

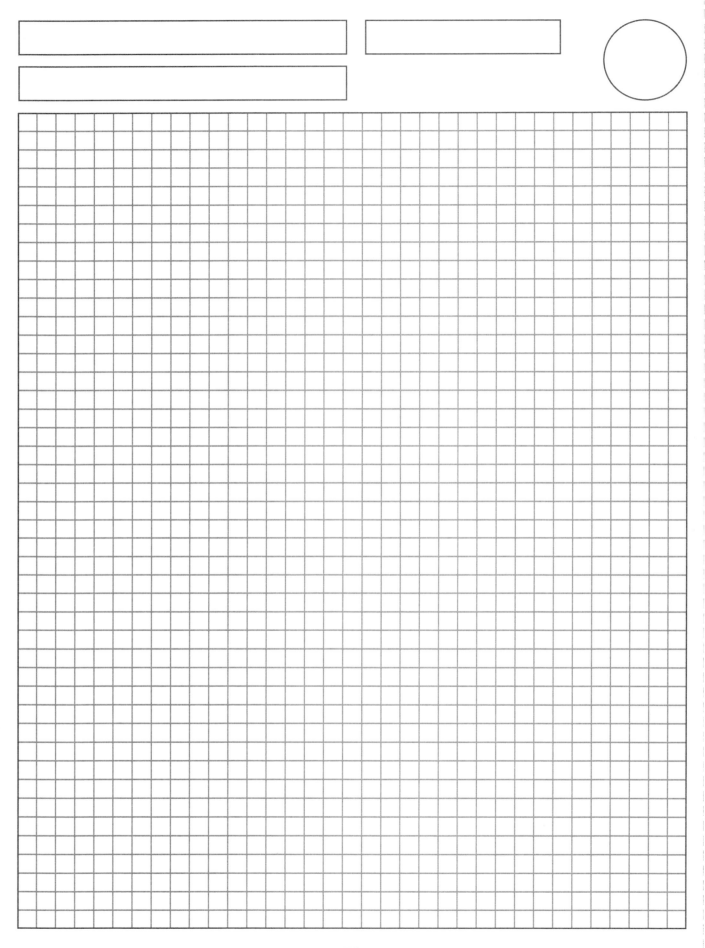

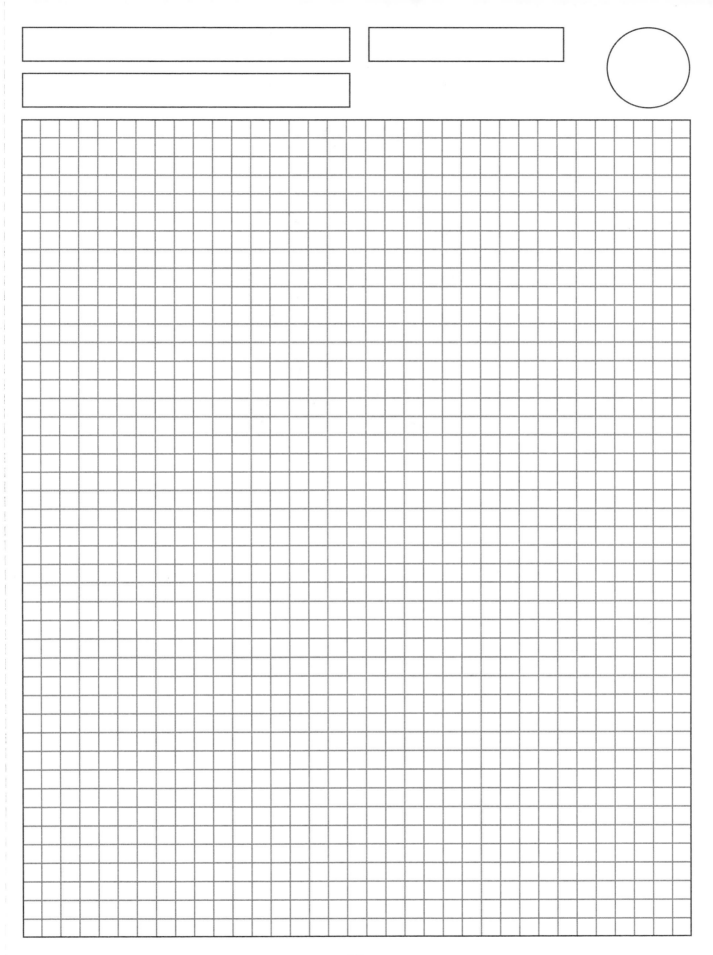

SECTOR 2

AVENUES OF APPROACH (AVP)

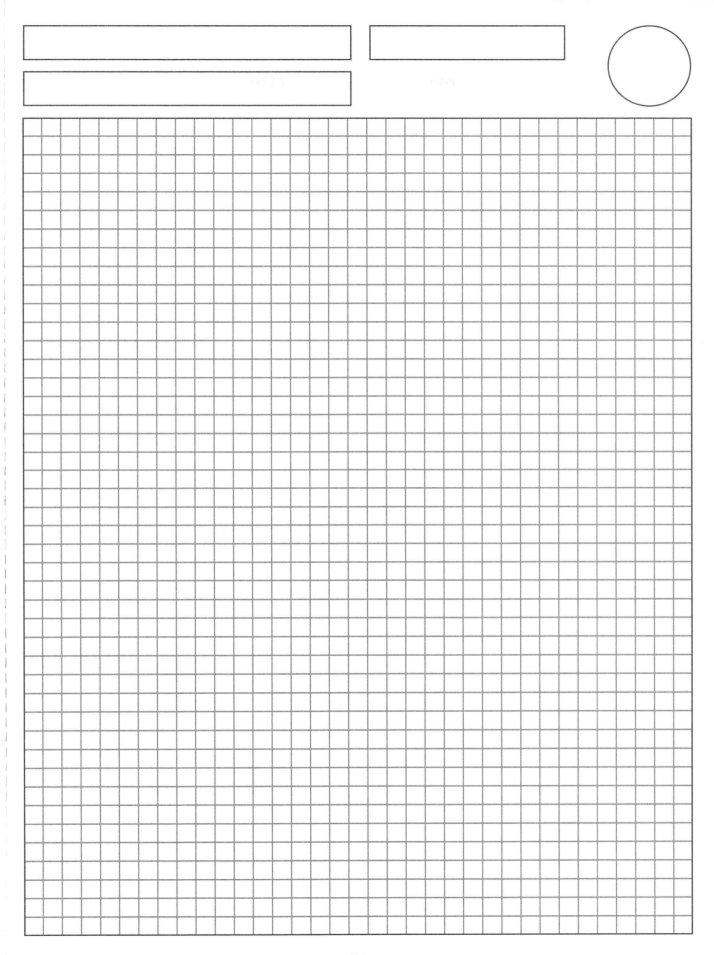

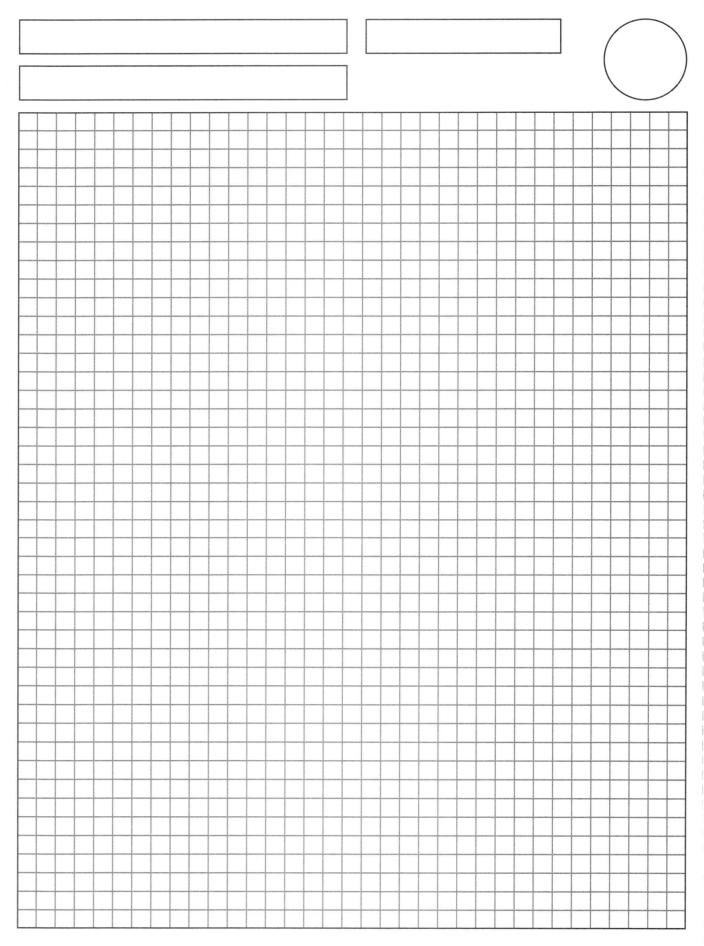

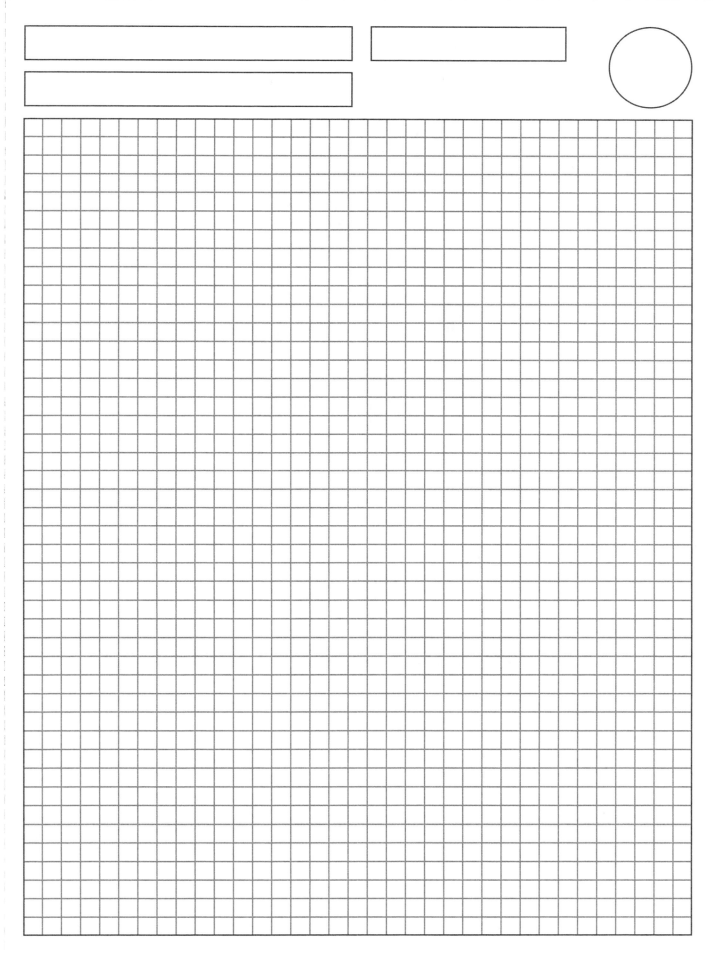

SECTOR 2

TARGET EQUATION

TARGET EQUATION WORKSHEET

Sector:	Date:

Type of attack:	Time of attack:

Avenues of Approach:

Vulnerabilities:

Type of attack:	Time of attack:

Avenues of Approach:

Vulnerabilities:

Type of attack:	Time of attack:

Avenues of Approach:

Vulnerabilities:

TARGET EQUATION WORKSHEET

Sector:	Date:

Type of attack:	Time of attack:

Avenues of Approach:

Vulnerabilities:

Type of attack:	Time of attack:

Avenues of Approach:

Vulnerabilities:

Type of attack:	Time of attack:

Avenues of Approach:

Vulnerabilities:

TARGET EQUATION WORKSHEET

Sector:

Date:

Type of attack:

Time of attack:

Avenues of Approach:

Vulnerabilities:

Type of attack:

Time of attack:

Avenues of Approach:

Vulnerabilities:

Type of attack:

Time of attack:

Avenues of Approach:

Vulnerabilities:

TARGET EQUATION WORKSHEET

Sector:	Date:

Type of attack:	Time of attack:

Avenues of Approach:

Vulnerabilities:

Type of attack:	Time of attack:

Avenues of Approach:

Vulnerabilities:

Type of attack:	Time of attack:

Avenues of Approach:

Vulnerabilities:

TARGET EQUATION WORKSHEET

Sector:

Date:

Type of attack:

Time of attack:

Avenues of Approach:

Vulnerabilities:

Type of attack:

Time of attack:

Avenues of Approach:

Vulnerabilities:

Type of attack:

Time of attack:

Avenues of Approach:

Vulnerabilities:

S3

SECTOR 3

SECTOR 3

OVERVIEW

THREAT ASSESSMENT SECTOR OVERVIEW

Sector:

Date:

Prepared by:

Situation:

Sector Overview:

Note: Make sure you print out map and directions to pertinent police precincts.

Police Departments:

PD Contact Information:

PD Response Times:

Crime Level:

Possible Threat Level:

Known Terror Threats:

Known Criminal Threats:

Note: Make sure you print out map and directions to all trauma centers. Always make the effort to proceed to a level 1 trauma center if the injury is life threatening.

Trauma Centers:

Trauma Center Level (I, II, III):

Response Times:

Weather Conditions:

Spring   Summer   Fall   Winter

SECTOR 3

CRITICAL ASSETS (CA)

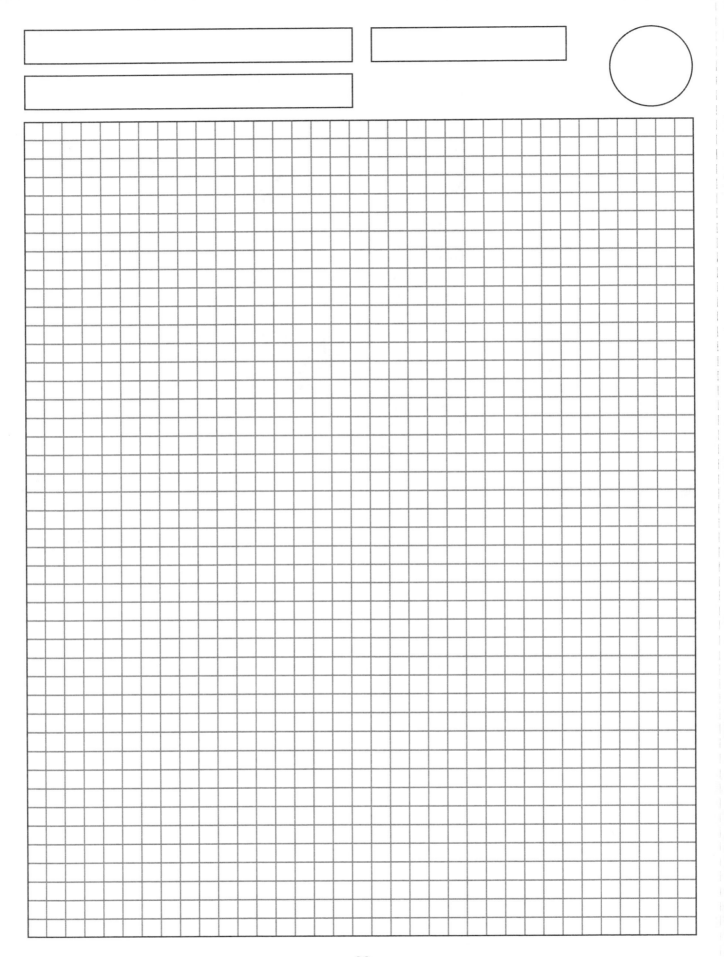

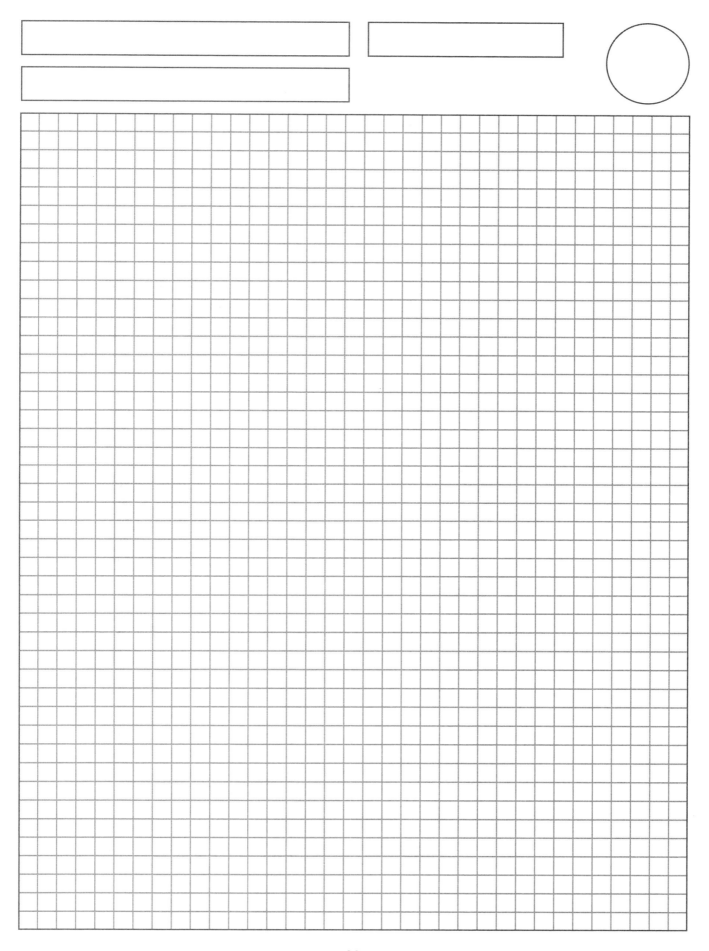

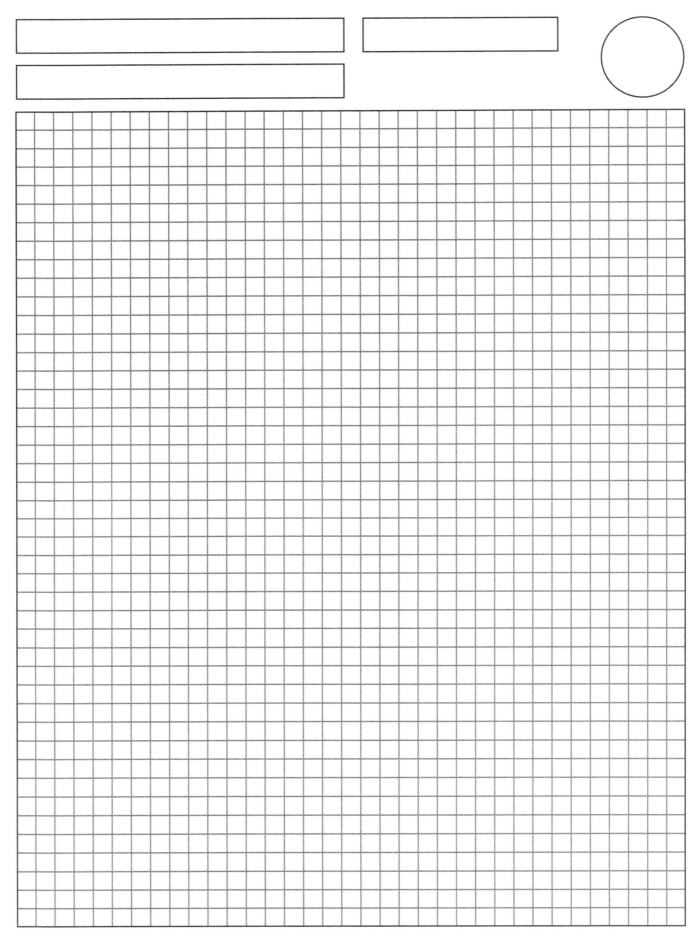

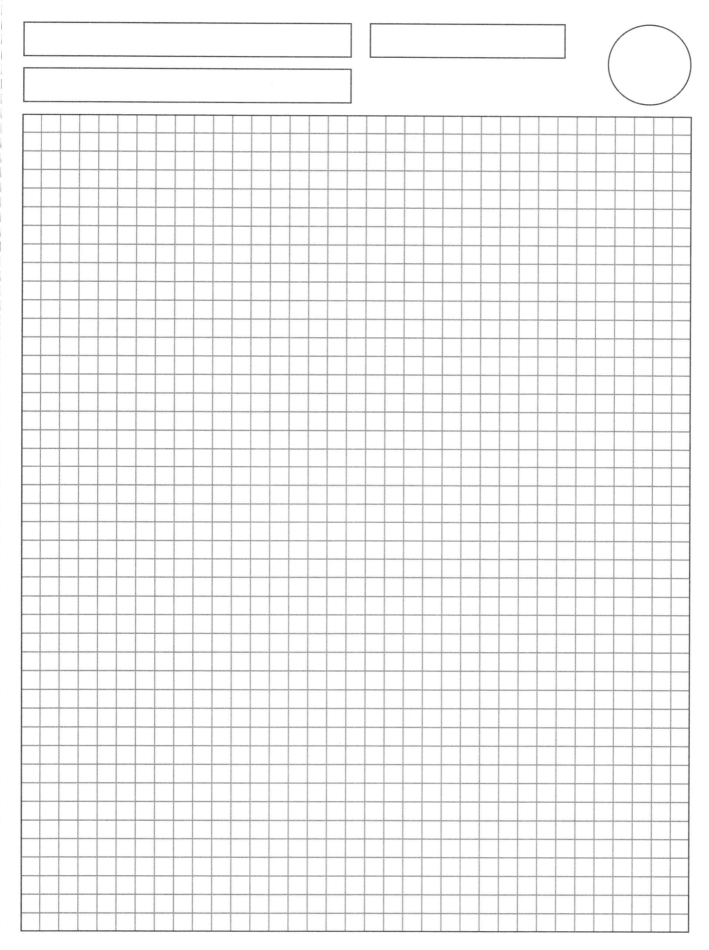

SECTOR 3

CRITICAL AREAS (CAR)

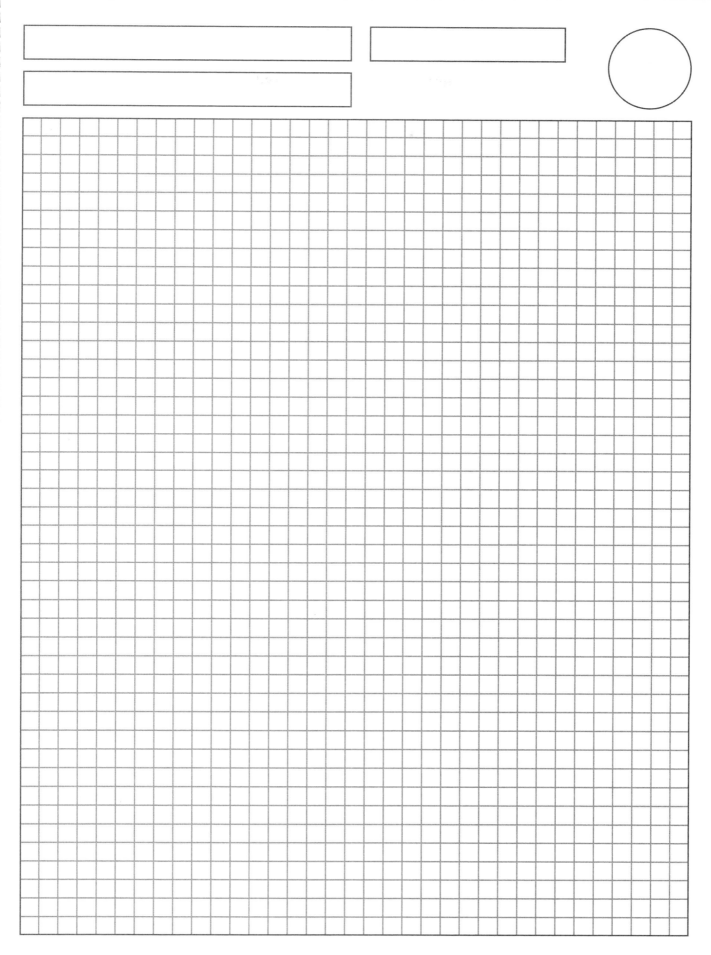

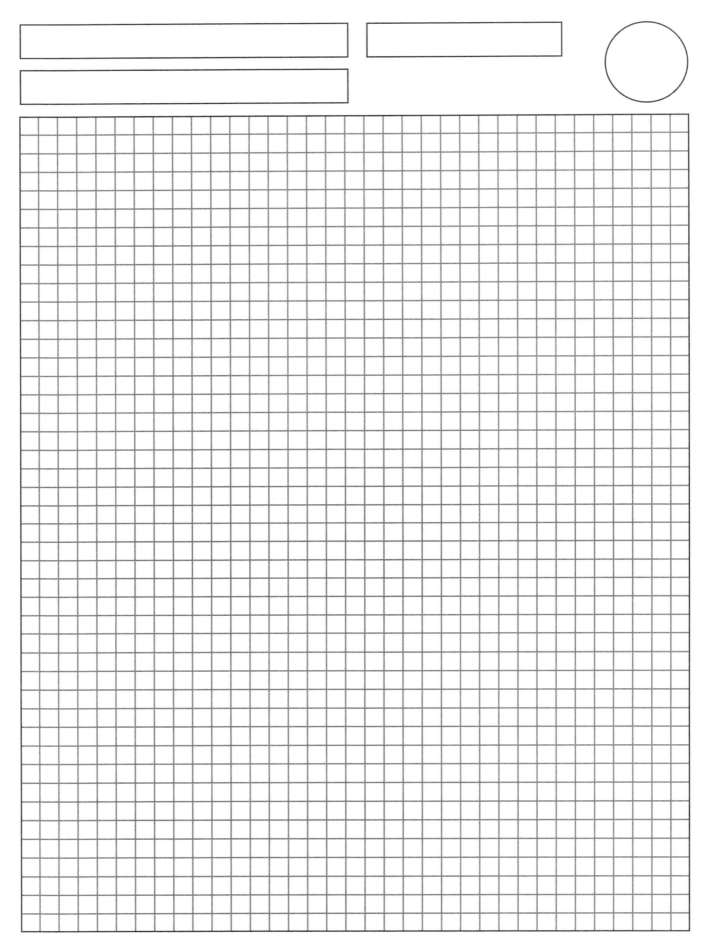

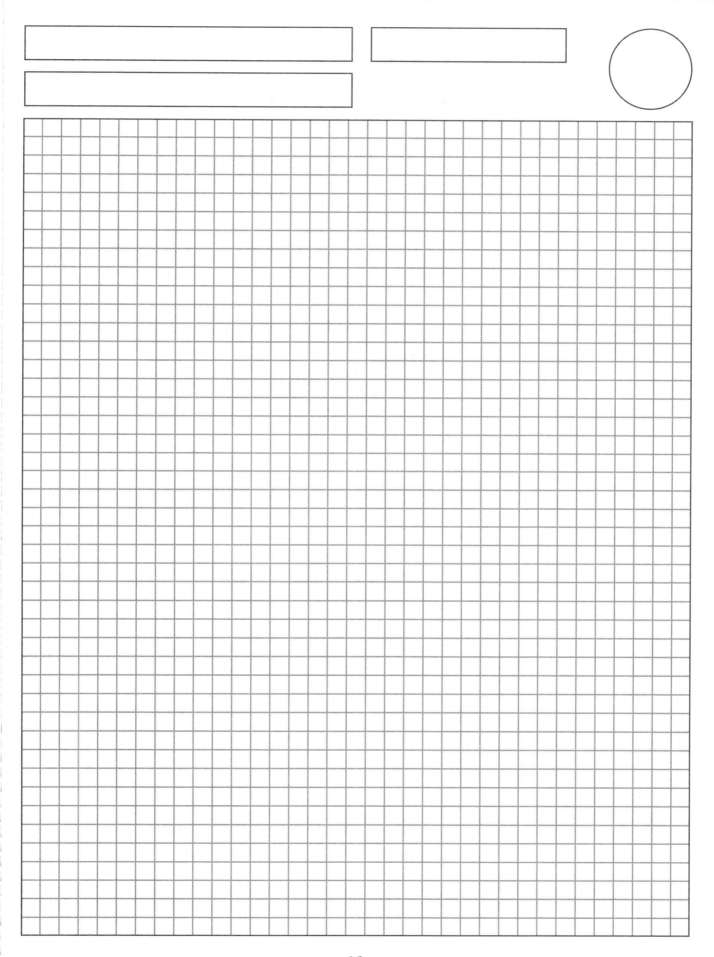

SECTOR 3
CRITICAL TIMES (CT)

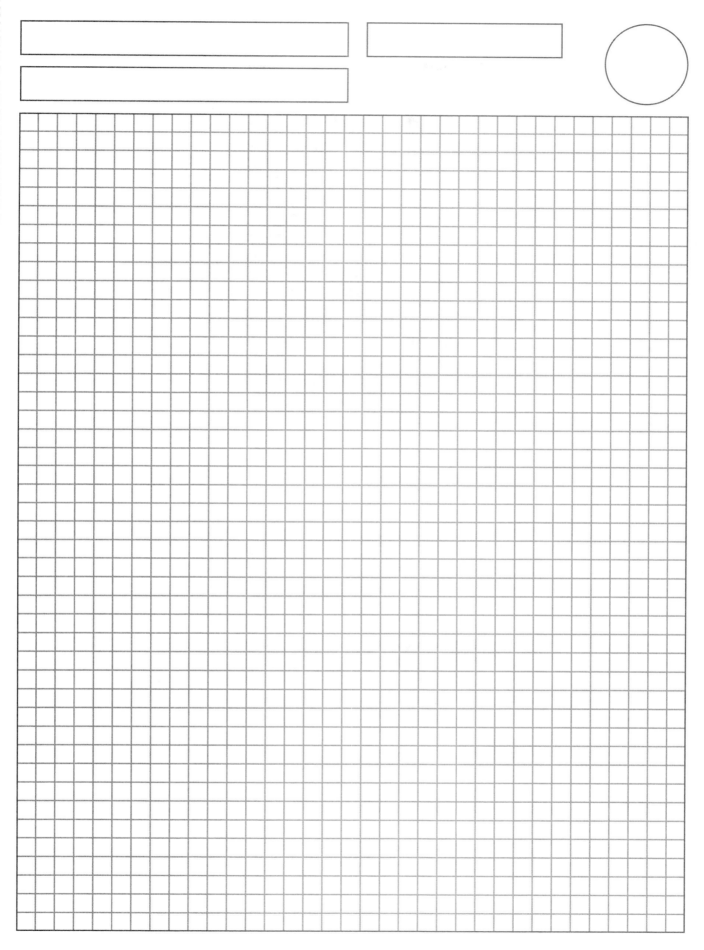

SECTOR 3

VULNERABILITIES

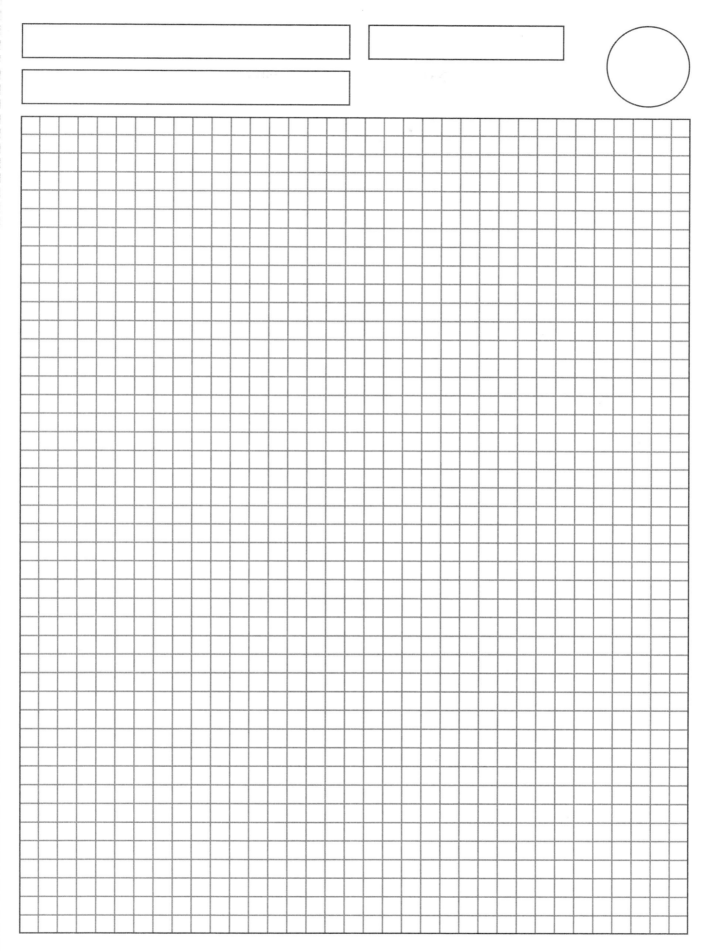

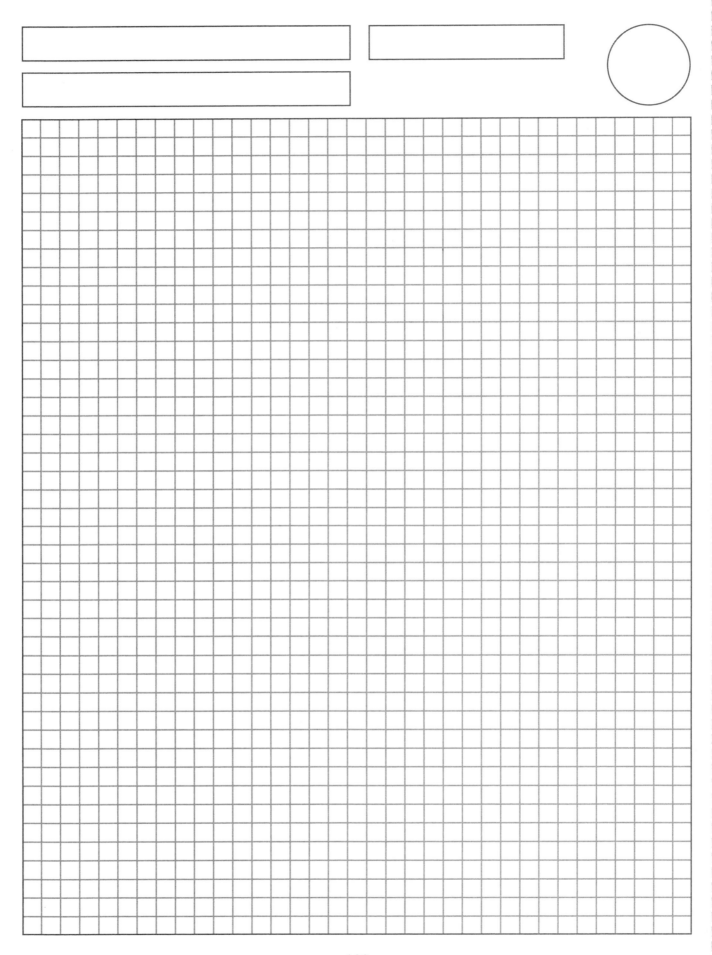

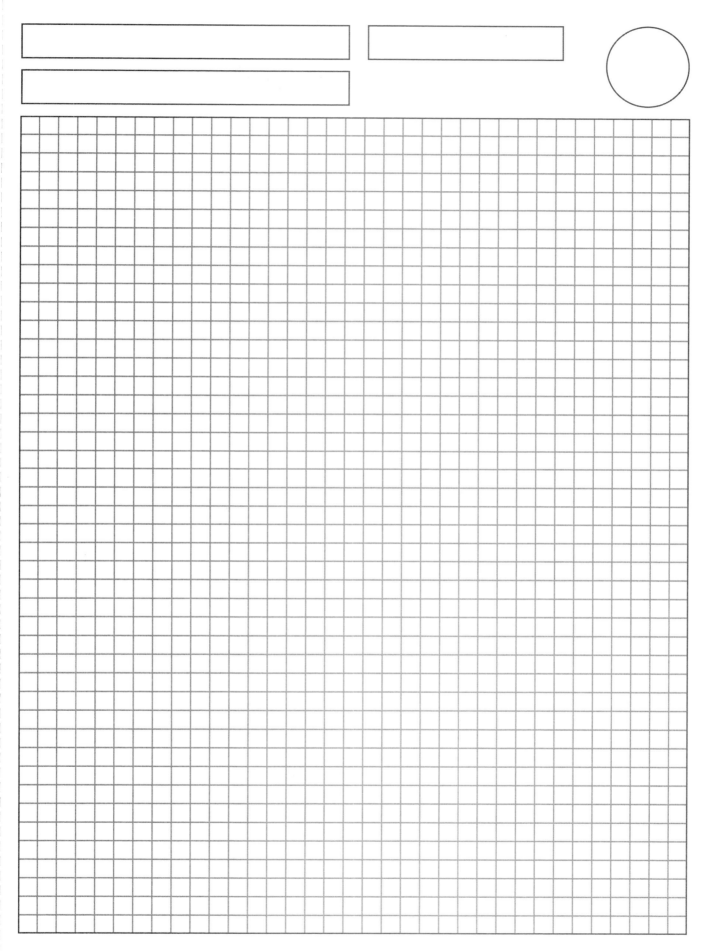

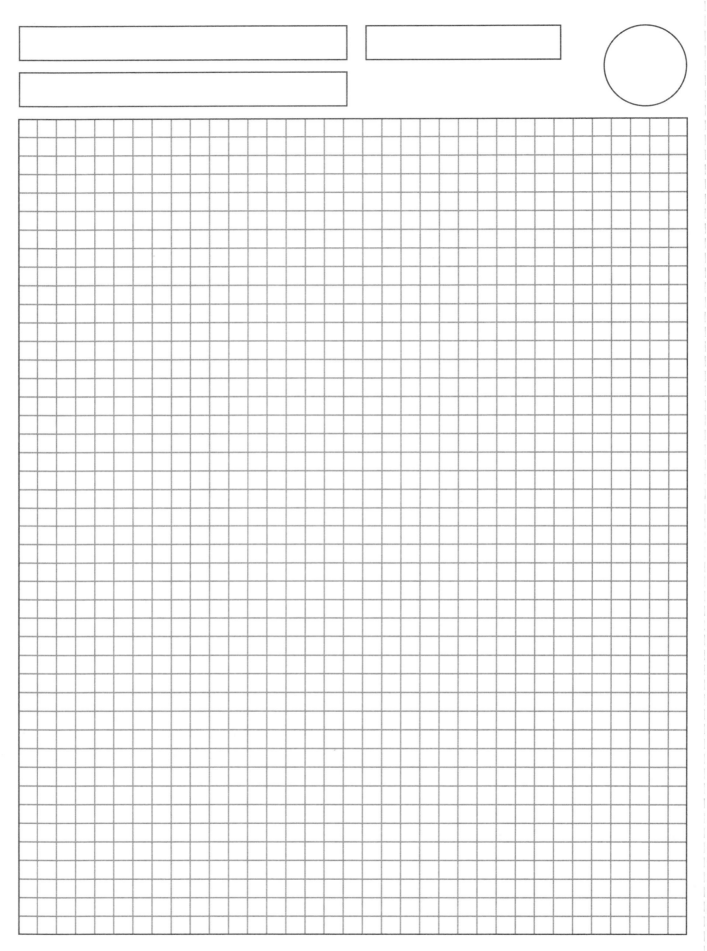

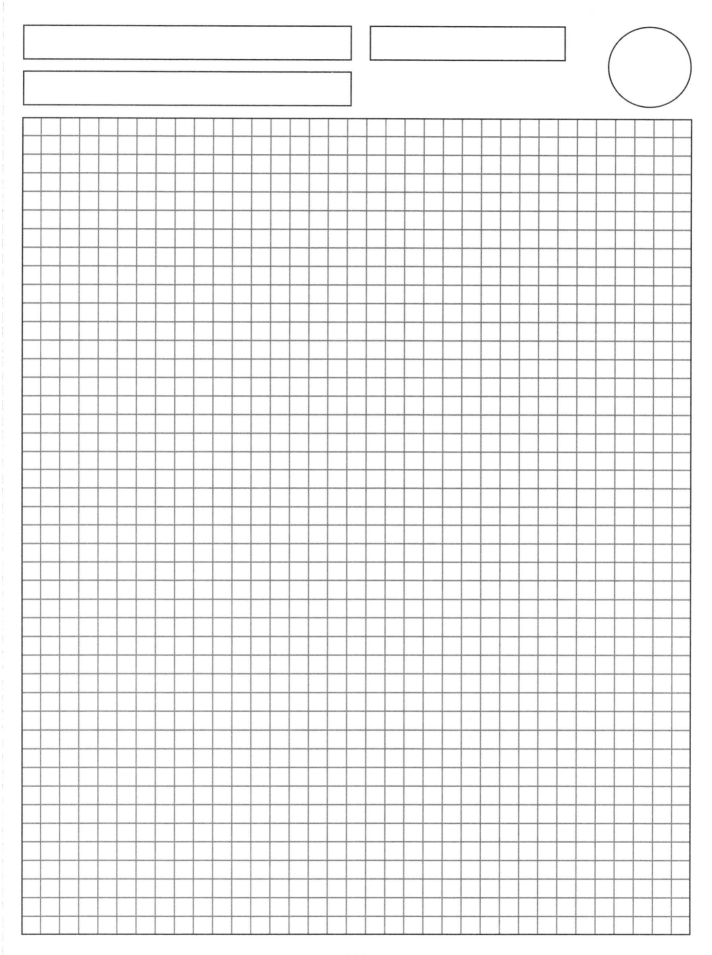

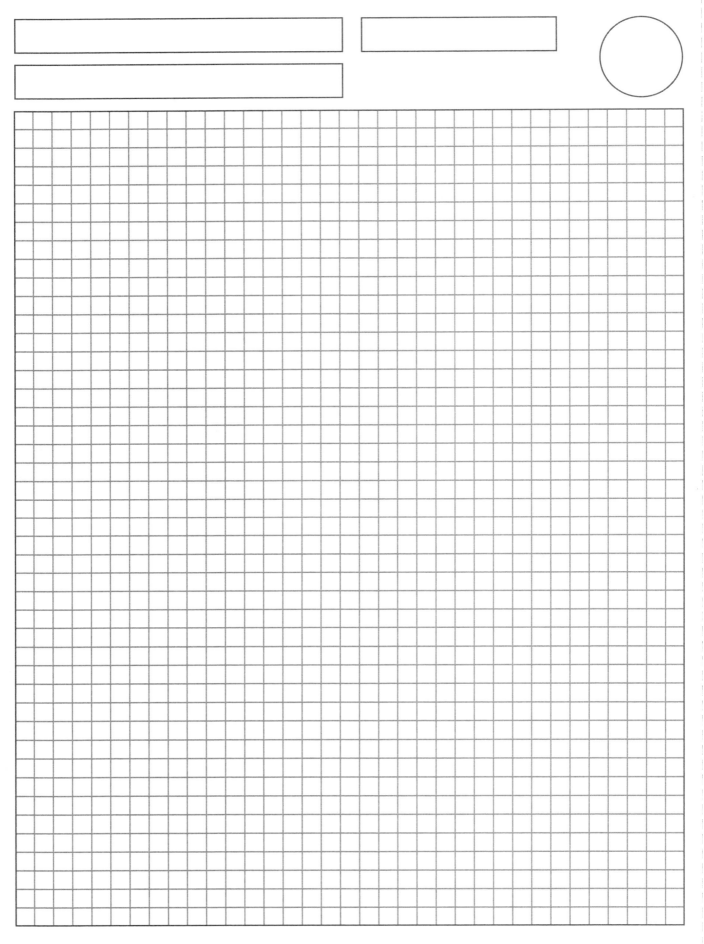

SECTOR 3

AVENUES OF APPROACH (AVP)

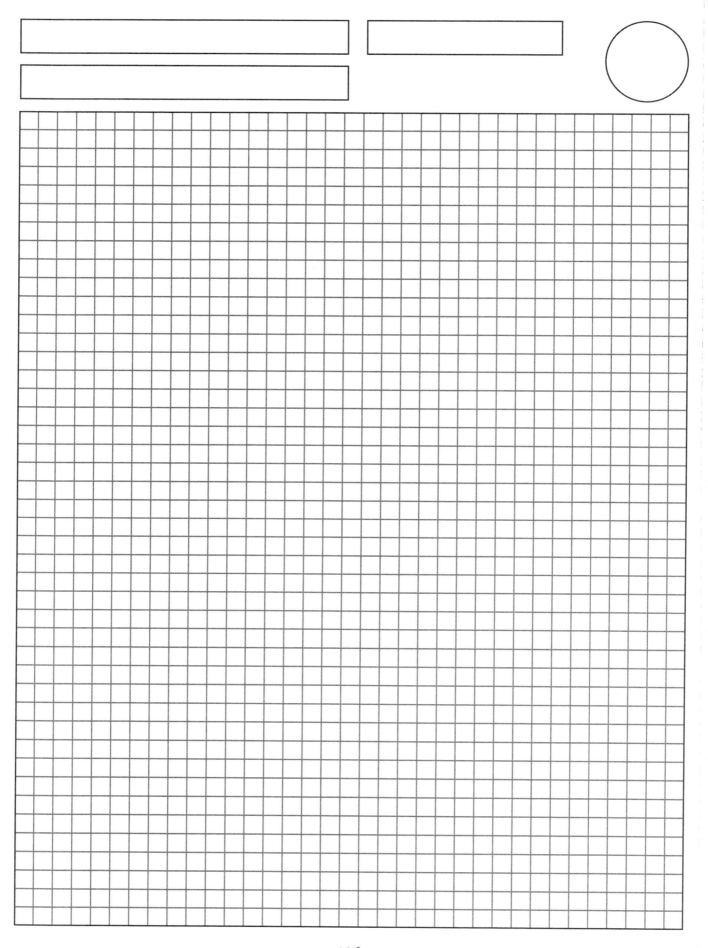

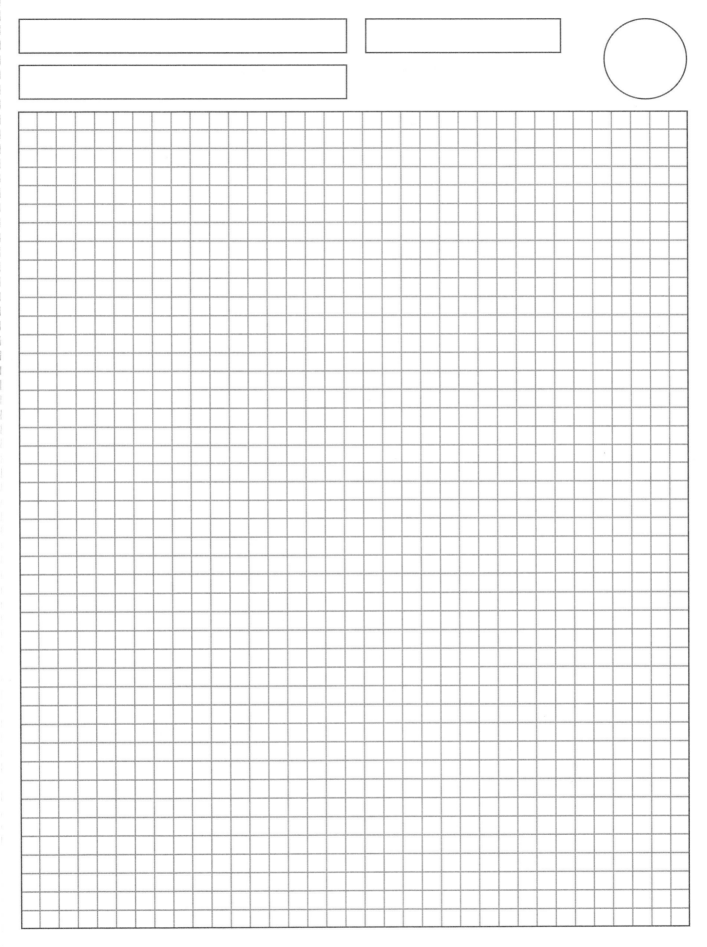

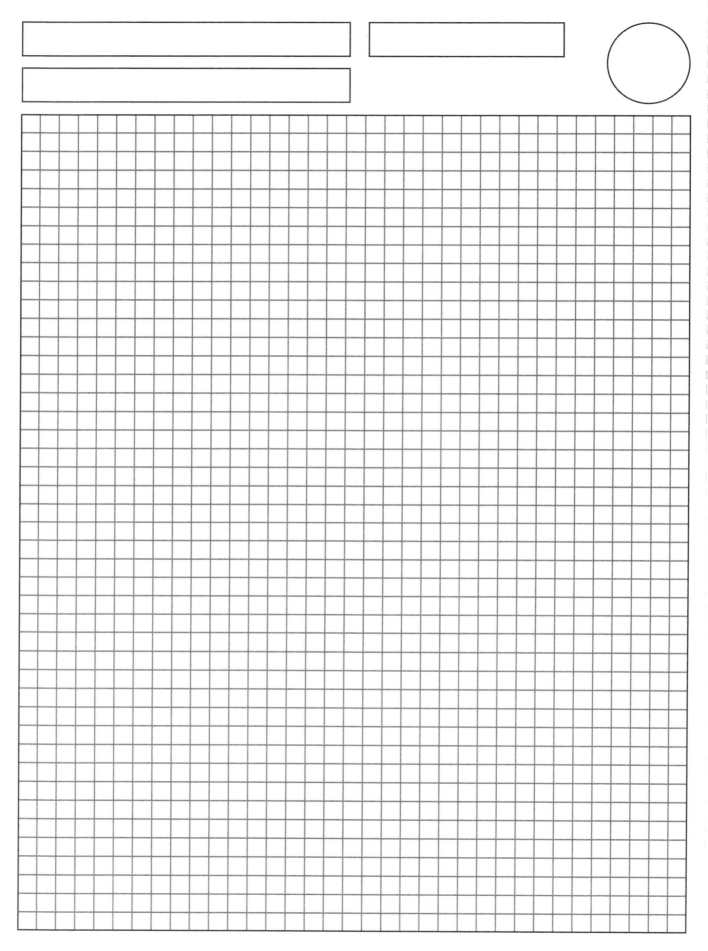

SECTOR 3

TARGET EQUATION

TARGET EQUATION WORKSHEET

Sector:

Date:

Type of attack:

Time of attack:

Avenues of Approach:

Vulnerabilities:

Type of attack:

Time of attack:

Avenues of Approach:

Vulnerabilities:

Type of attack:

Time of attack:

Avenues of Approach:

Vulnerabilities:

TARGET EQUATION WORKSHEET

Sector:

Date:

Type of attack:

Time of attack:

Avenues of Approach:

Vulnerabilities:

Type of attack:

Time of attack:

Avenues of Approach:

Vulnerabilities:

Type of attack:

Time of attack:

Avenues of Approach:

Vulnerabilities:

TARGET EQUATION WORKSHEET

Sector:

Date:

Type of attack:

Time of attack:

Avenues of Approach:

Vulnerabilities:

Type of attack:

Time of attack:

Avenues of Approach:

Vulnerabilities:

Type of attack:

Time of attack:

Avenues of Approach:

Vulnerabilities:

TARGET EQUATION WORKSHEET

Sector:

Date:

Type of attack:

Time of attack:

Avenues of Approach:

Vulnerabilities:

Type of attack:

Time of attack:

Avenues of Approach:

Vulnerabilities:

Type of attack:

Time of attack:

Avenues of Approach:

Vulnerabilities:

TARGET EQUATION WORKSHEET

Sector:	Date:

Type of attack:	Time of attack:

Avenues of Approach:

Vulnerabilities:

Type of attack:	Time of attack:

Avenues of Approach:

Vulnerabilities:

Type of attack:	Time of attack:

Avenues of Approach:

Vulnerabilities:

S4

SECTOR 4

SECTOR 4

OVERVIEW

THREAT ASSESSMENT SECTOR OVERVIEW

Sector:

Date:

Prepared by:

Situation:

Sector Overview:

Note: Make sure you print out map and directions to pertinent police precincts.

Police Departments:

PD Contact Information:

PD Response Times:

Crime Level:

Possible Threat Level:

Known Terror Threats:

Known Criminal Threats:

Note: Make sure you print out map and directions to all trauma centers. Always make the effort to proceed to a level 1 trauma center if the injury is life threatening.

Trauma Centers:

Trauma Center Level (I, II, III):

Response Times:

Weather Conditions:

Spring   Summer   Fall   Winter

SECTOR 4

CRITICAL ASSETS (CA)

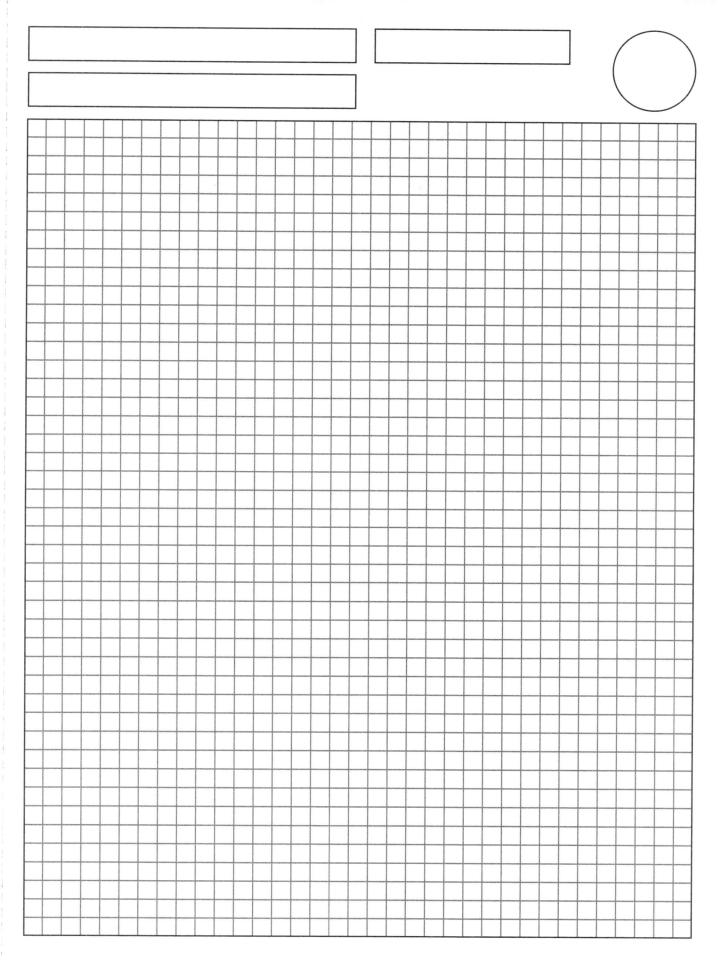

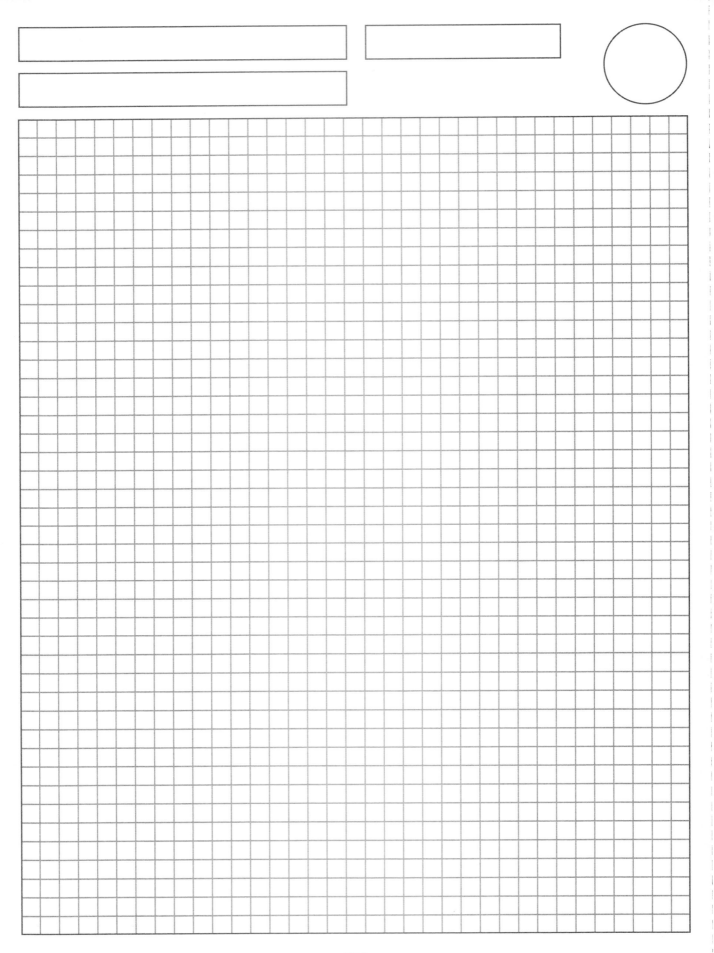

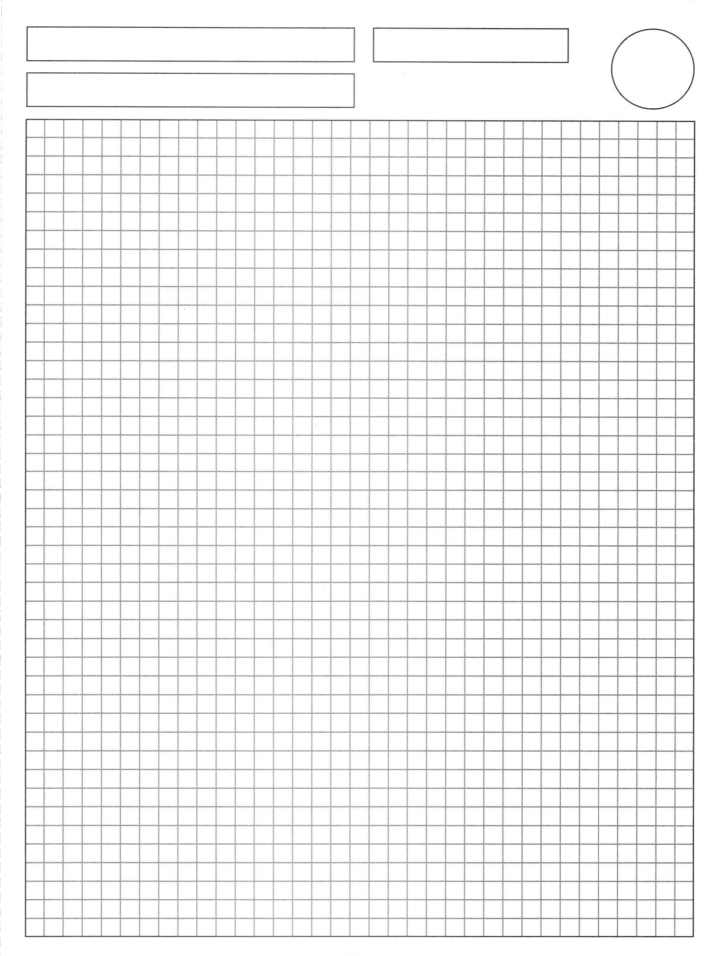

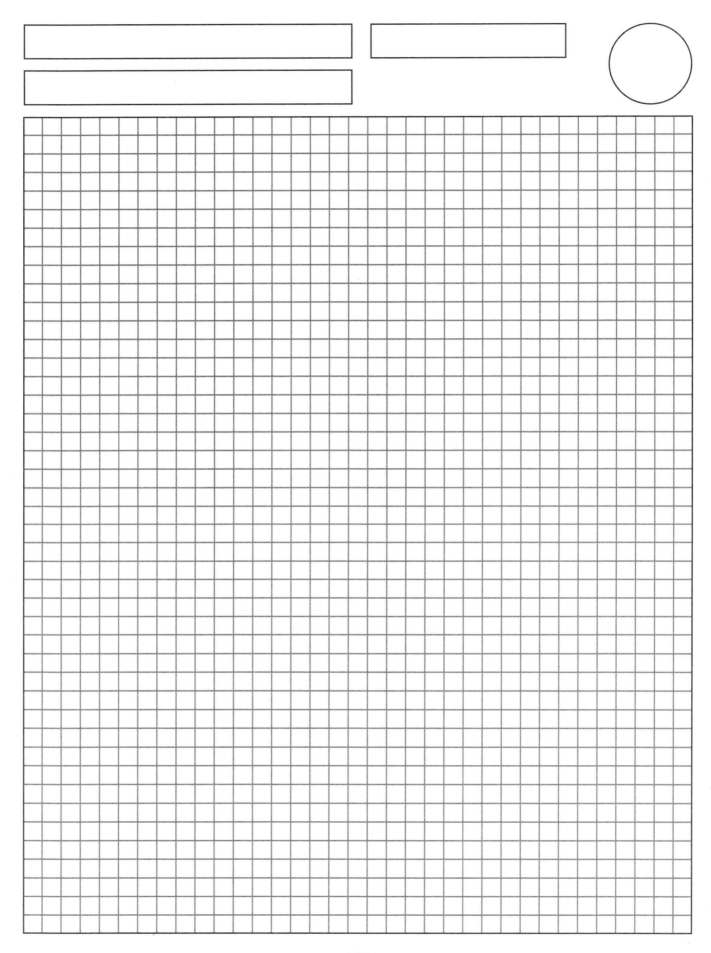

SECTOR 4

CRITICAL AREAS (CAR)

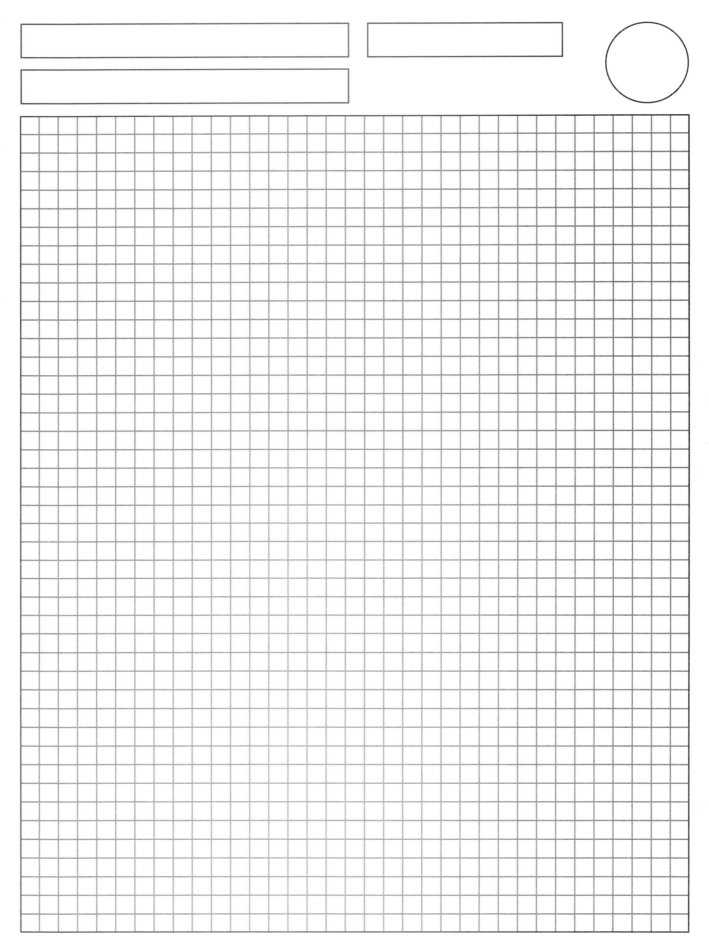

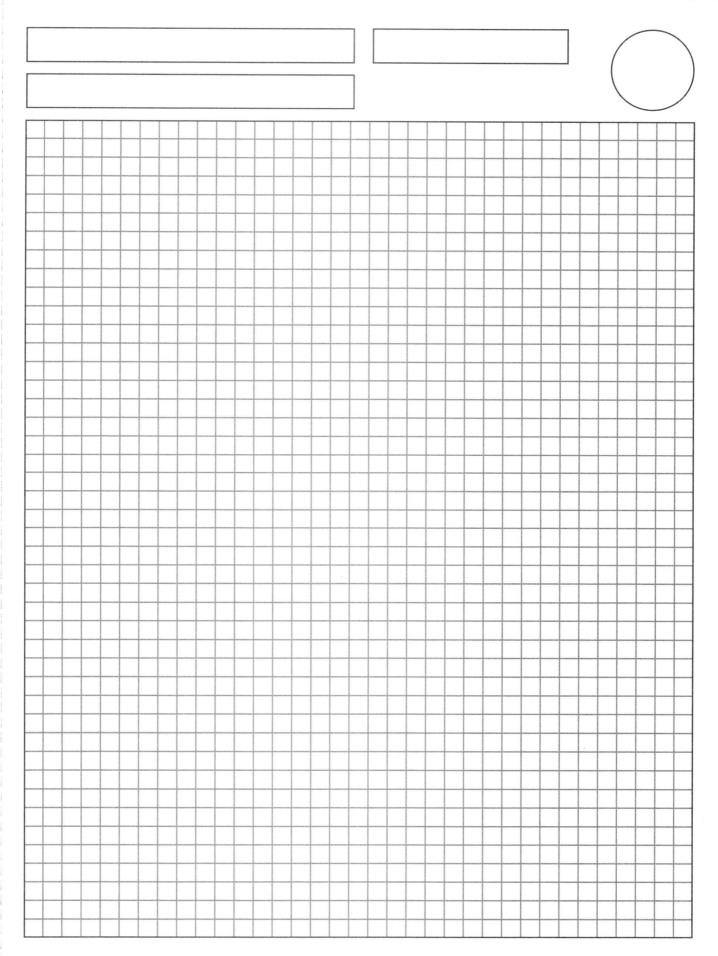

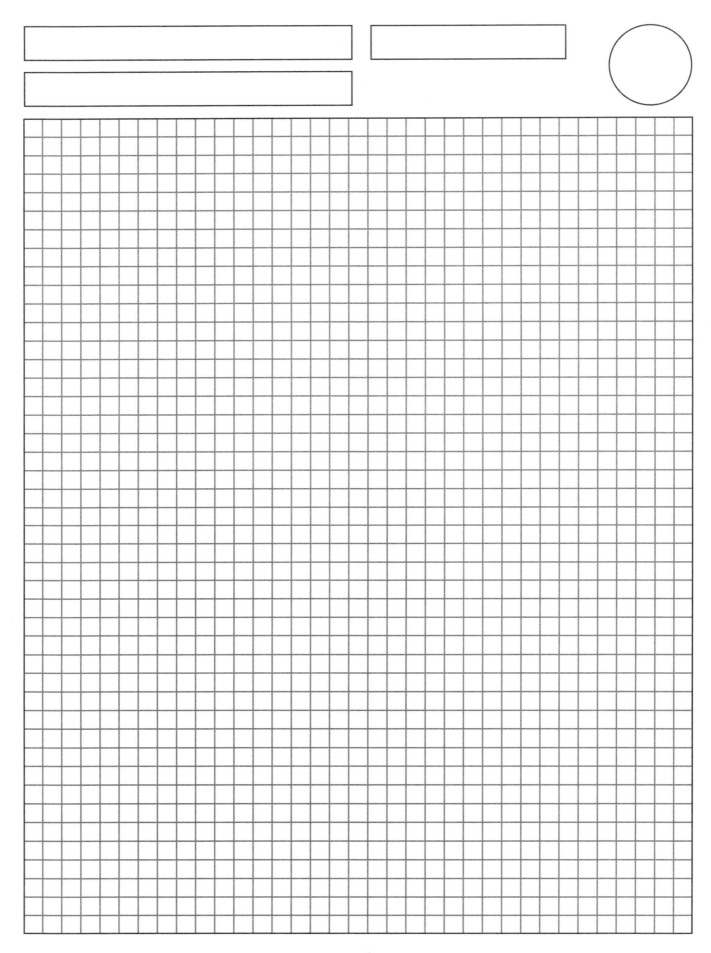

SECTOR 4

CRITICAL TIMES (CT)

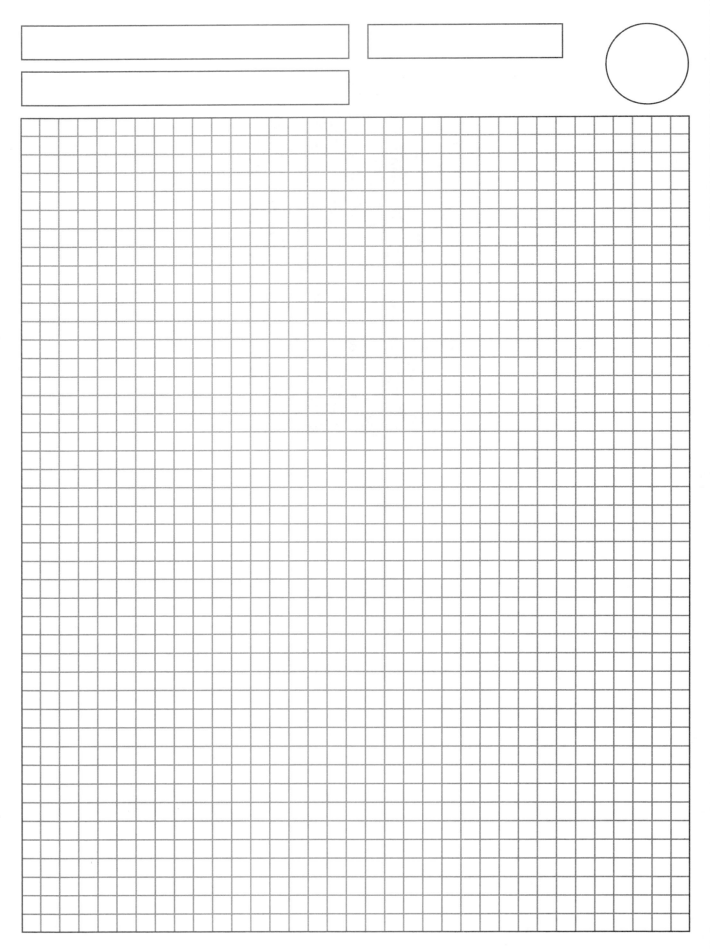

SECTOR 4

VULNERABILITIES

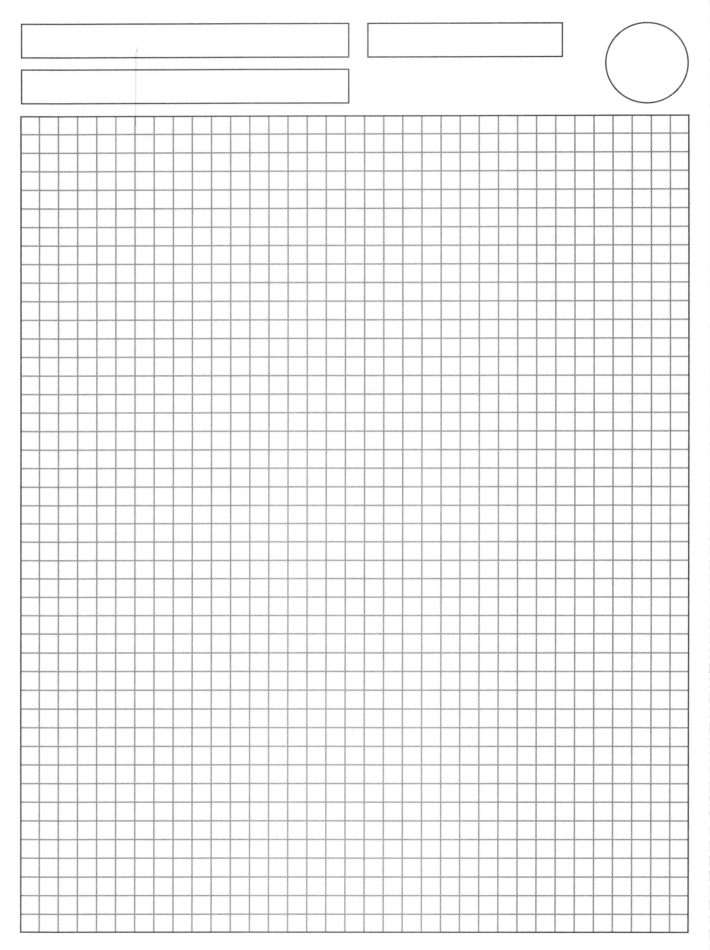

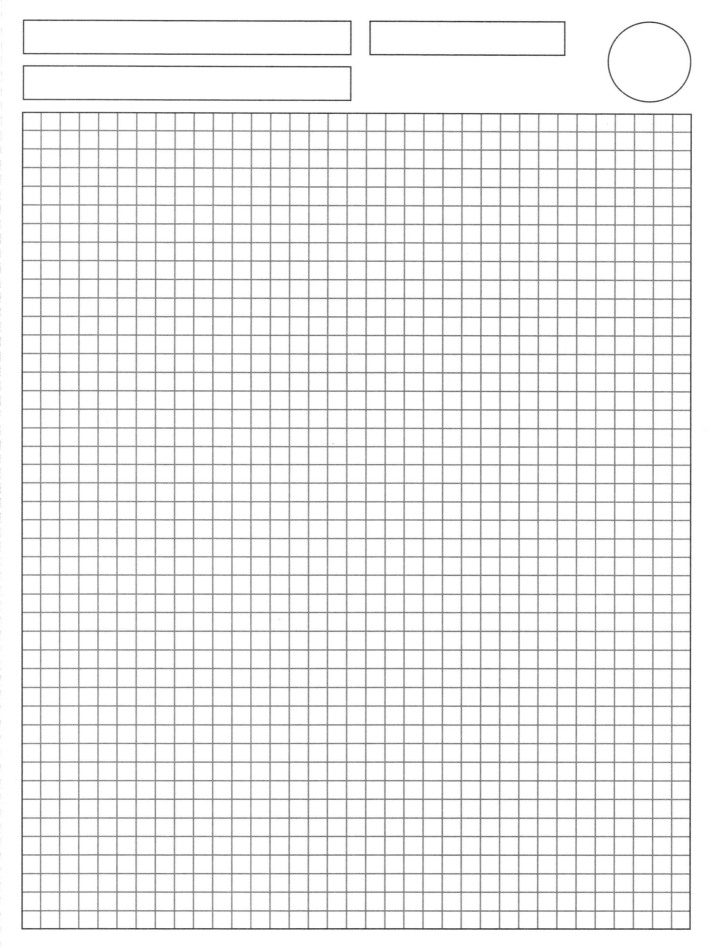

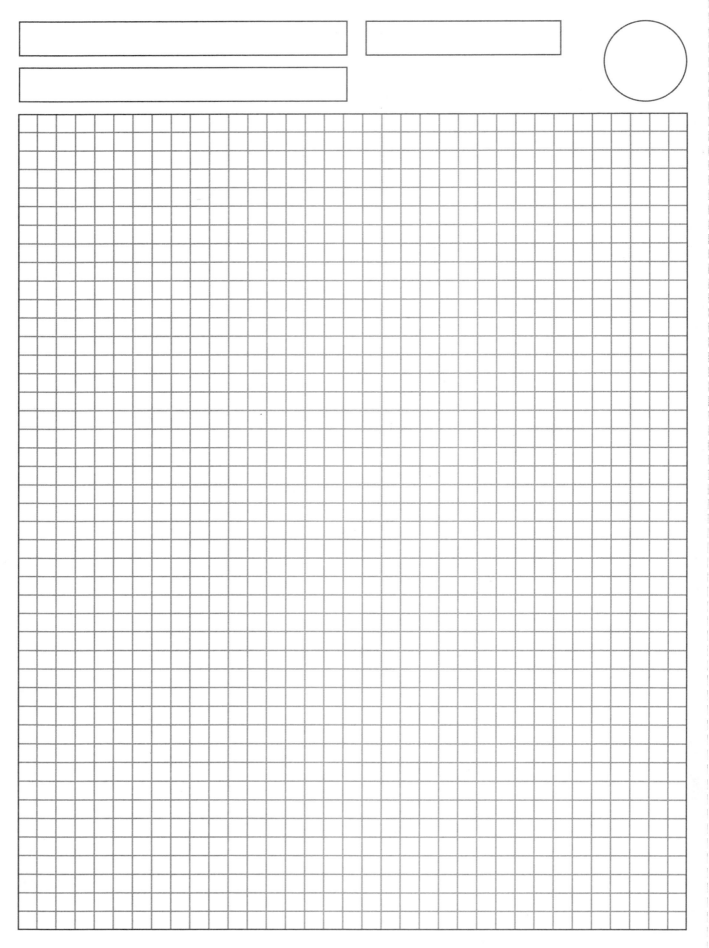

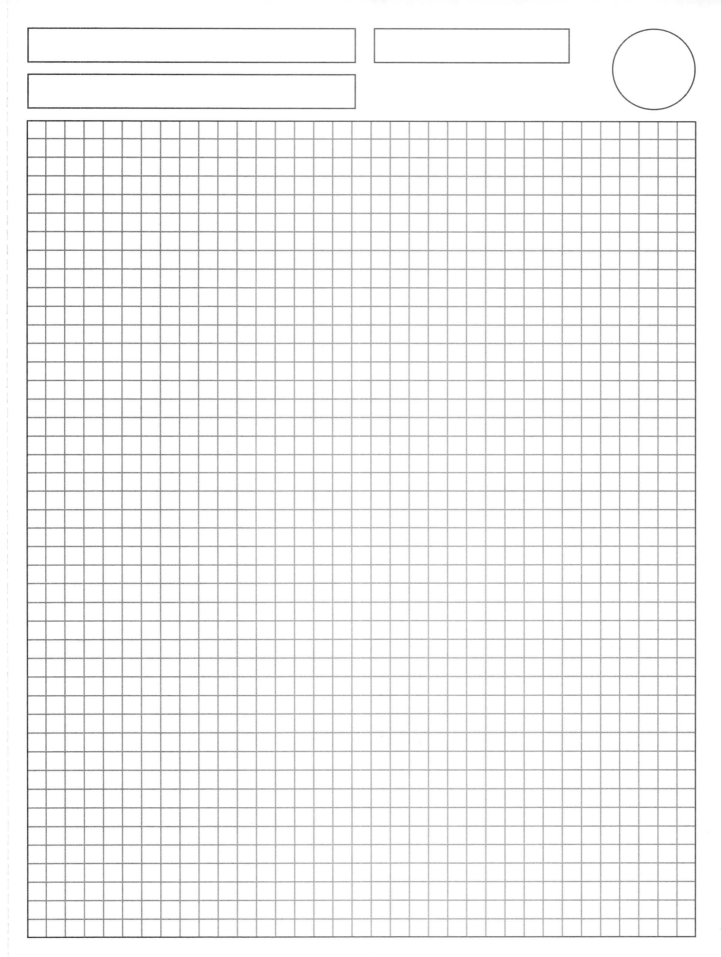

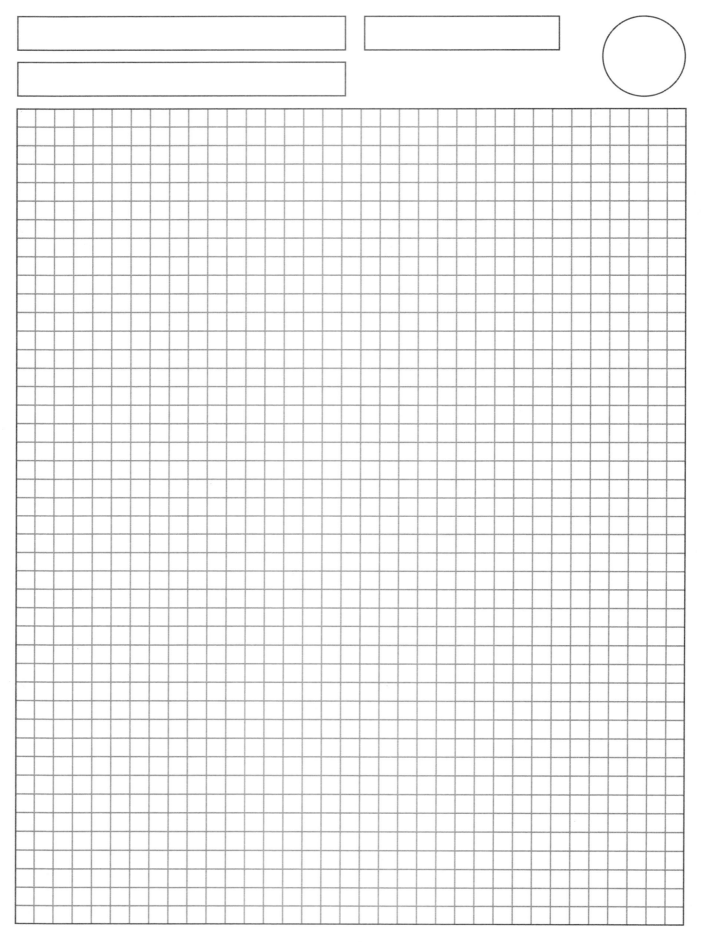

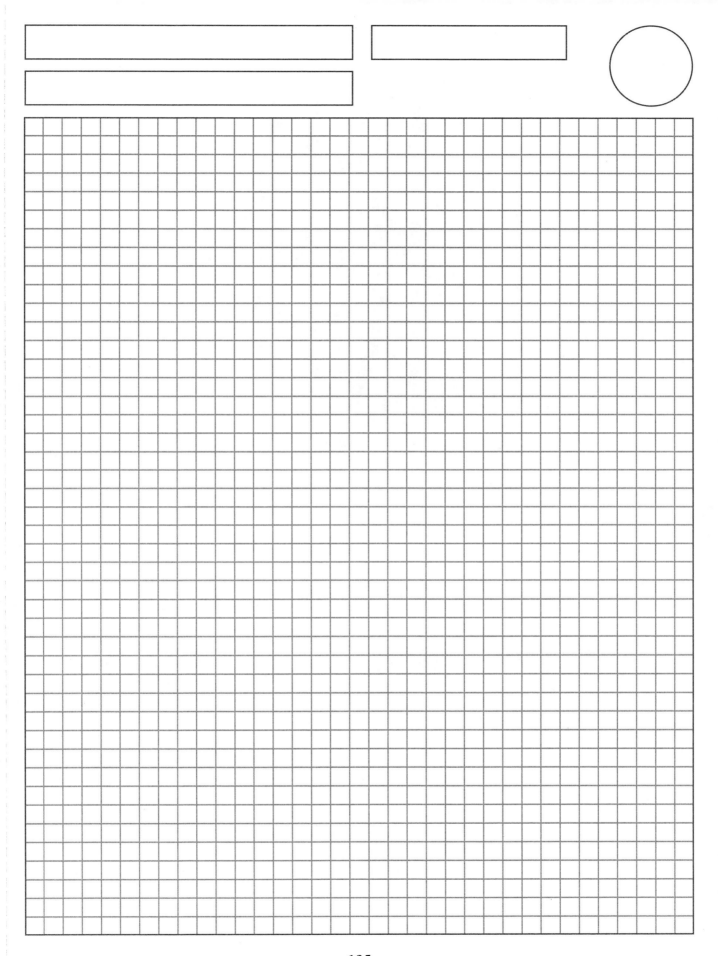

SECTOR 4

AVENUES OF APPROACH (AVP)

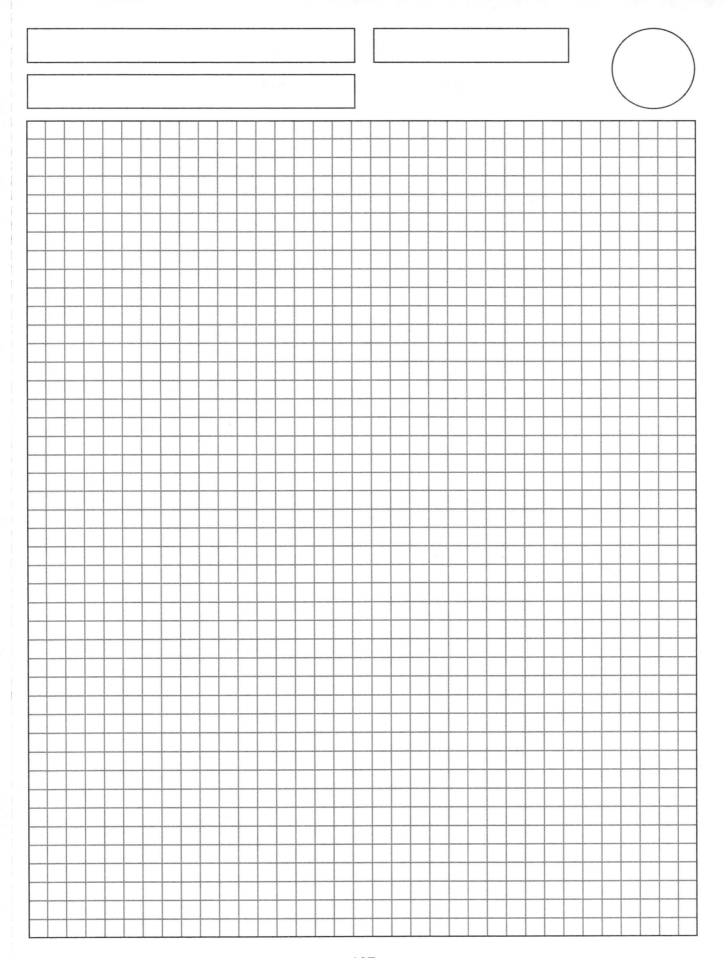

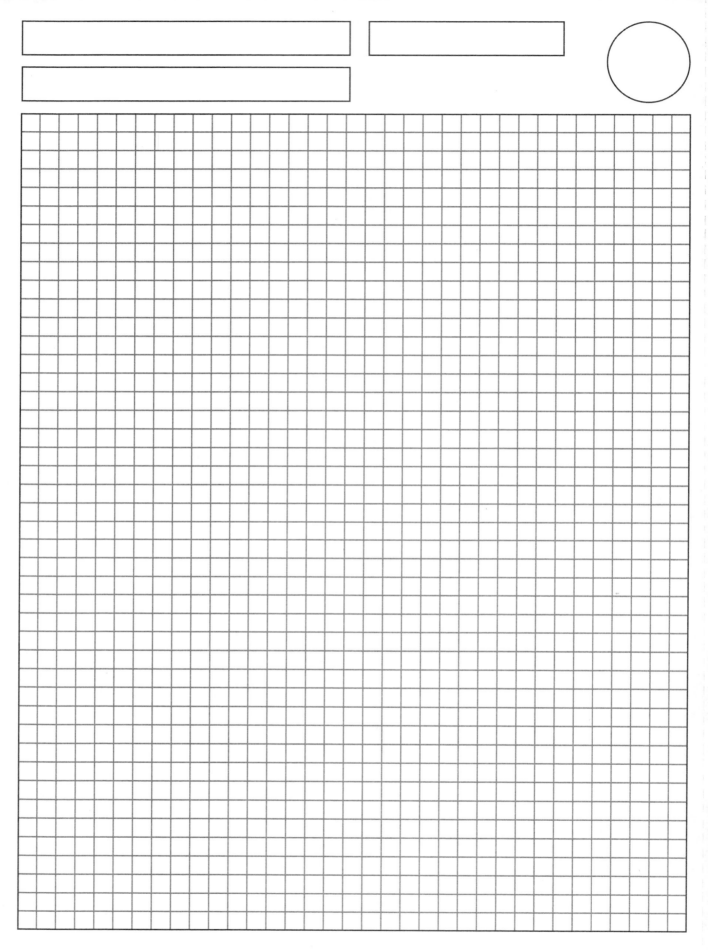

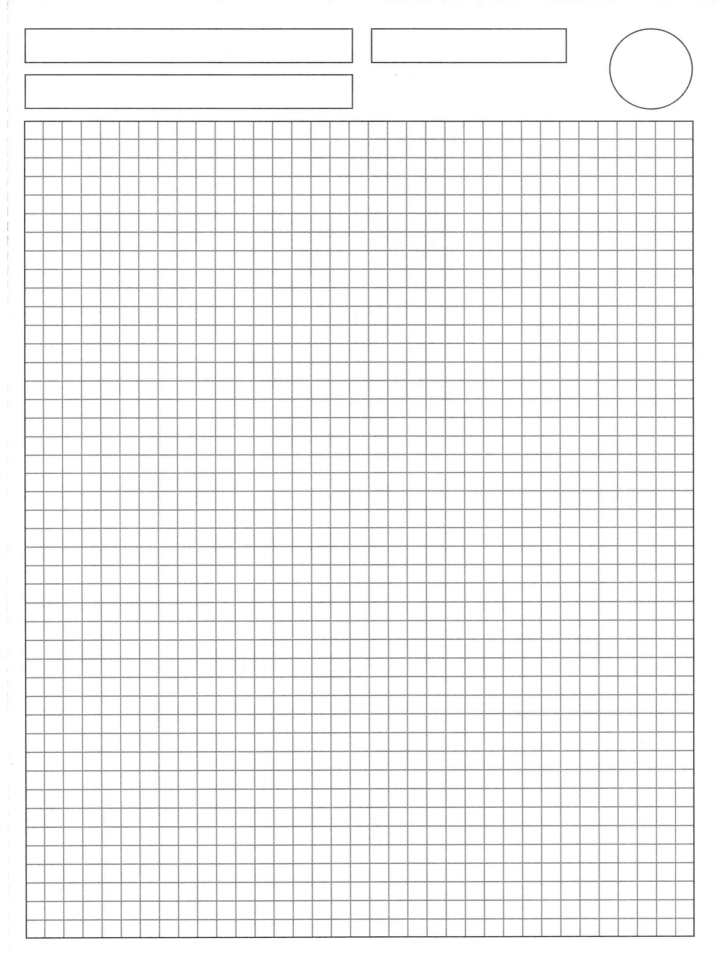

SECTOR 4

TARGET EQUATION

TARGET EQUATION WORKSHEET

Sector:	Date:

Type of attack:	Time of attack:

Avenues of Approach:

Vulnerabilities:

Type of attack:	Time of attack:

Avenues of Approach:

Vulnerabilities:

Type of attack:	Time of attack:

Avenues of Approach:

Vulnerabilities:

TARGET EQUATION WORKSHEET

Sector:

Date:

Type of attack:

Time of attack:

Avenues of Approach:

Vulnerabilities:

Type of attack:

Time of attack:

Avenues of Approach:

Vulnerabilities:

Type of attack:

Time of attack:

Avenues of Approach:

Vulnerabilities:

TARGET EQUATION WORKSHEET

Sector:

Date:

Type of attack:

Time of attack:

Avenues of Approach:

Vulnerabilities:

Type of attack:

Time of attack:

Avenues of Approach:

Vulnerabilities:

Type of attack:

Time of attack:

Avenues of Approach:

Vulnerabilities:

TARGET EQUATION WORKSHEET

Sector:

Date:

Type of attack:

Time of attack:

Avenues of Approach:

Vulnerabilities:

Type of attack:

Time of attack:

Avenues of Approach:

Vulnerabilities:

Type of attack:

Time of attack:

Avenues of Approach:

Vulnerabilities:

TARGET EQUATION WORKSHEET

Sector:

Date:

Type of attack:

Time of attack:

Avenues of Approach:

Vulnerabilities:

Type of attack:

Time of attack:

Avenues of Approach:

Vulnerabilities:

Type of attack:

Time of attack:

Avenues of Approach:

Vulnerabilities:

S5

SECTOR 5

SECTOR 5

OVERVIEW

THREAT ASSESSMENT SECTOR OVERVIEW

Sector:	Date:

Prepared by:

Situation:

Sector Overview:

Note: Make sure you print out map and directions to pertinent police precincts.

Police Departments:	PD Contact Information:	PD Response Times:

Crime Level:	Possible Threat Level:

Known Terror Threats:

Known Criminal Threats:

Note: Make sure you print out map and directions to all trauma centers. Always make the effort to proceed to a level 1 trauma center if the injury is life threatening.

Trauma Centers:	Trauma Center Level (I, II, III):	Response Times:

Weather Conditions:			
Spring	Summer	Fall	Winter

SECTOR 5

CRITICAL ASSETS (CA)

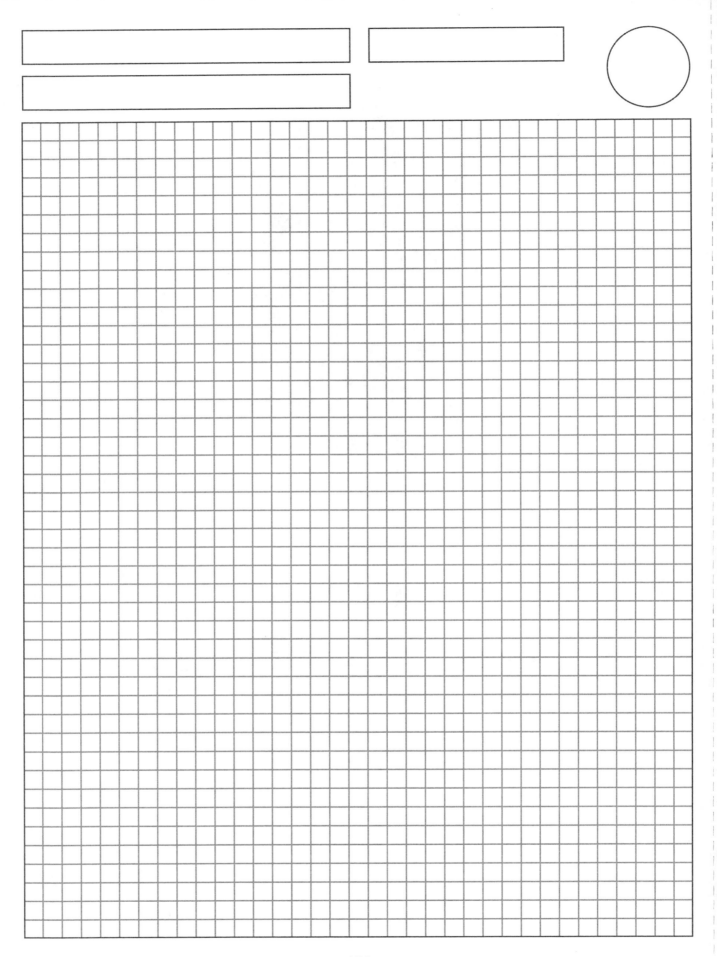

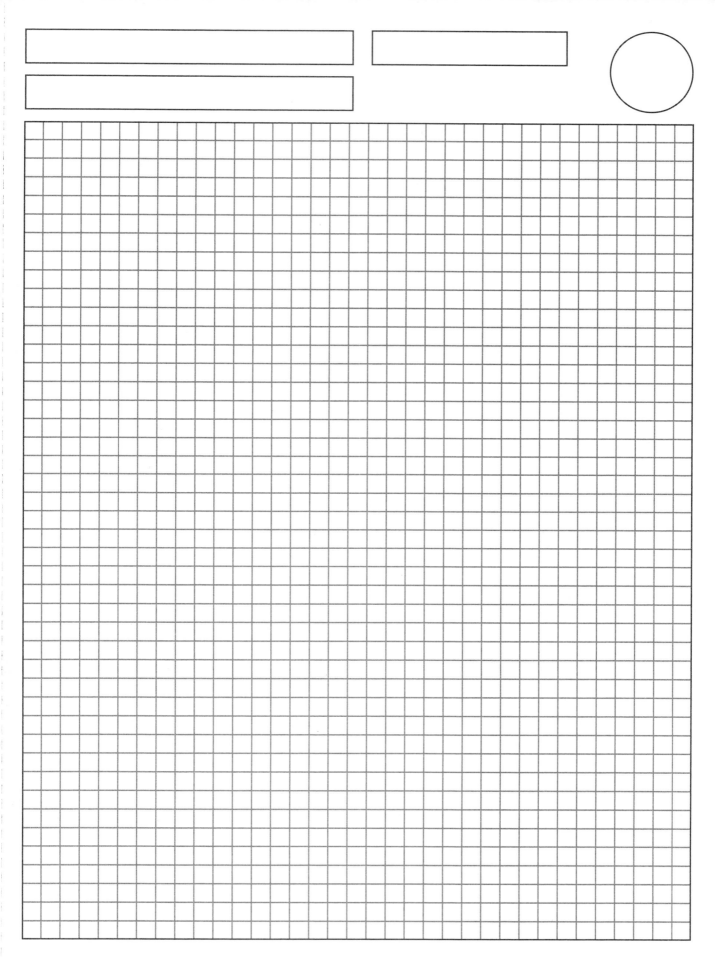

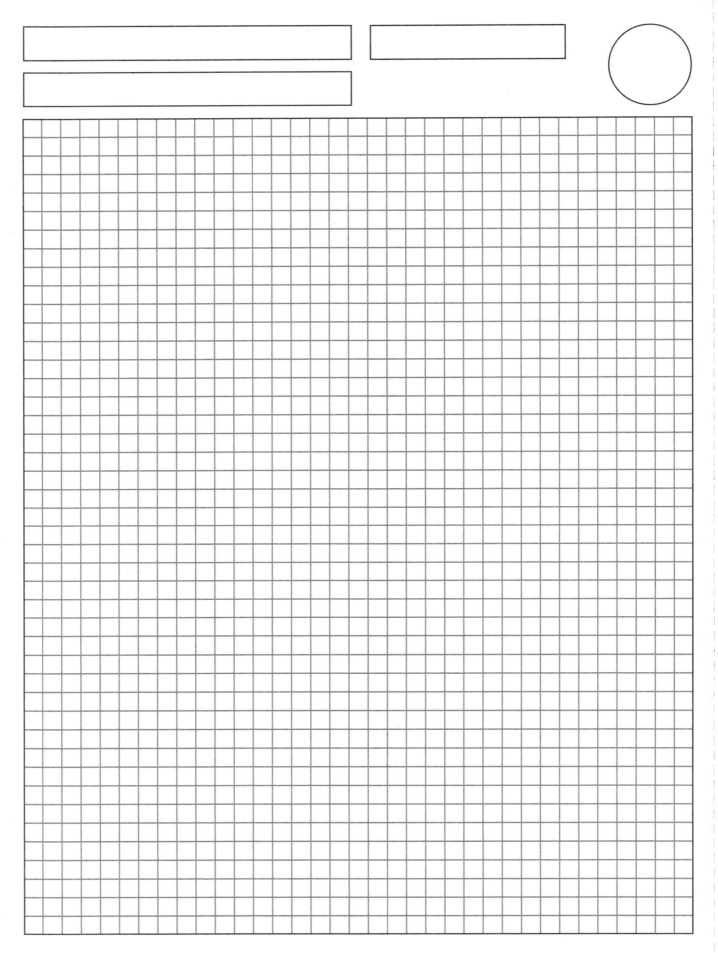

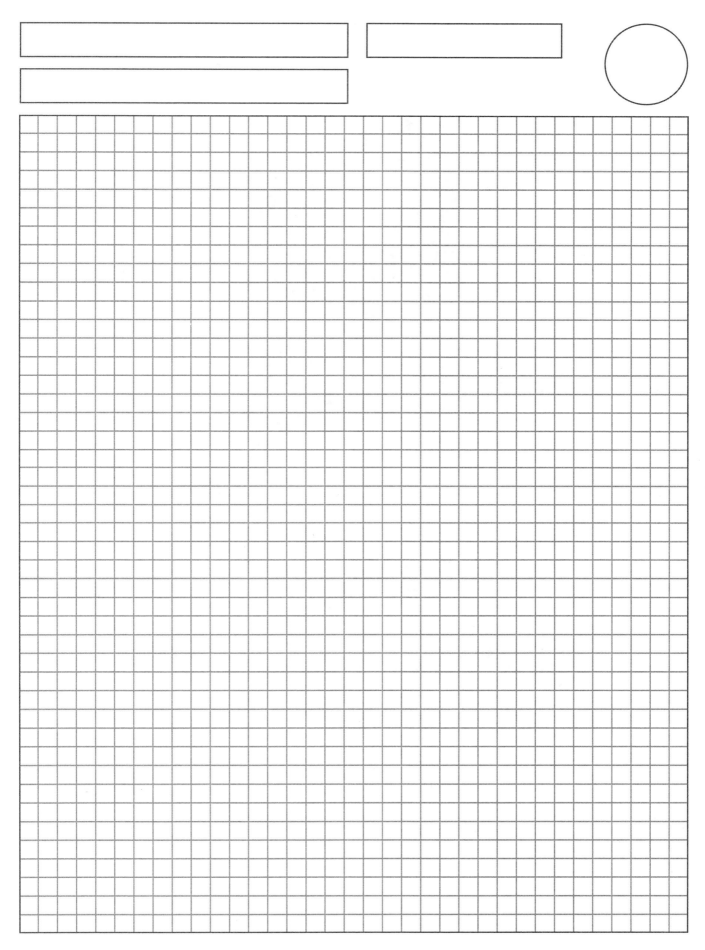

SECTOR 5

CRITICAL AREAS (CAR)

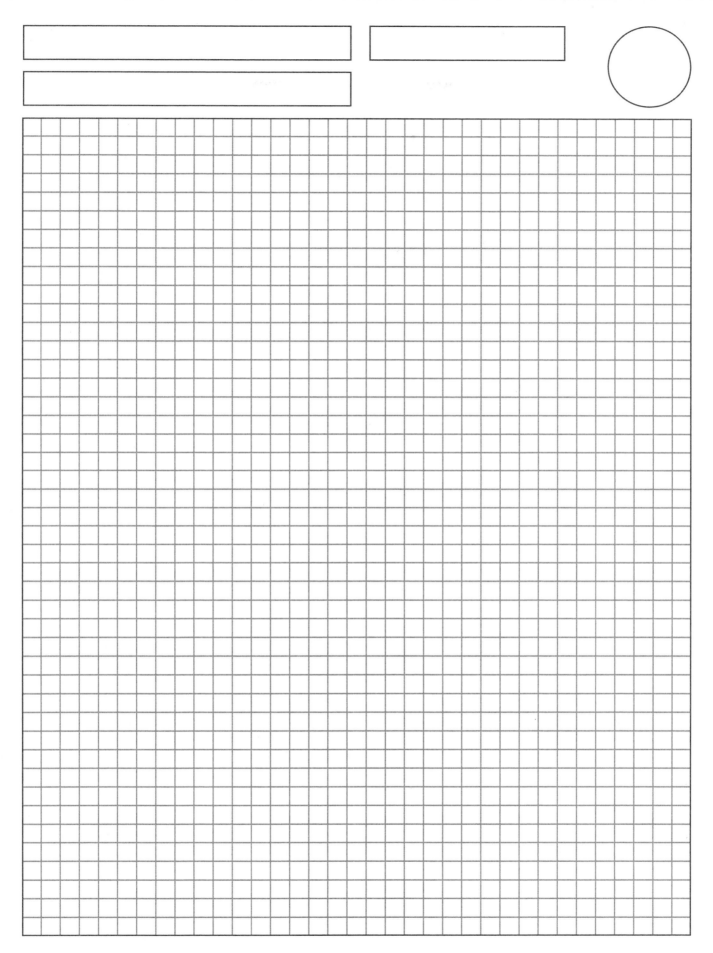

155

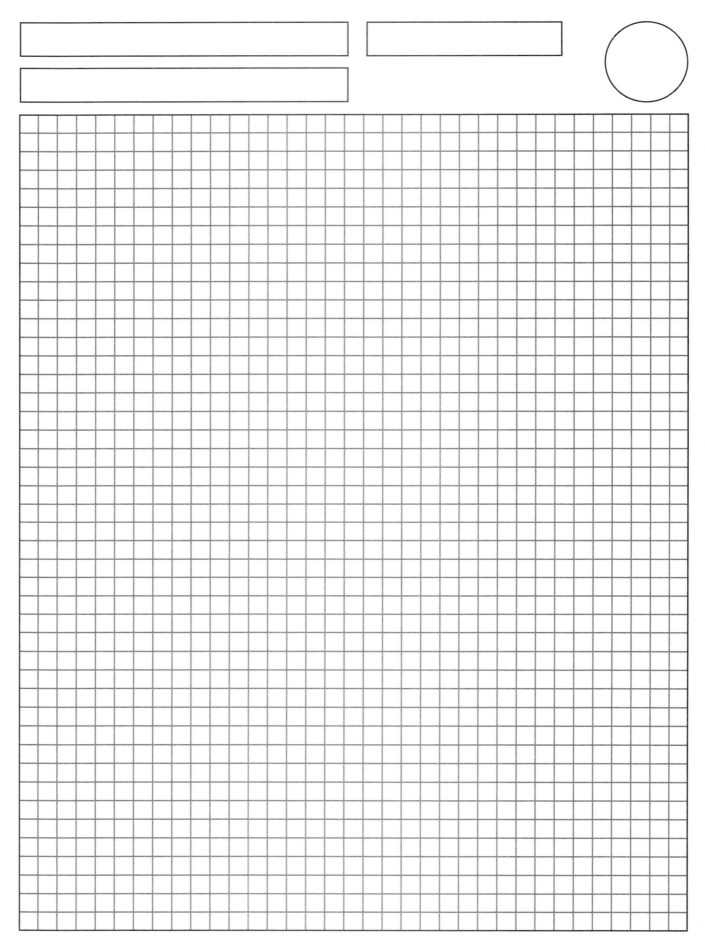

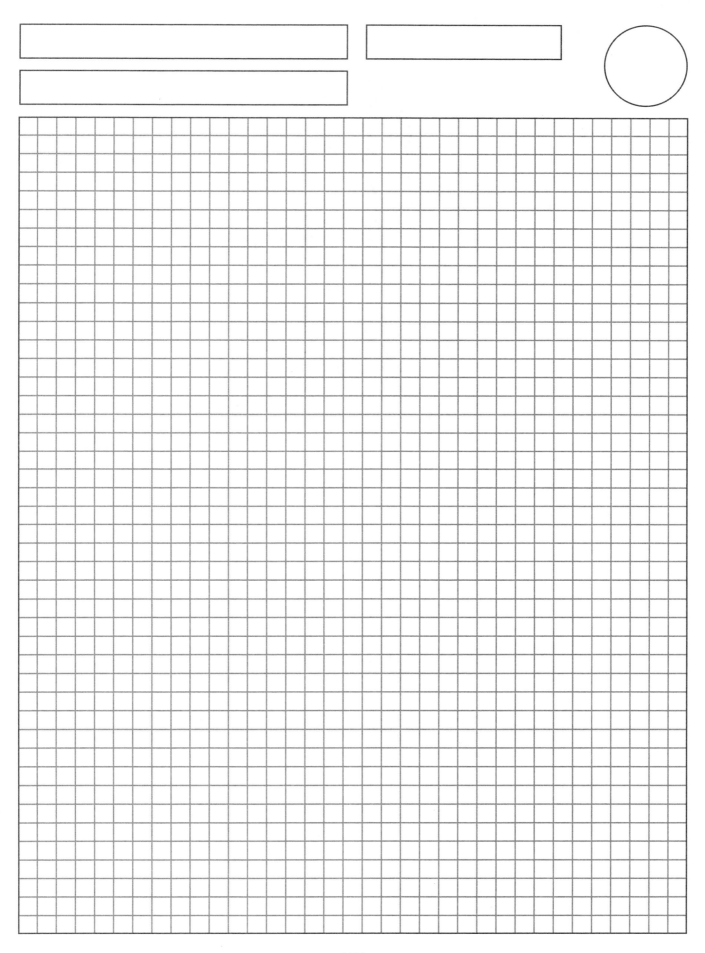

SECTOR 5

CRITICAL TIMES (CT)

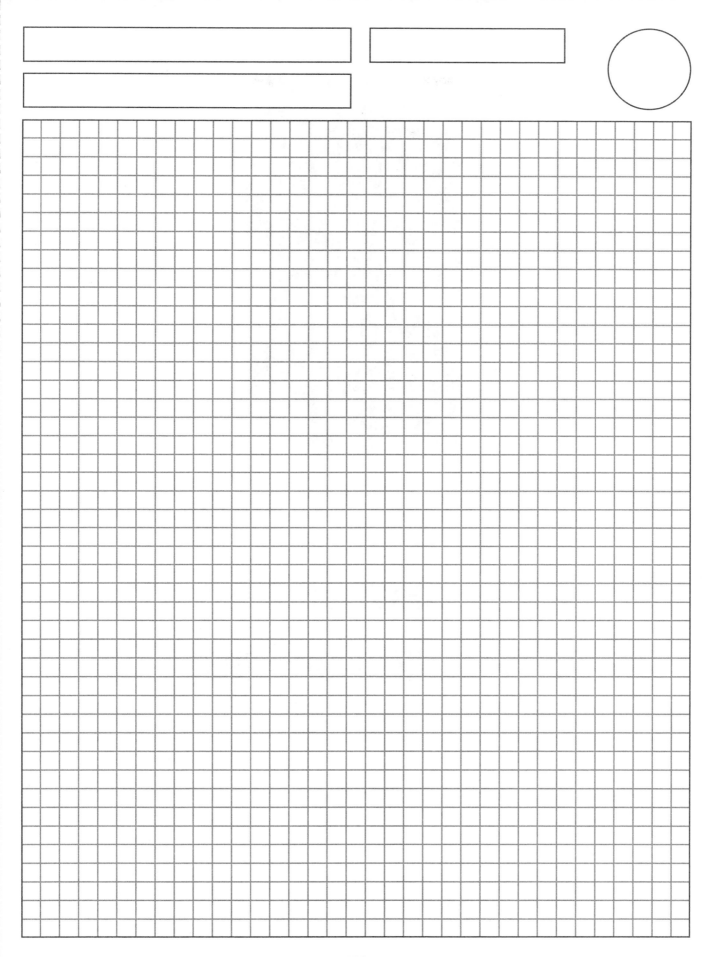

SECTOR 5

VULNERABILITIES

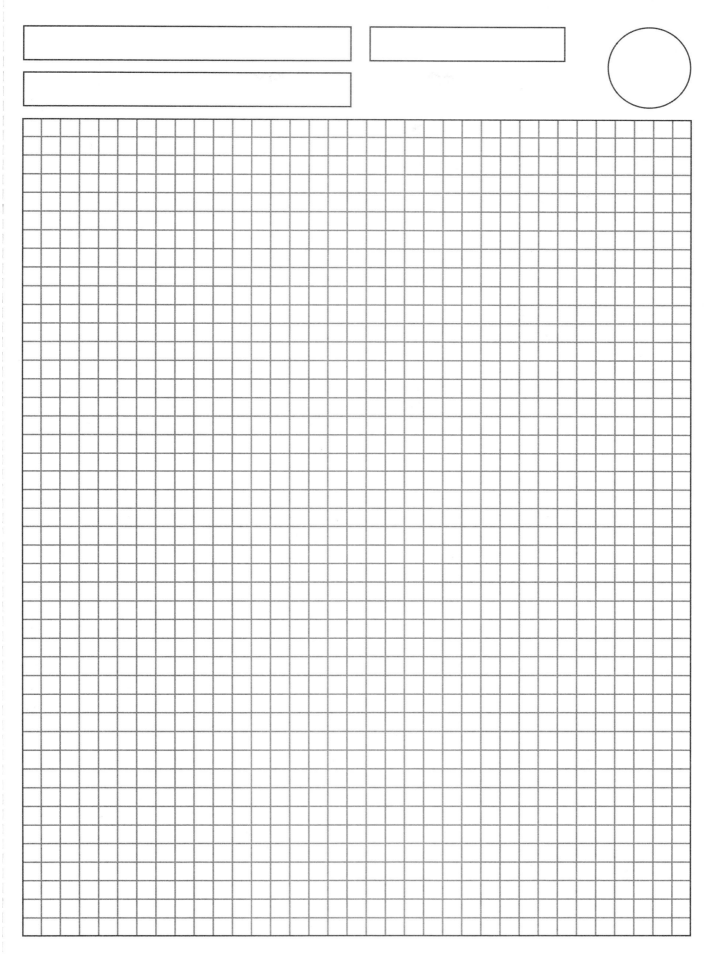

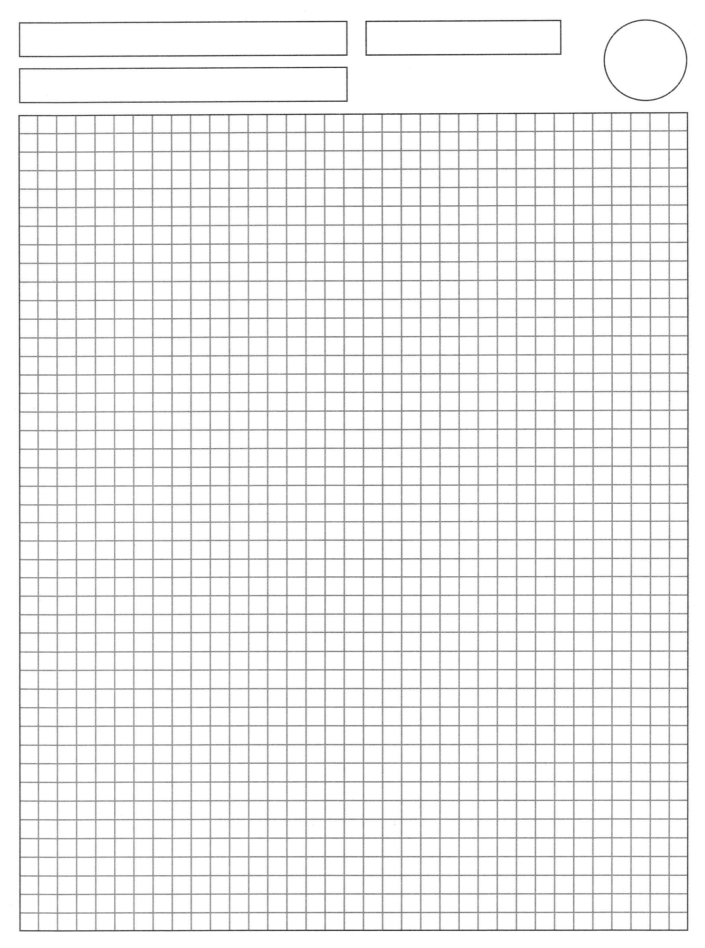

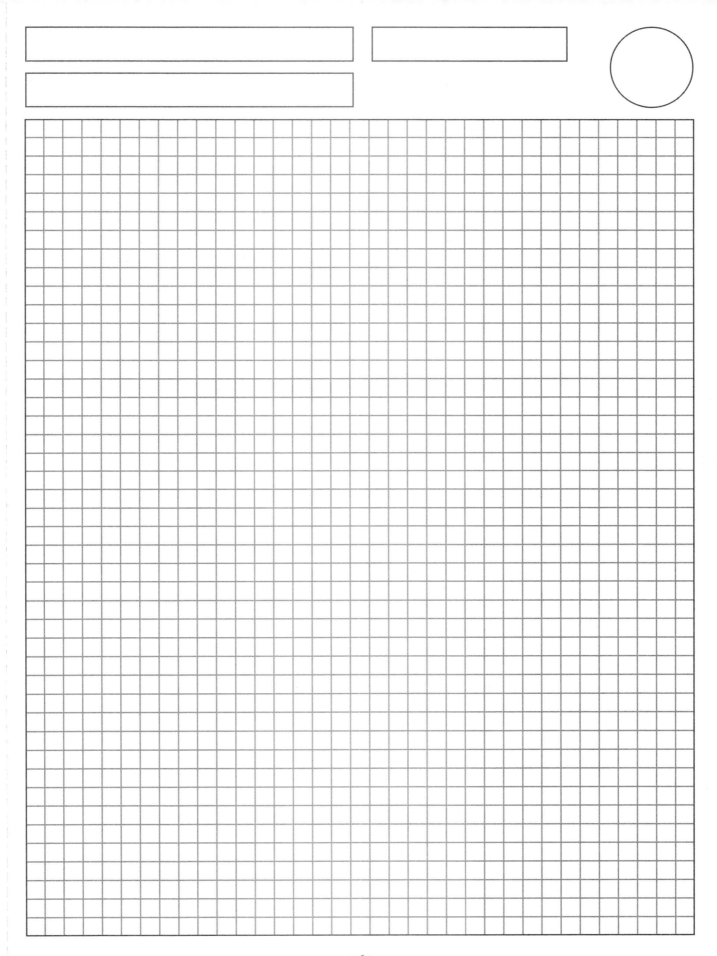

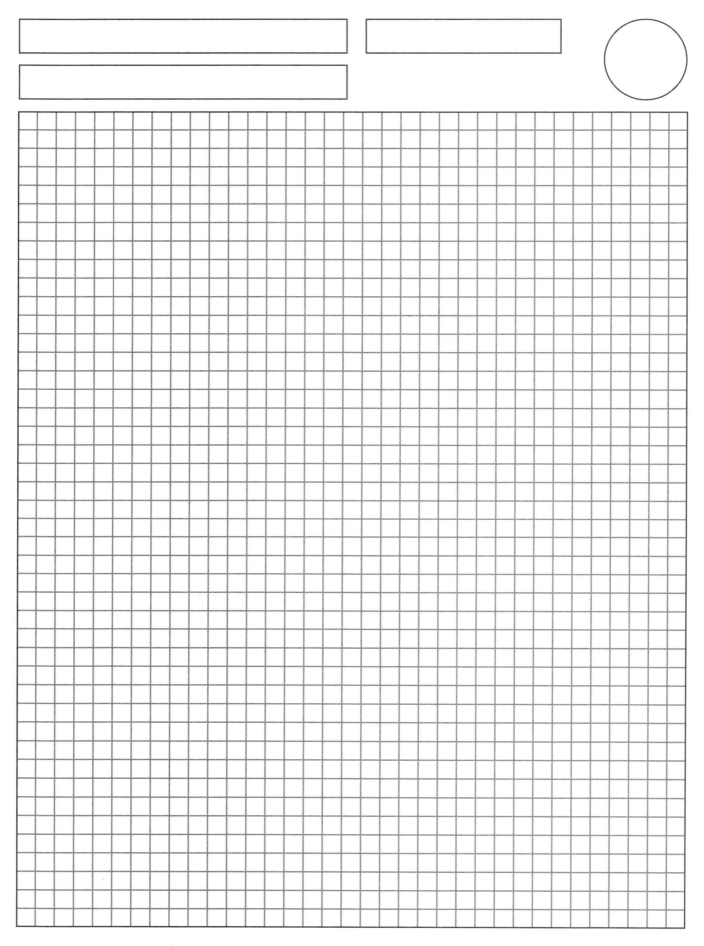

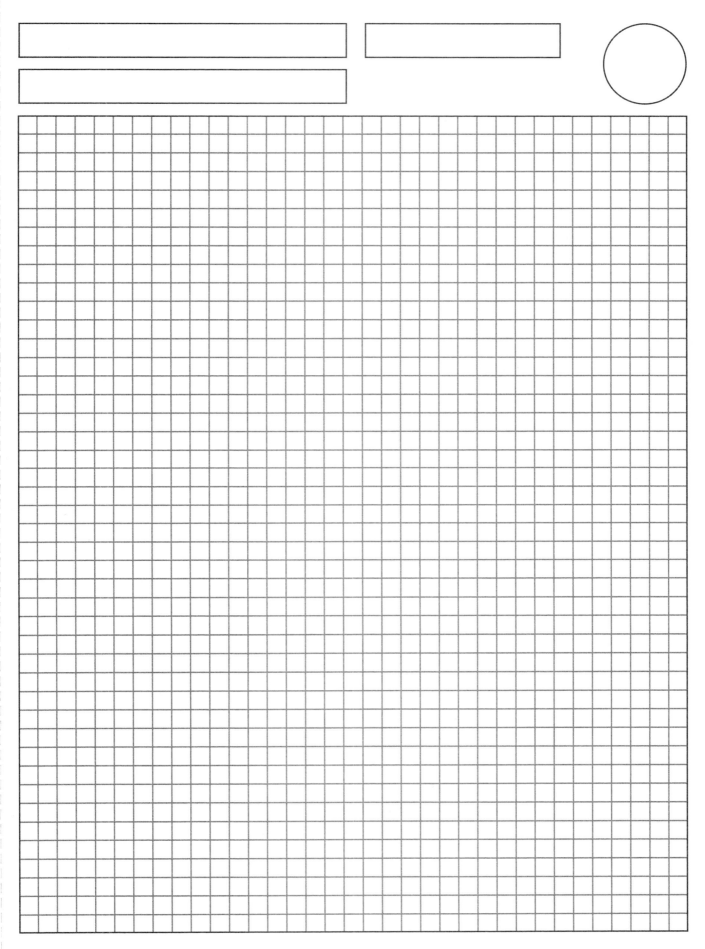

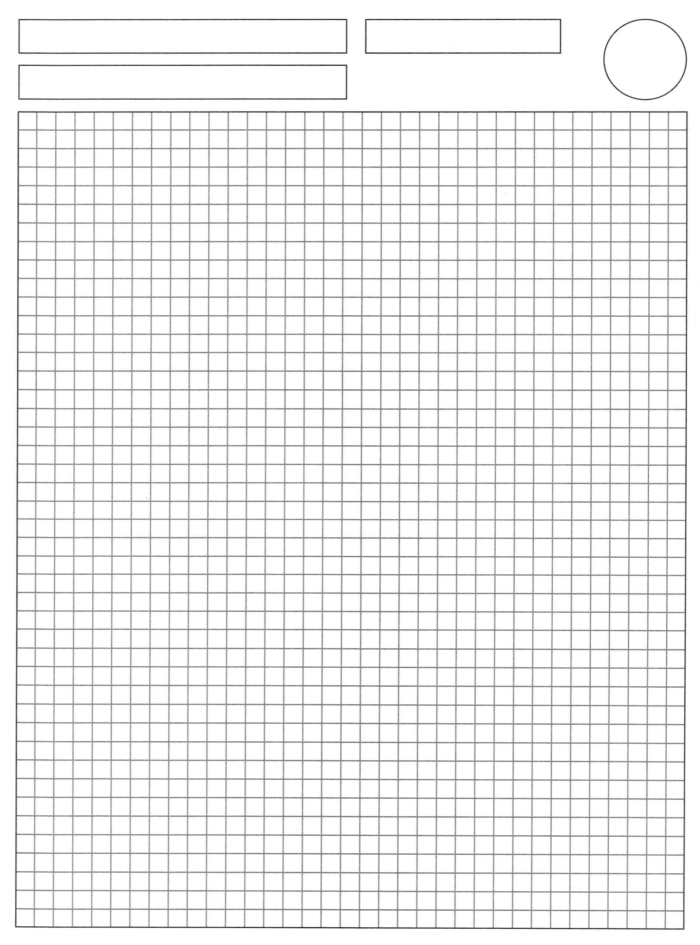

SECTOR 5

AVENUES OF APPROACH (AVP)

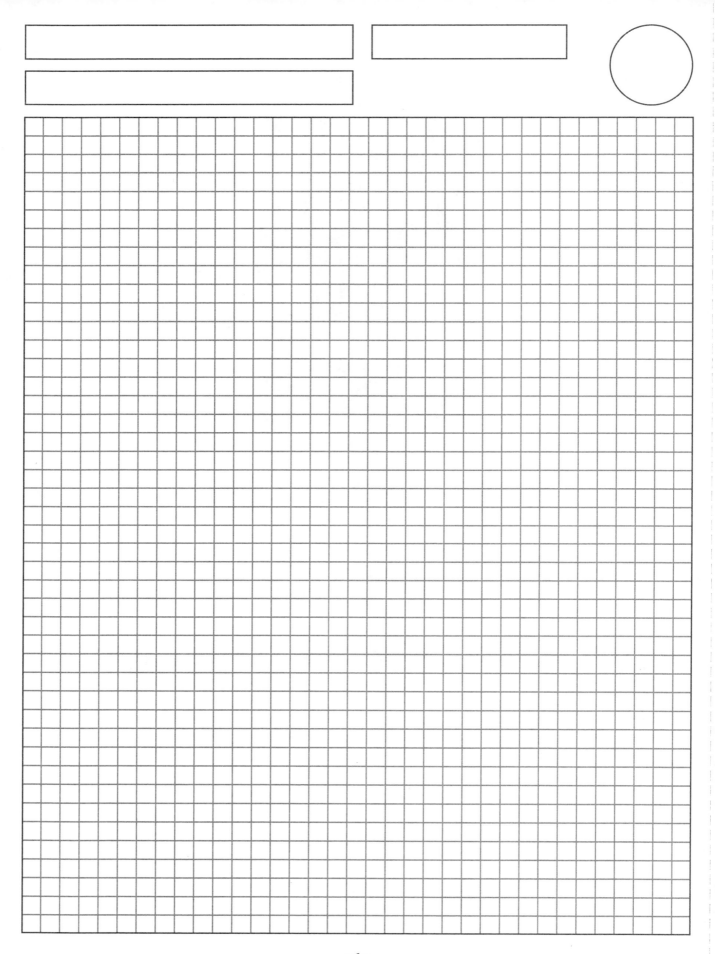

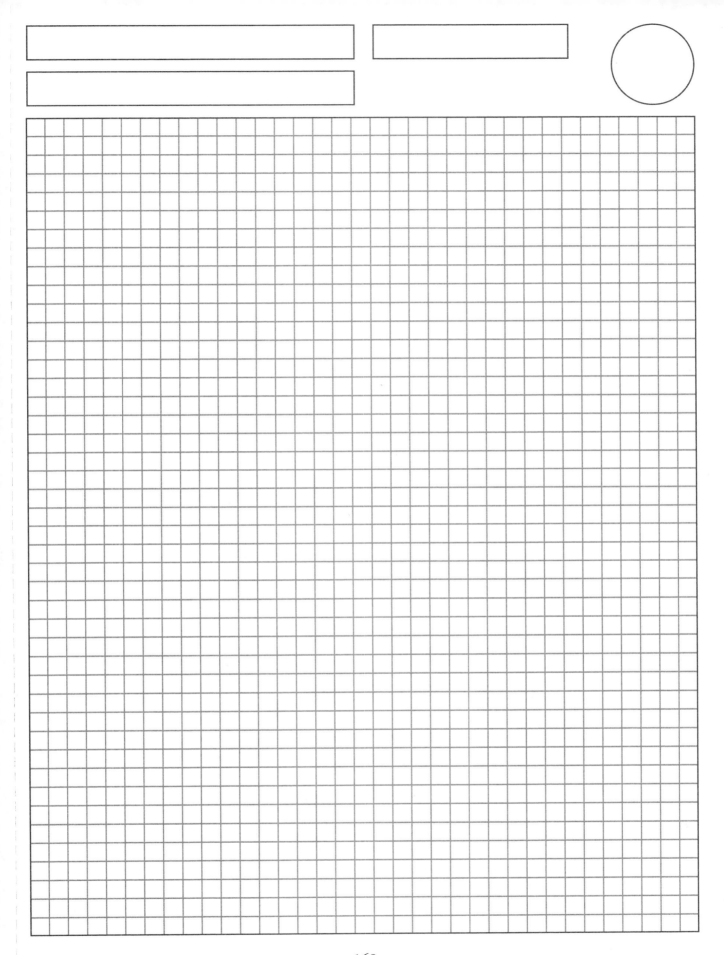

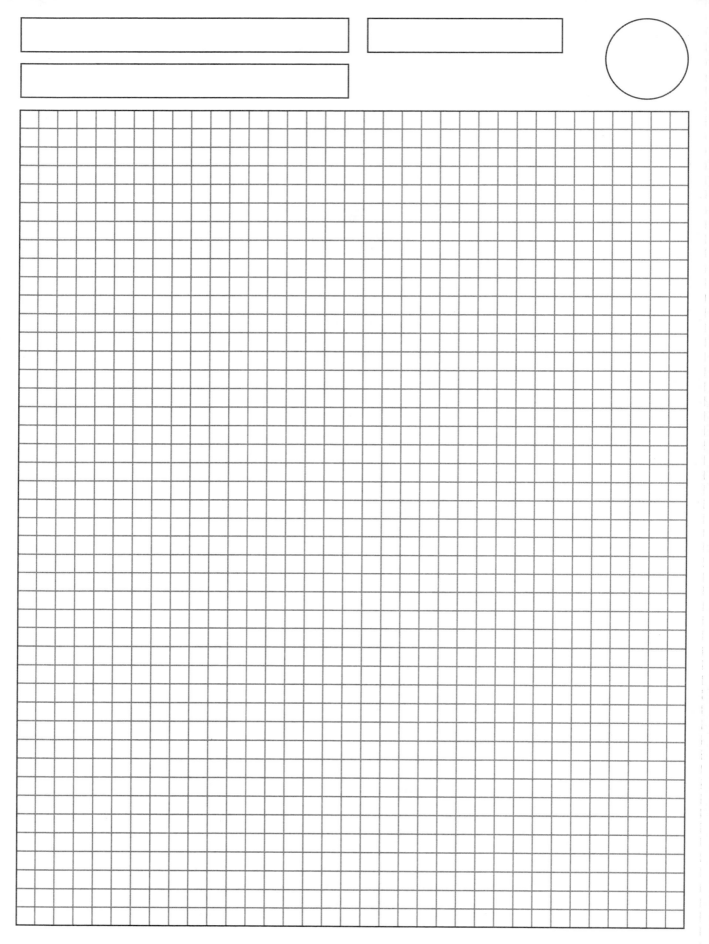

SECTOR 5

TARGET EQUATION

TARGET EQUATION WORKSHEET

Sector:

Date:

Type of attack:

Time of attack:

Avenues of Approach:

Vulnerabilities:

Type of attack:

Time of attack:

Avenues of Approach:

Vulnerabilities:

Type of attack:

Time of attack:

Avenues of Approach:

Vulnerabilities:

TARGET EQUATION WORKSHEET

Sector:	Date:

Type of attack:	Time of attack:

Avenues of Approach:

Vulnerabilities:

Type of attack:	Time of attack:

Avenues of Approach:

Vulnerabilities:

Type of attack:	Time of attack:

Avenues of Approach:

Vulnerabilities:

TARGET EQUATION WORKSHEET

Sector:	Date:

Type of attack:	Time of attack:

Avenues of Approach:

Vulnerabilities:

Type of attack:	Time of attack:

Avenues of Approach:

Vulnerabilities:

Type of attack:	Time of attack:

Avenues of Approach:

Vulnerabilities:

TARGET EQUATION WORKSHEET

Sector:

Date:

Type of attack:

Time of attack:

Avenues of Approach:

Vulnerabilities:

Type of attack:

Time of attack:

Avenues of Approach:

Vulnerabilities:

Type of attack:

Time of attack:

Avenues of Approach:

Vulnerabilities:

TARGET EQUATION WORKSHEET

Sector:	Date:

Type of attack:	Time of attack:

Avenues of Approach:

Vulnerabilities:

Type of attack:	Time of attack:

Avenues of Approach:

Vulnerabilities:

Type of attack:	Time of attack:

Avenues of Approach:

Vulnerabilities:

S6

SECTOR 6

SECTOR 6

OVERVIEW

THREAT ASSESSMENT SECTOR OVERVIEW

Sector:

Date:

Prepared by:

Situation:

Sector Overview:

Note: Make sure you print out map and directions to pertinent police precincts.

Police Departments:

PD Contact Information:

PD Response Times:

Crime Level:

Possible Threat Level:

Known Terror Threats:

Known Criminal Threats:

Note: Make sure you print out map and directions to all trauma centers. Always make the effort to proceed to a level 1 trauma center if the injury is life threatening.

Trauma Centers:

Trauma Center Level (I, II, III):

Response Times:

Weather Conditions:

Spring   Summer   Fall   Winter

SECTOR 6

CRITICAL ASSETS (CA)

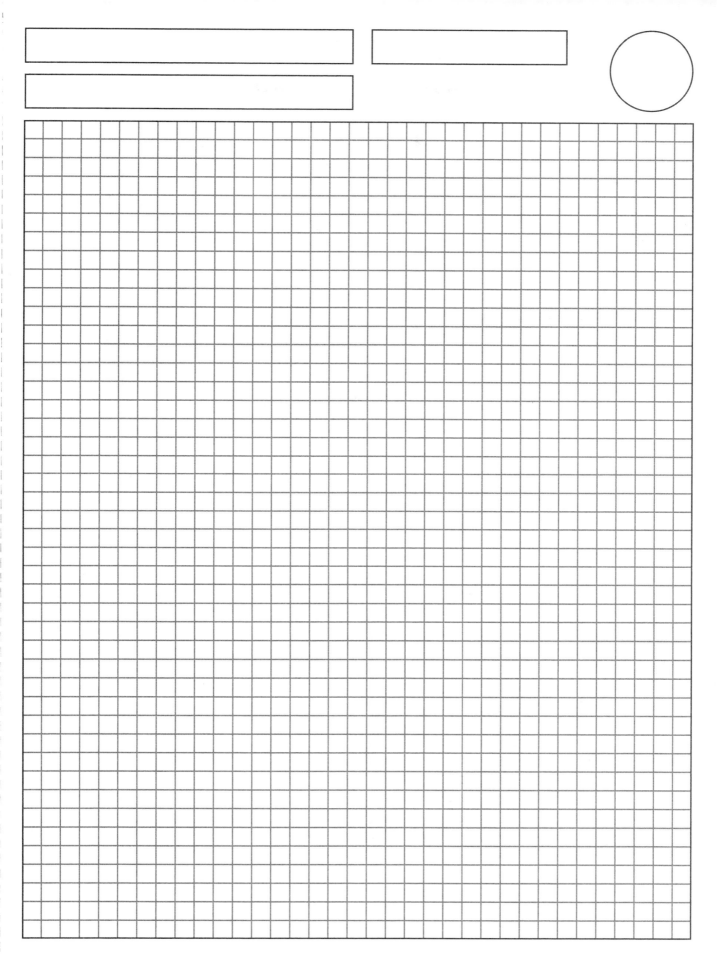

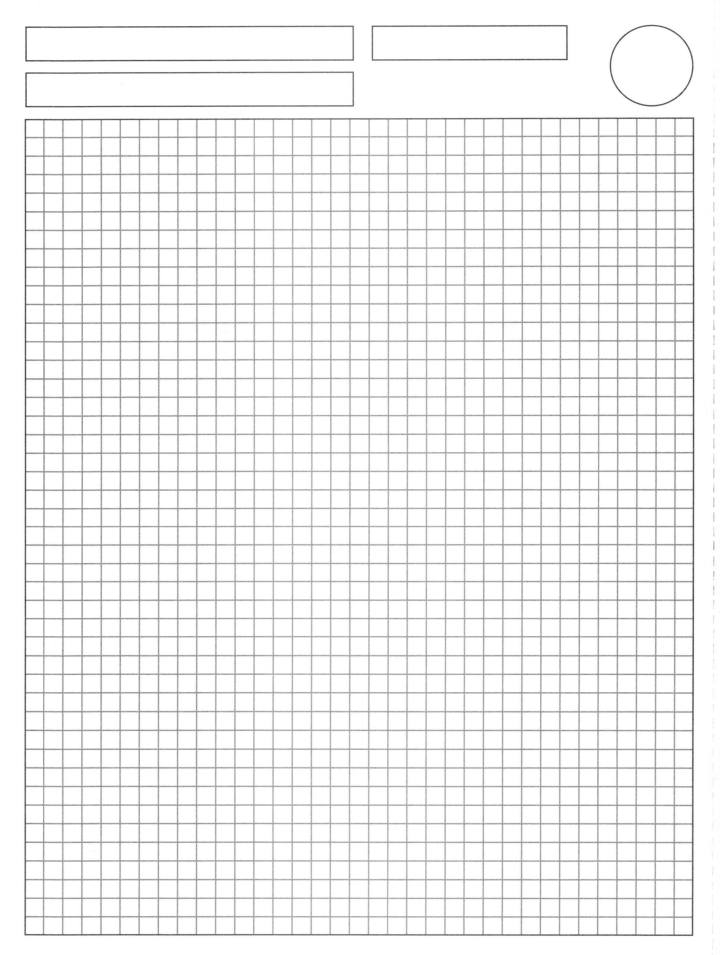

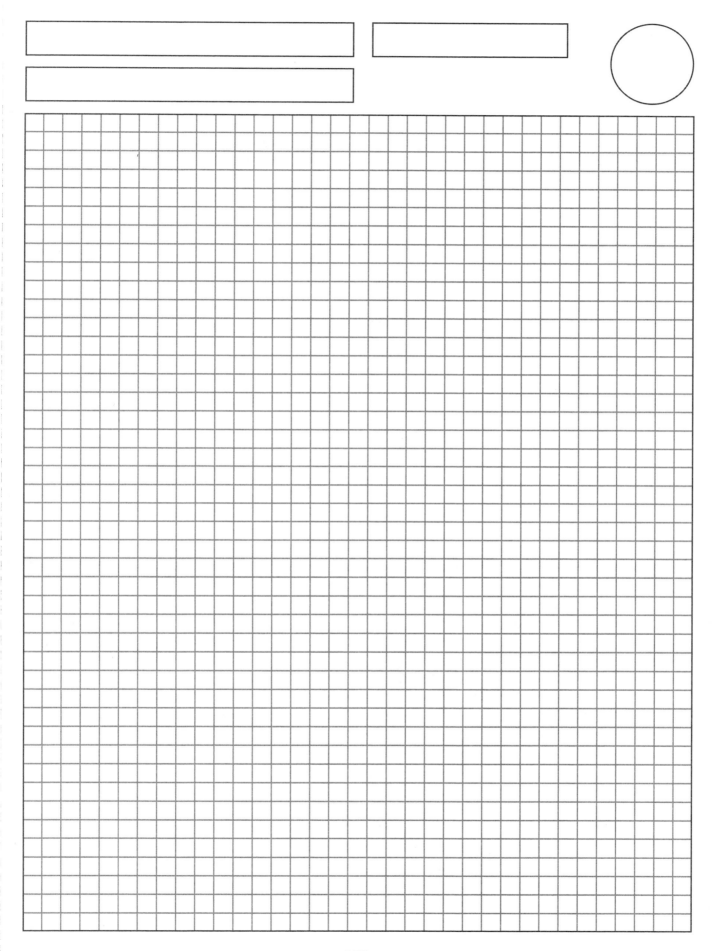

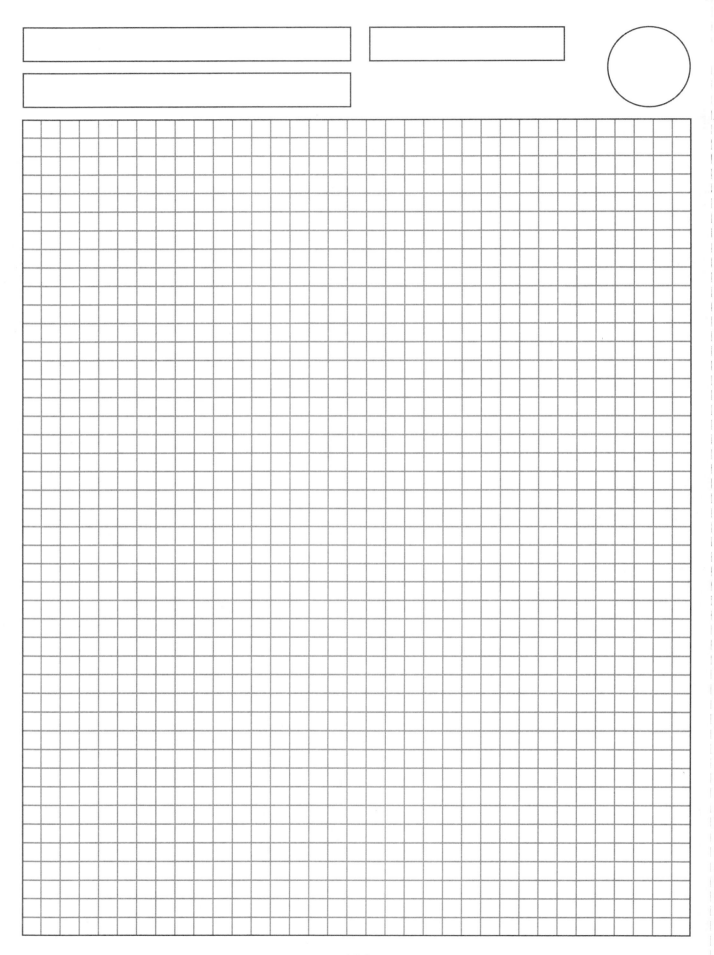

SECTOR 6

CRITICAL AREAS (CAR)

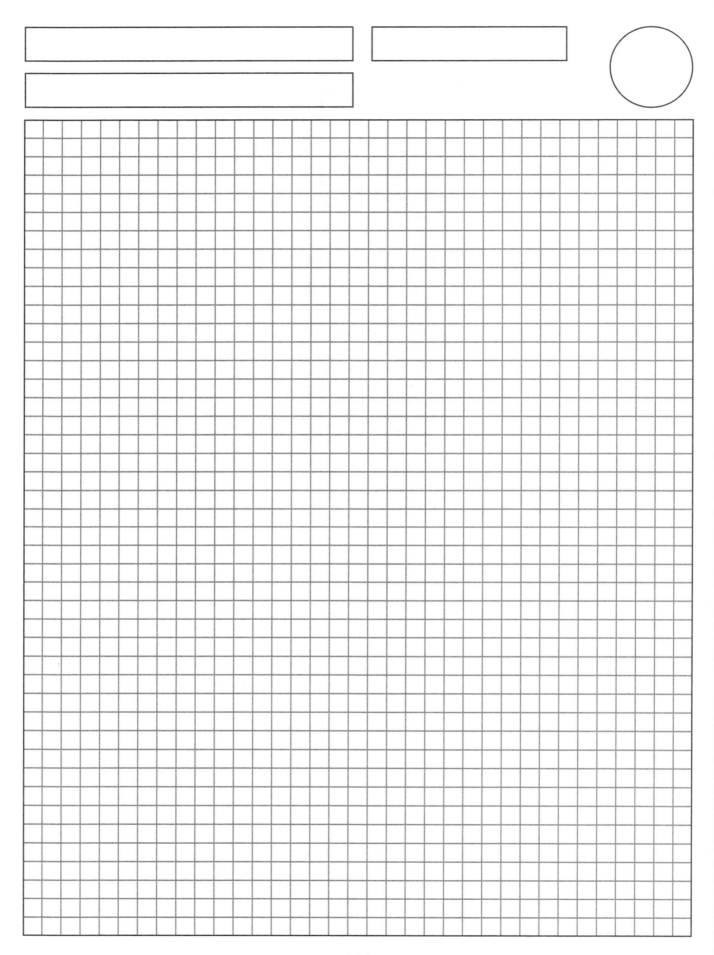

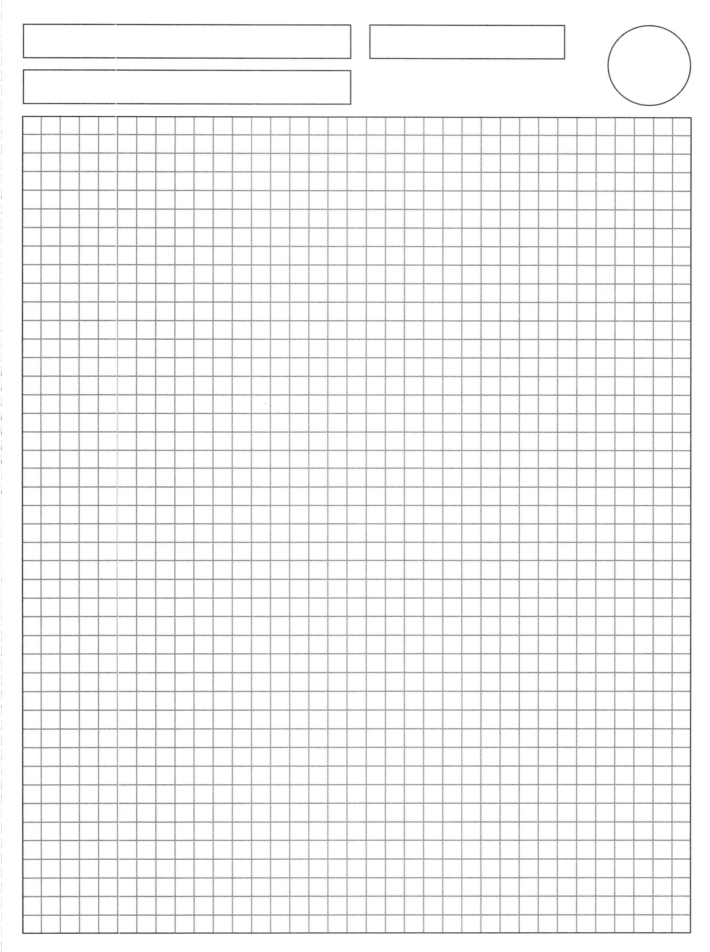

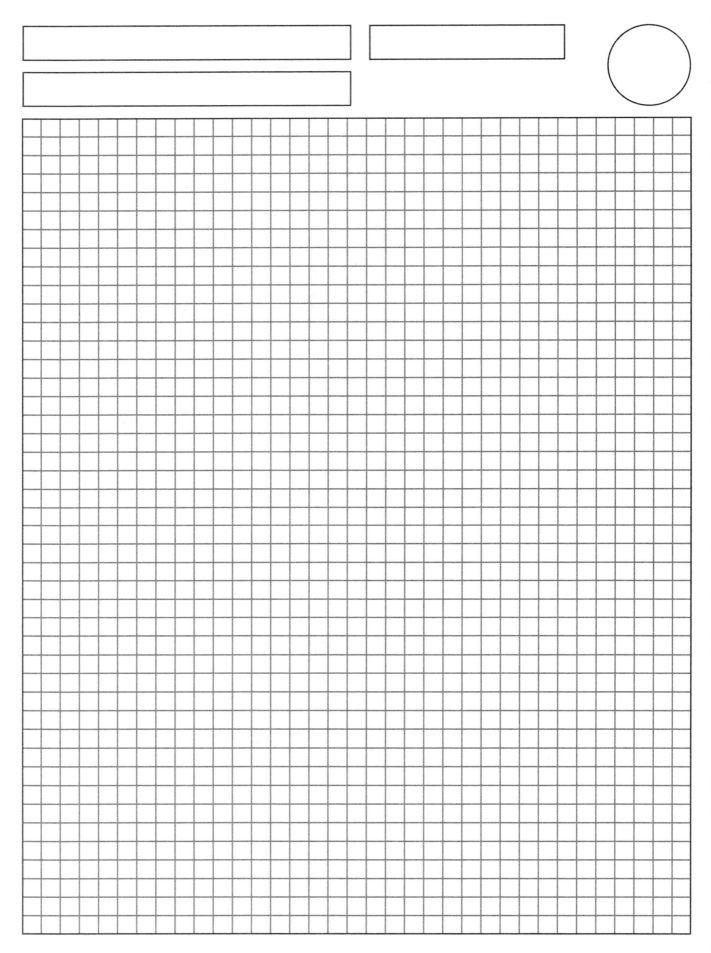

SECTOR 6

CRITICAL TIMES (CT)

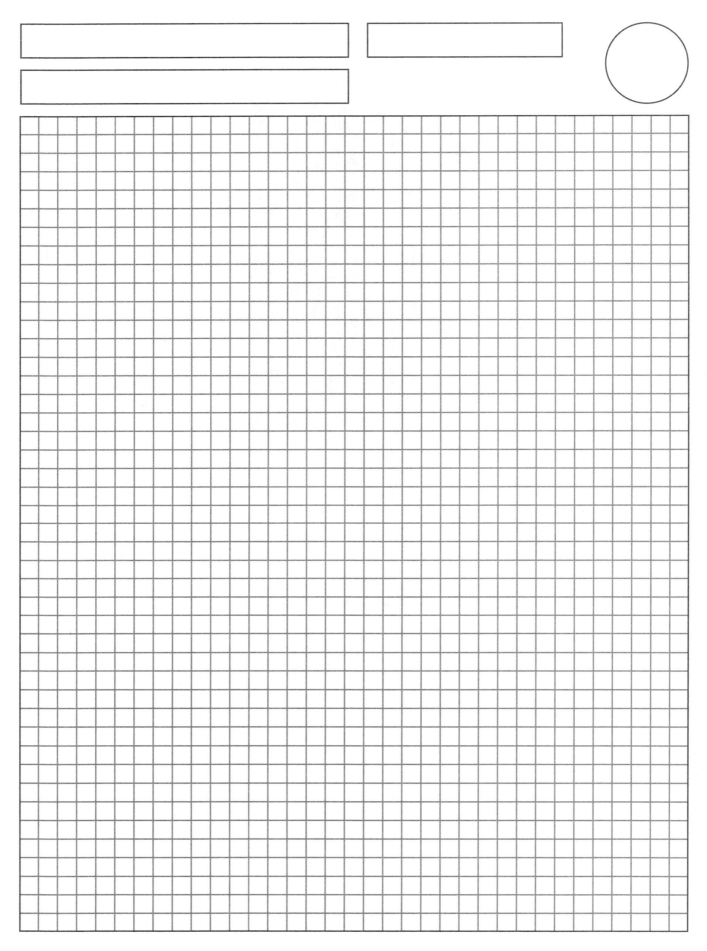

SECTOR 6

VULNERABILITIES

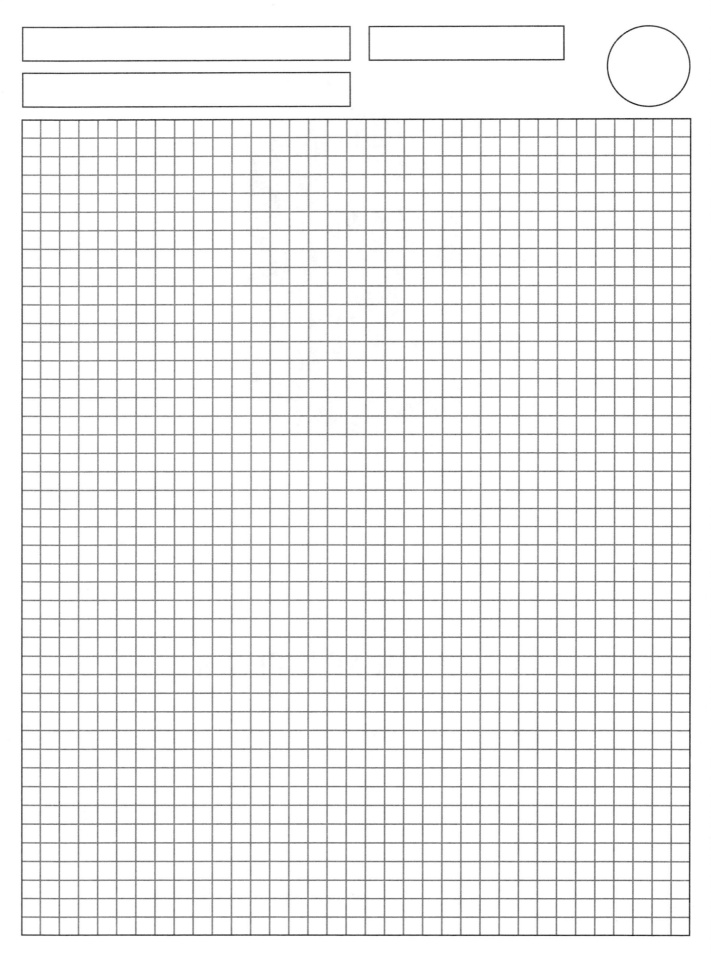

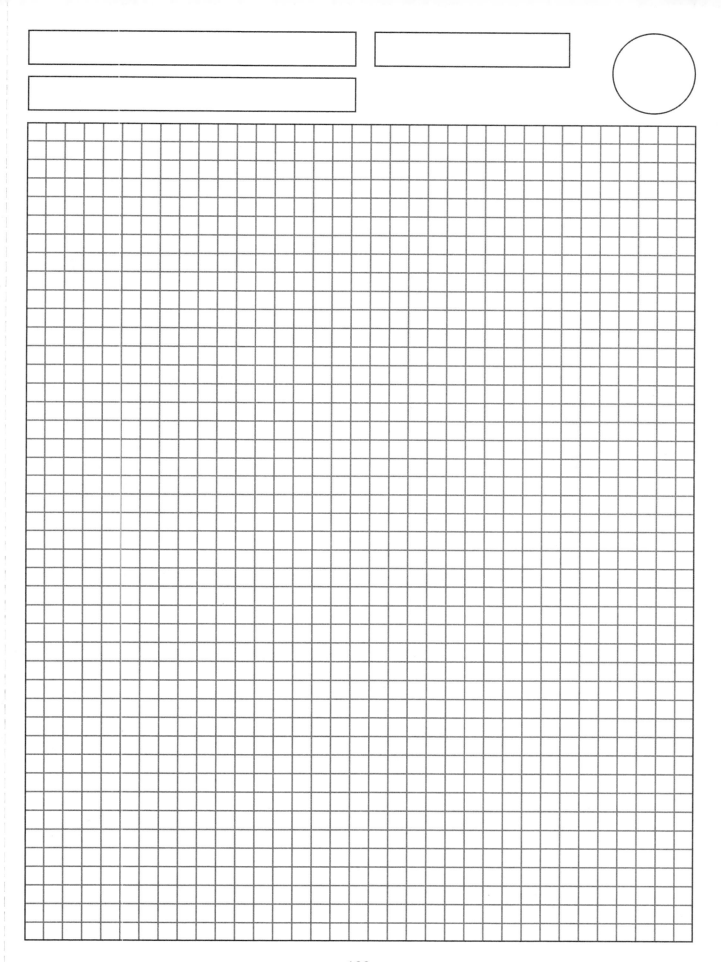

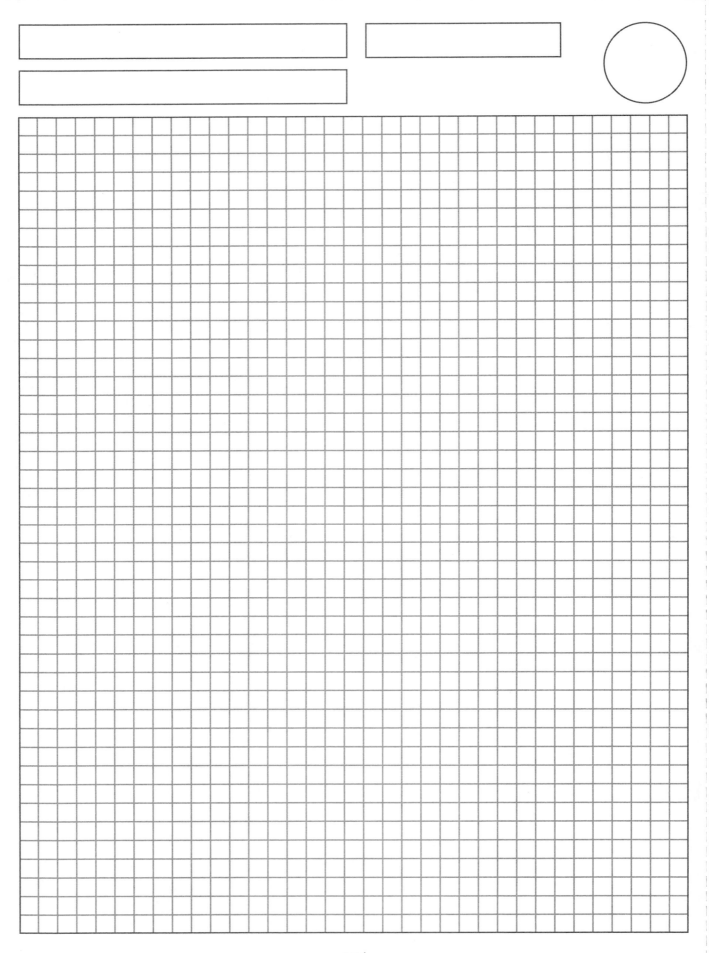

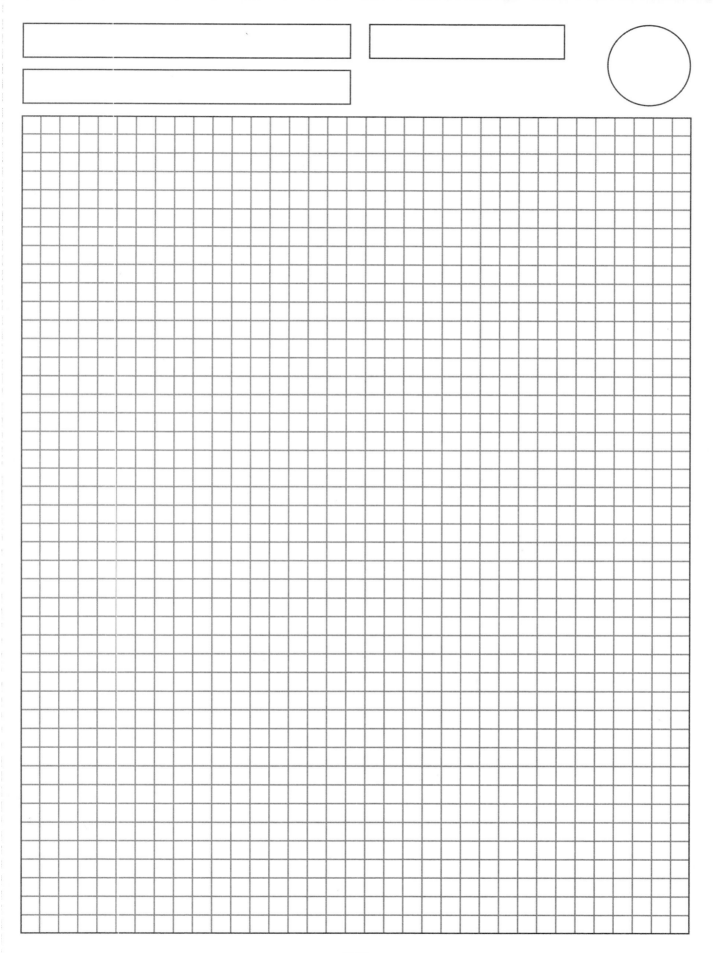

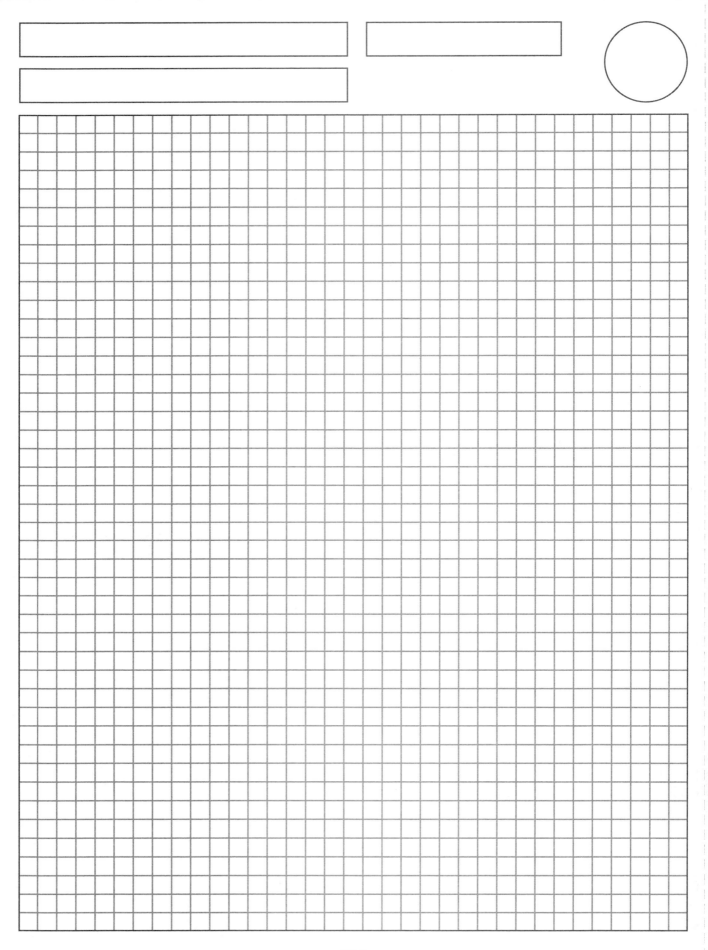

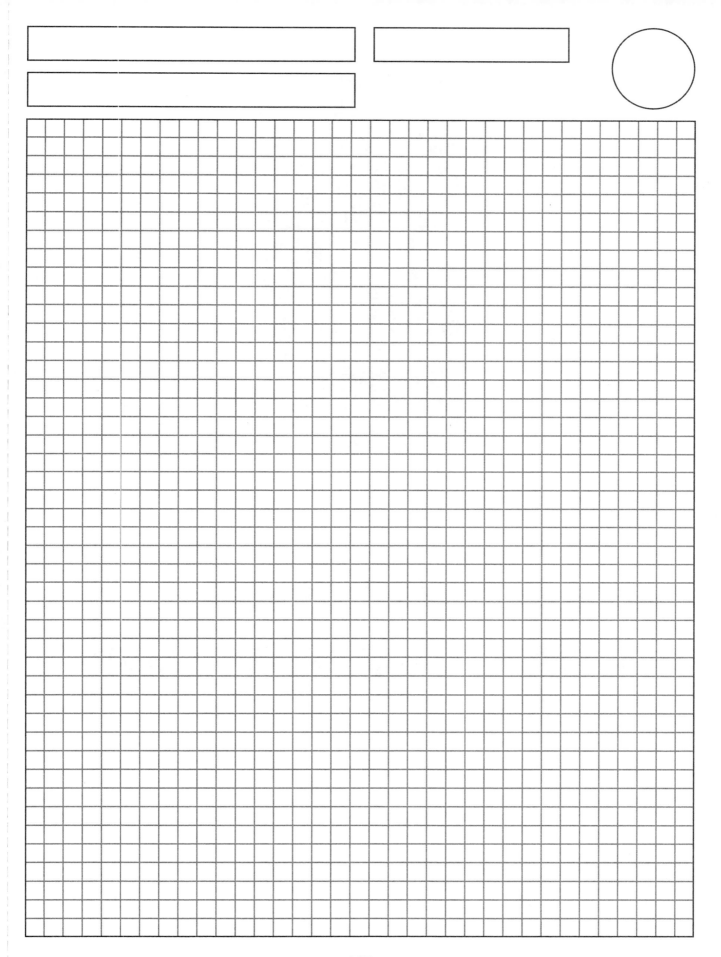

SECTOR 6

AVENUES OF APPROACH (AVP)

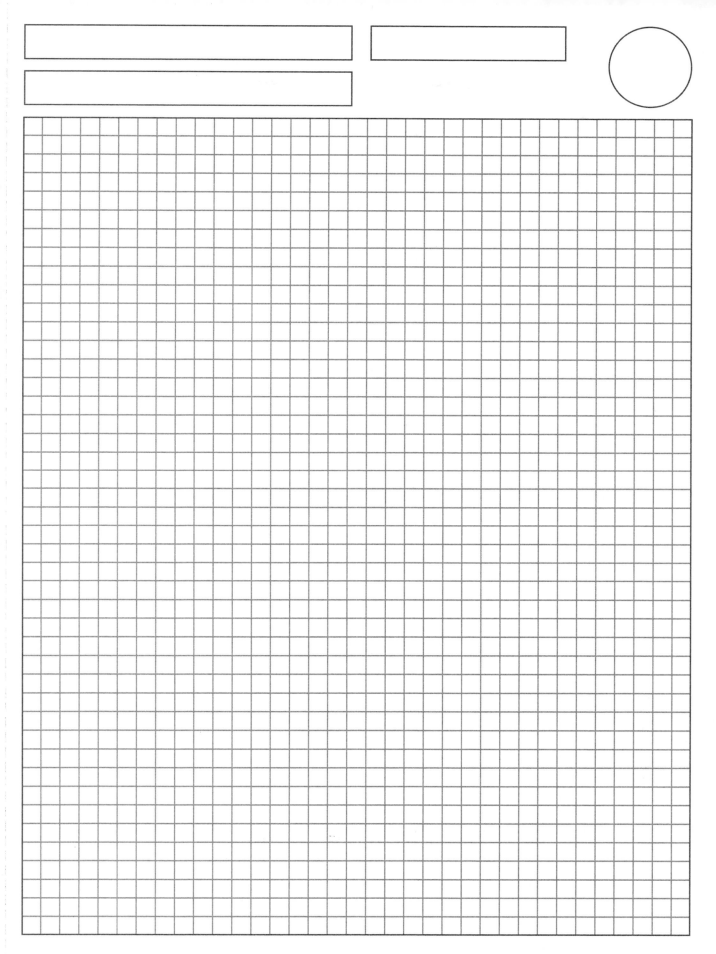

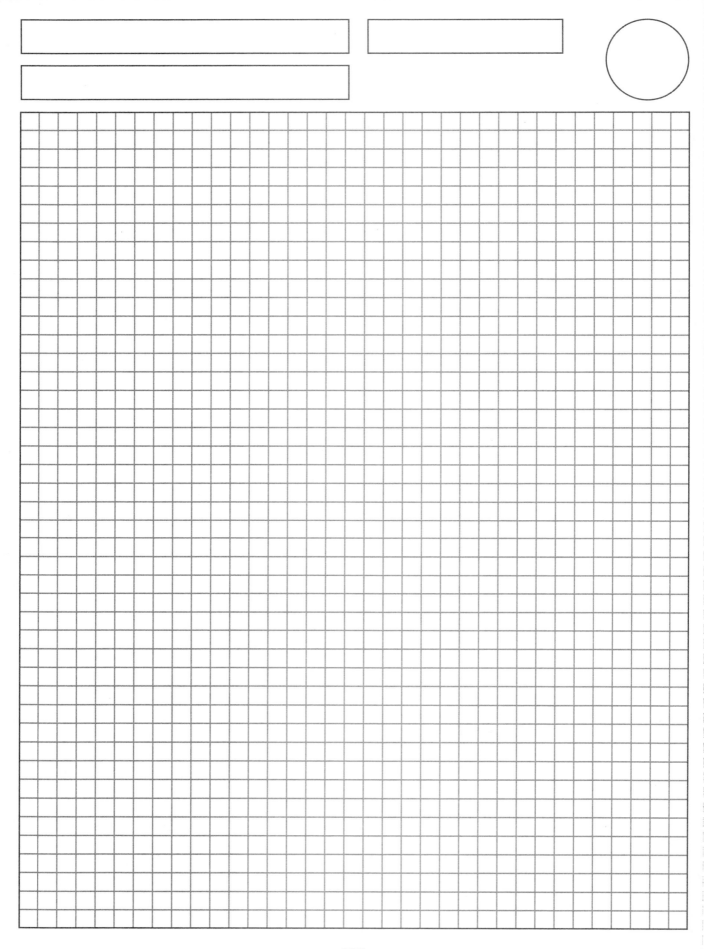

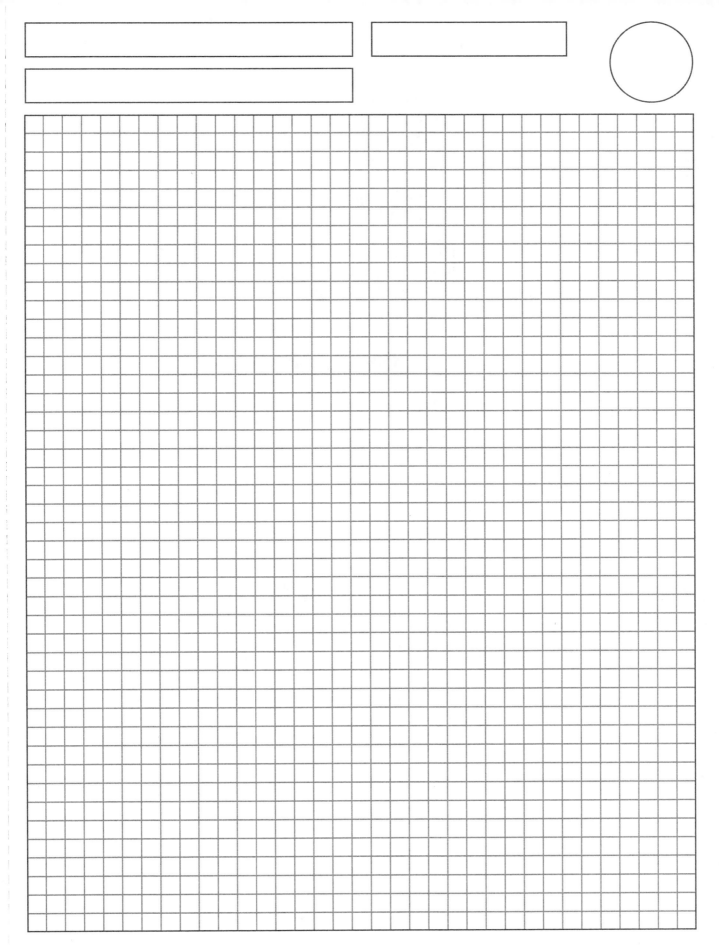

SECTOR 6
TARGET EQUATION

TARGET EQUATION WORKSHEET

Sector:

Date:

Type of attack:

Time of attack:

Avenues of Approach:

Vulnerabilities:

Type of attack:

Time of attack:

Avenues of Approach:

Vulnerabilities:

Type of attack:

Time of attack:

Avenues of Approach:

Vulnerabilities:

TARGET EQUATION WORKSHEET

Sector:

Date:

Type of attack:

Time of attack:

Avenues of Approach:

Vulnerabilities:

Type of attack:

Time of attack:

Avenues of Approach:

Vulnerabilities:

Type of attack:

Time of attack:

Avenues of Approach:

Vulnerabilities:

TARGET EQUATION WORKSHEET

Sector:	Date:

Type of attack:	Time of attack:

Avenues of Approach:

Vulnerabilities:

Type of attack:	Time of attack:

Avenues of Approach:

Vulnerabilities:

Type of attack:	Time of attack:

Avenues of Approach:

Vulnerabilities:

TARGET EQUATION WORKSHEET

Sector:

Date:

Type of attack:

Time of attack:

Avenues of Approach:

Vulnerabilities:

Type of attack:

Time of attack:

Avenues of Approach:

Vulnerabilities:

Type of attack:

Time of attack:

Avenues of Approach:

Vulnerabilities:

TARGET EQUATION WORKSHEET

Sector:

Date:

Type of attack:

Time of attack:

Avenues of Approach:

Vulnerabilities:

Type of attack:

Time of attack:

Avenues of Approach:

Vulnerabilities:

Type of attack:

Time of attack:

Avenues of Approach:

Vulnerabilities:

S7

SECTOR 7

SECTOR 7

OVERVIEW

THREAT ASSESSMENT SECTOR OVERVIEW

Sector:

Date:

Prepared by:

Situation:

Sector Overview:

Note: Make sure you print out map and directions to pertinent police precincts.

Police Departments:

PD Contact Information:

PD Response Times:

Crime Level:

Possible Threat Level:

Known Terror Threats:

Known Criminal Threats:

Note: Make sure you print out map and directions to all trauma centers. Always make the effort to proceed to a level 1 trauma center if the injury is life threatening.

Trauma Centers:

Trauma Center Level (I, II, III):

Response Times:

Weather Conditions:

| Spring | Summer | Fall | Winter |

SECTOR 7

CRITICAL ASSETS (CA)

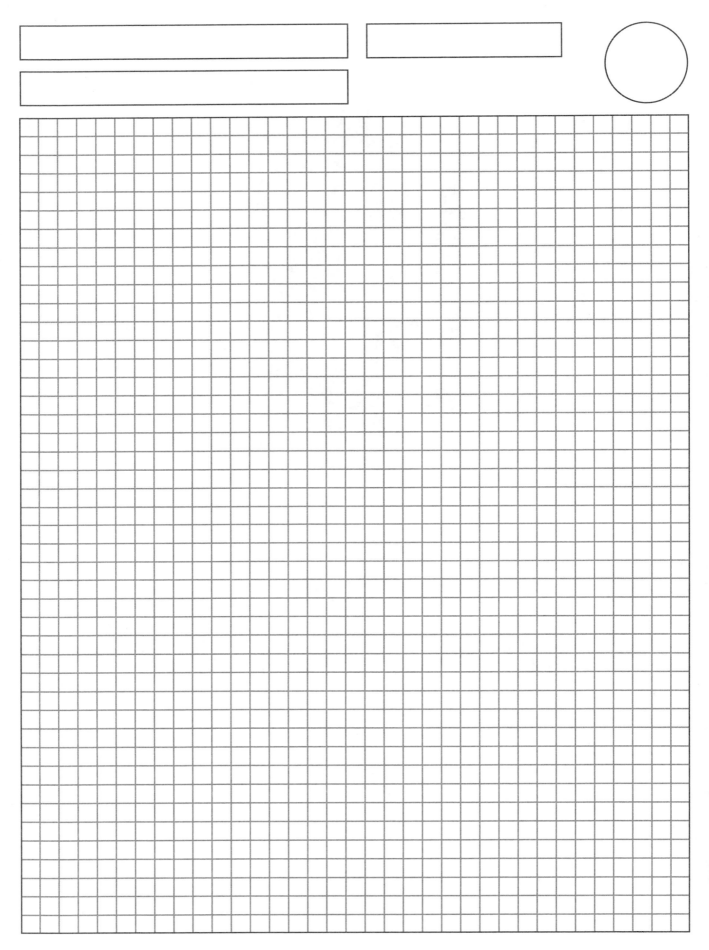

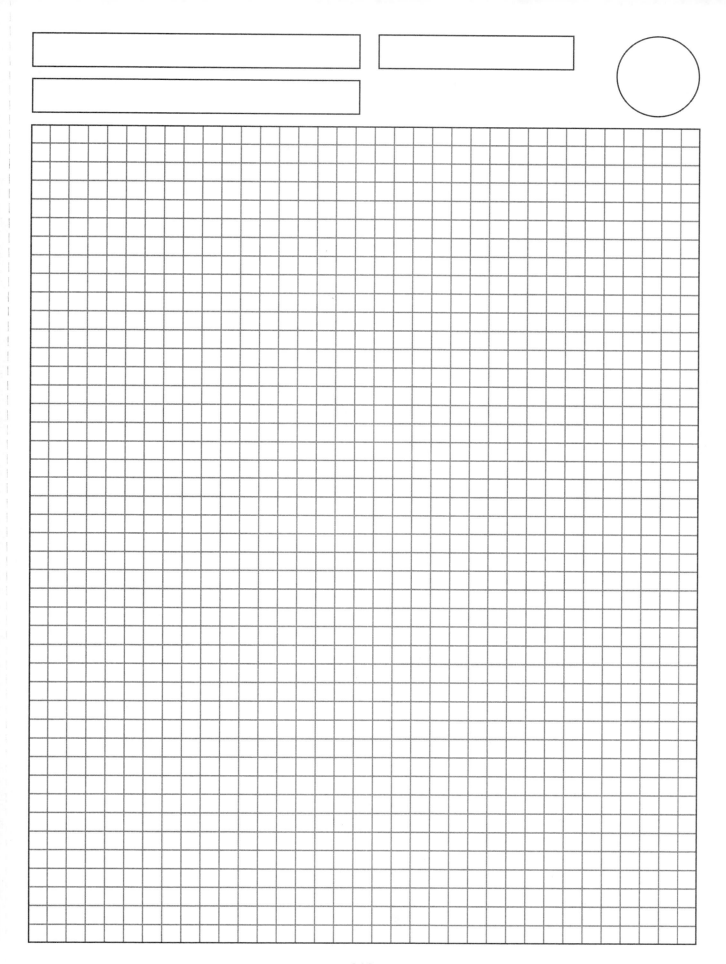

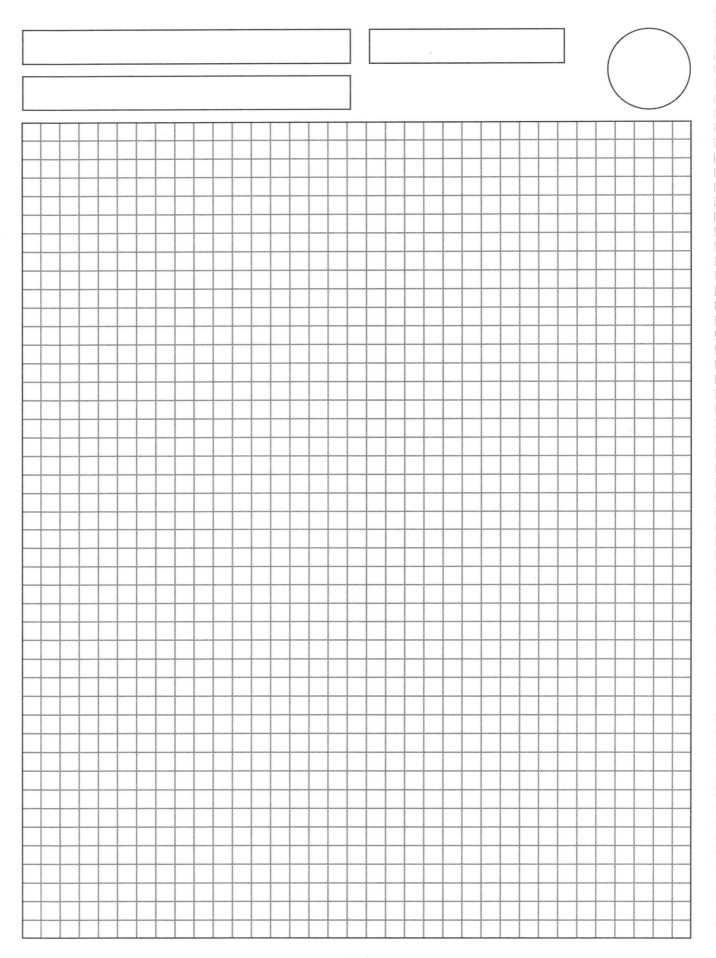

SECTOR 7

CRITICAL AREAS (CAR)

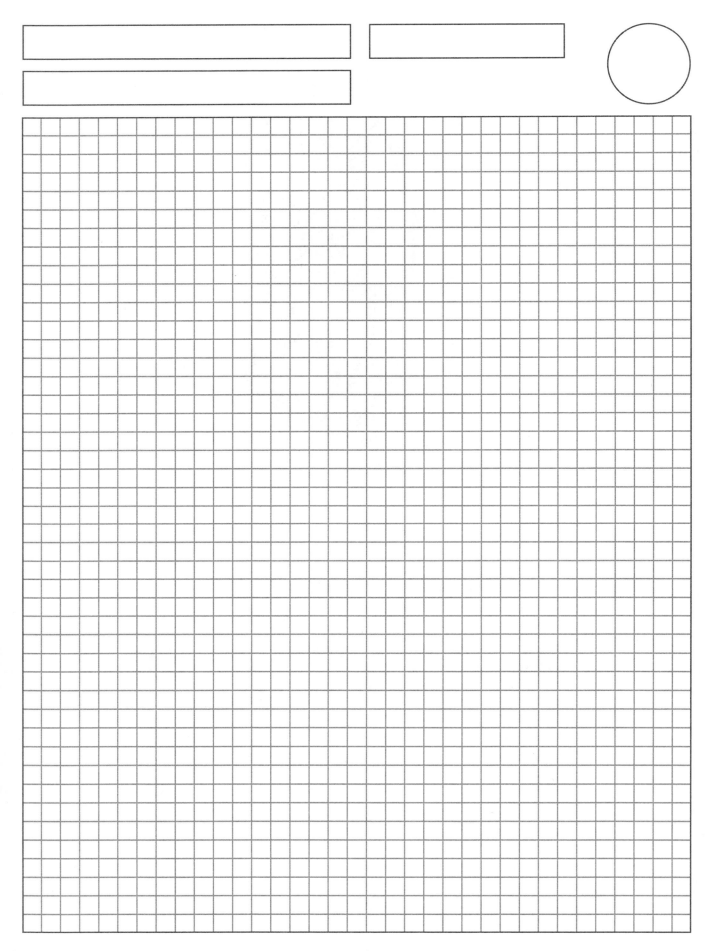

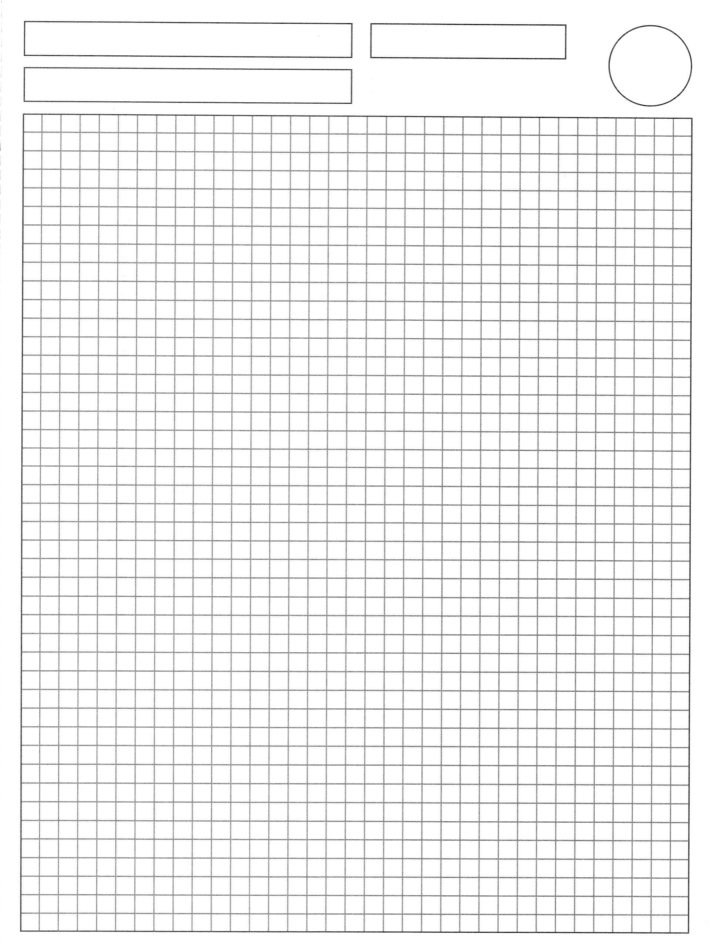

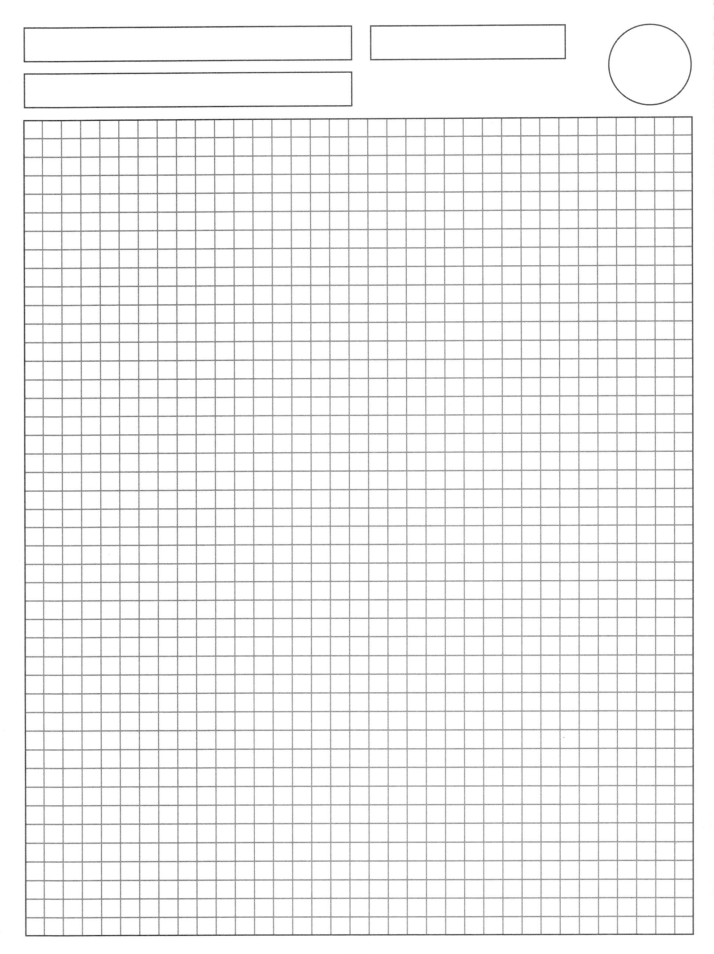

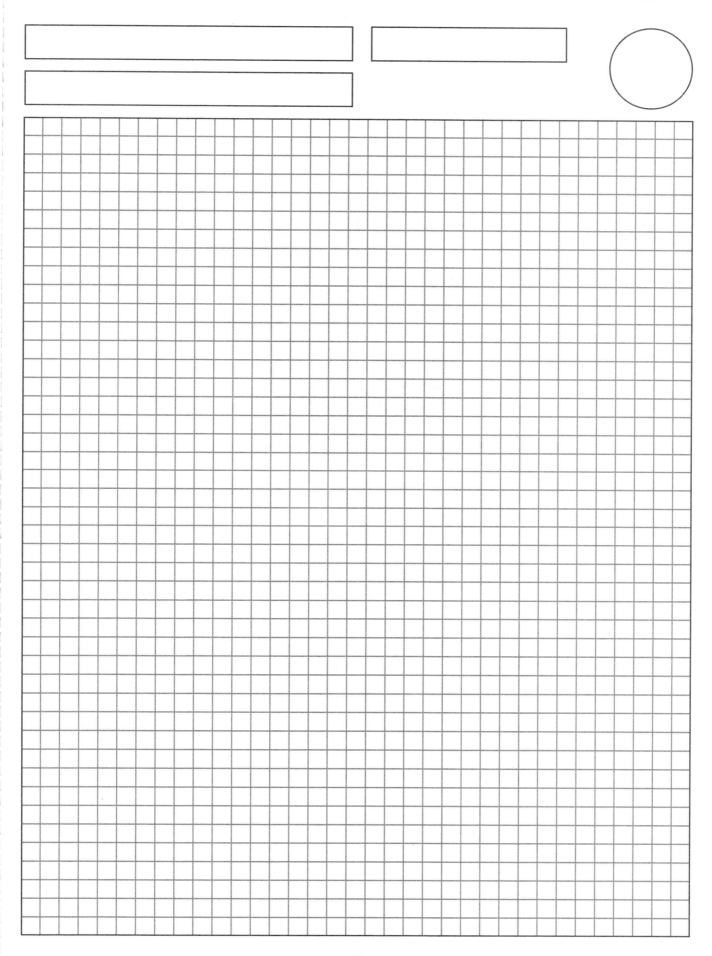

SECTOR 7

CRITICAL TIMES (CT)

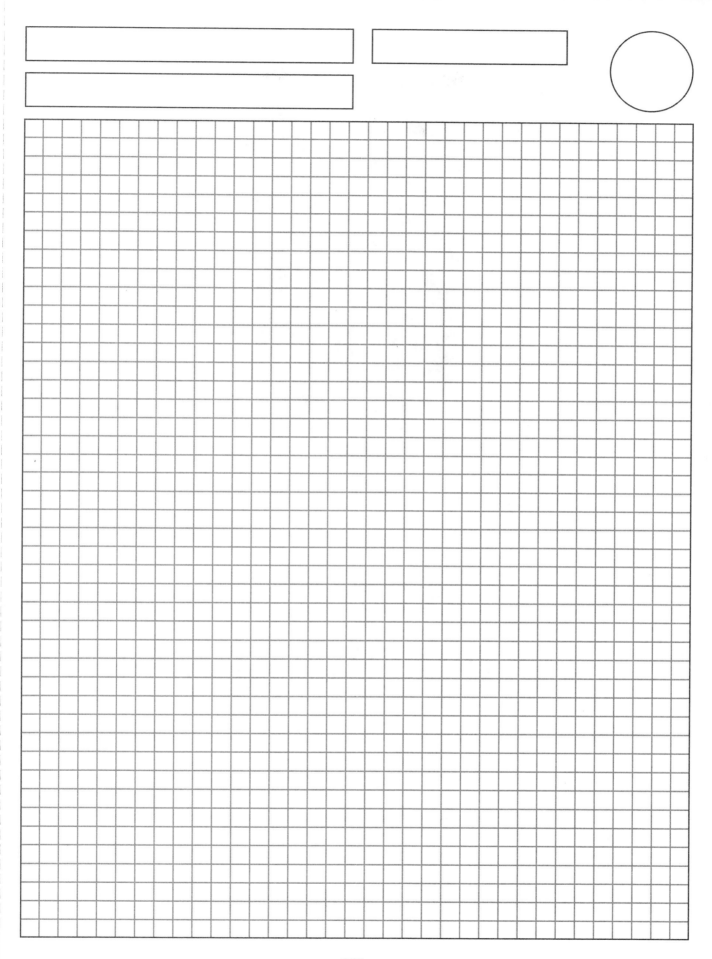

SECTOR 7

VULNERABILITIES

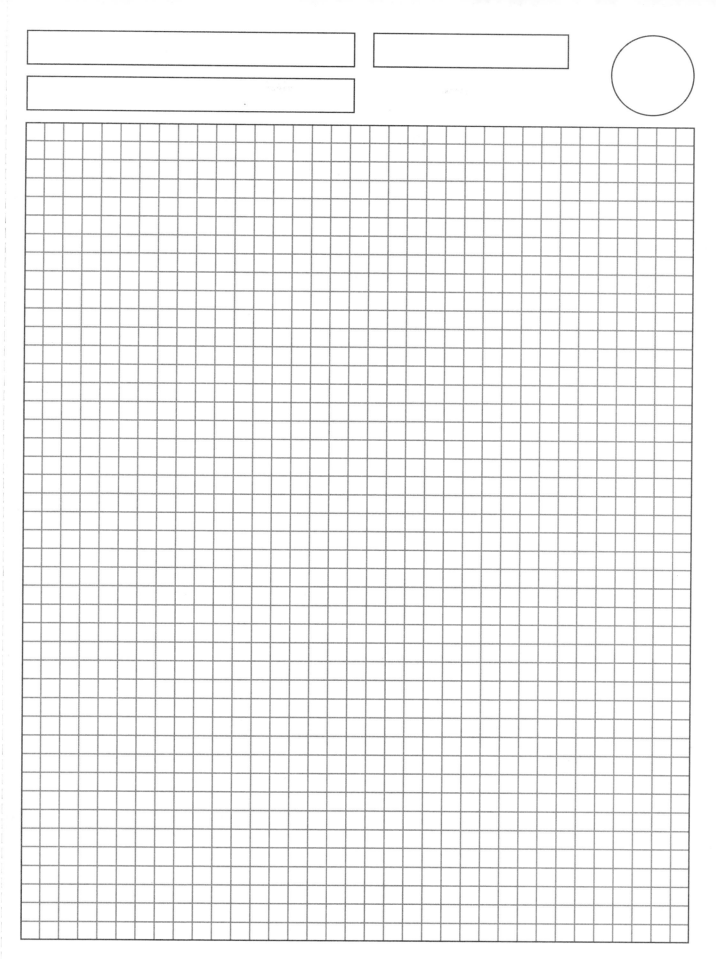

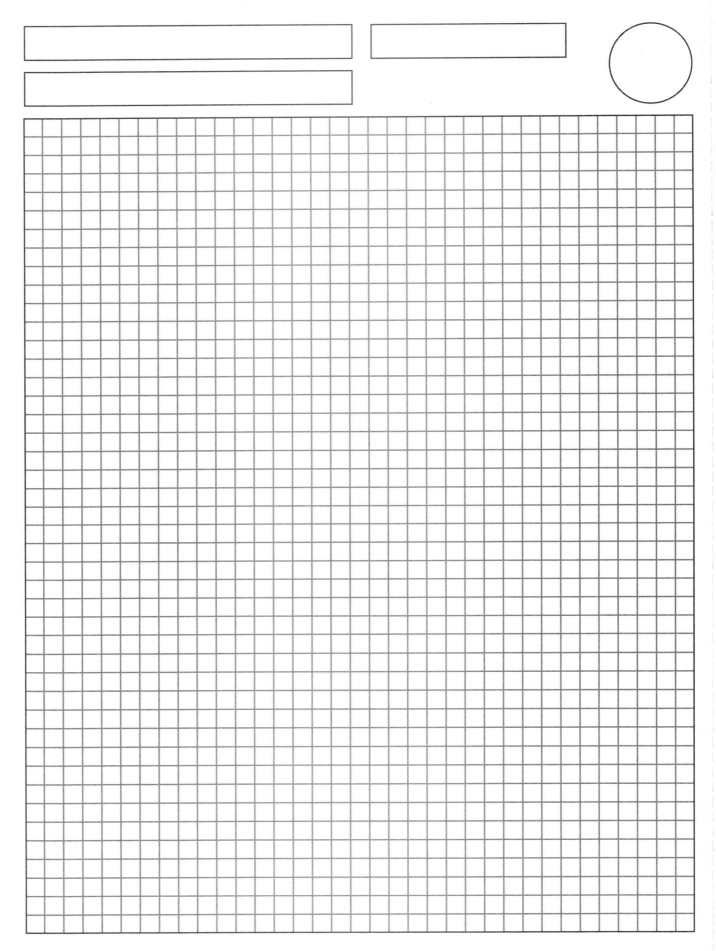

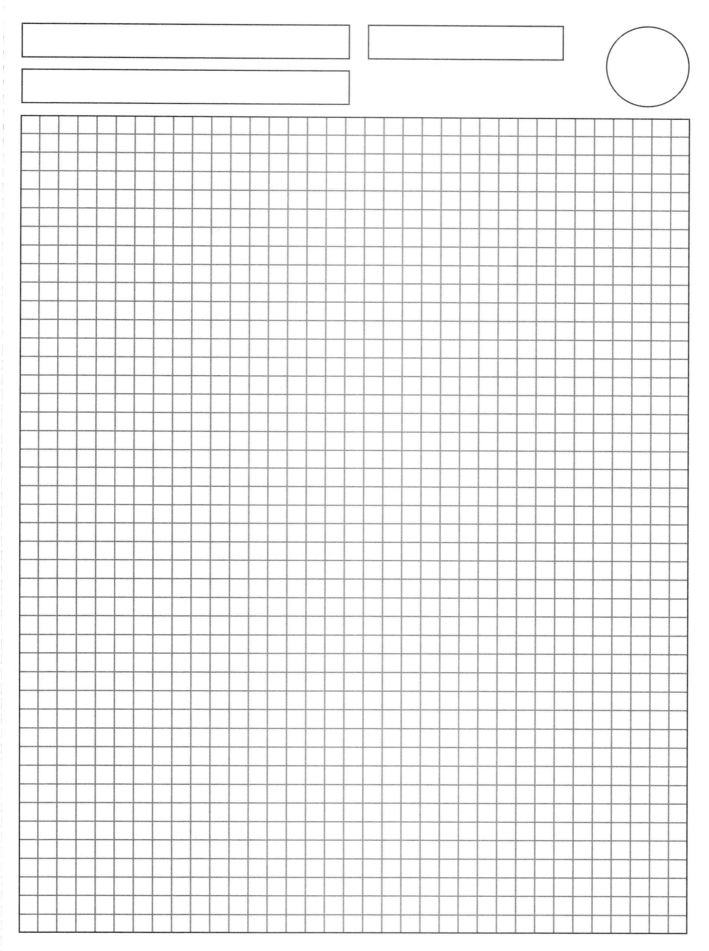

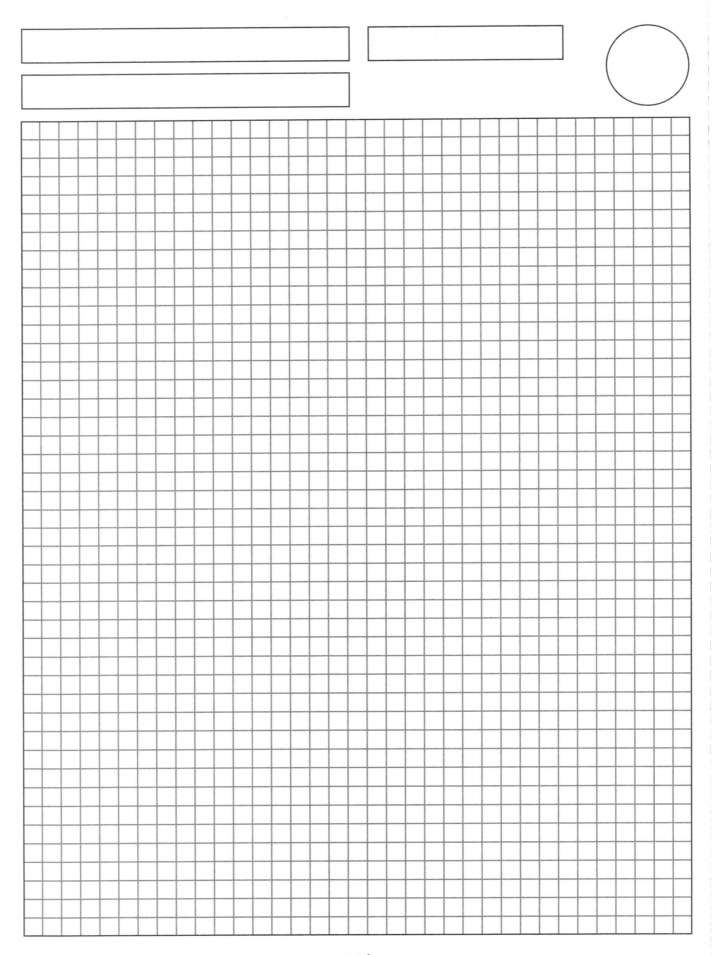

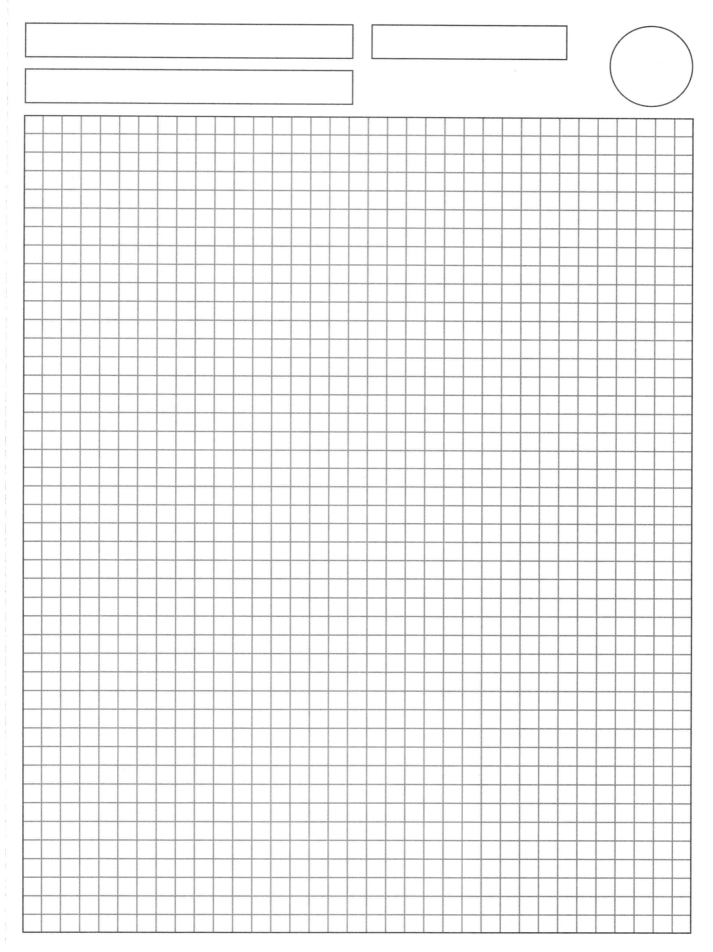

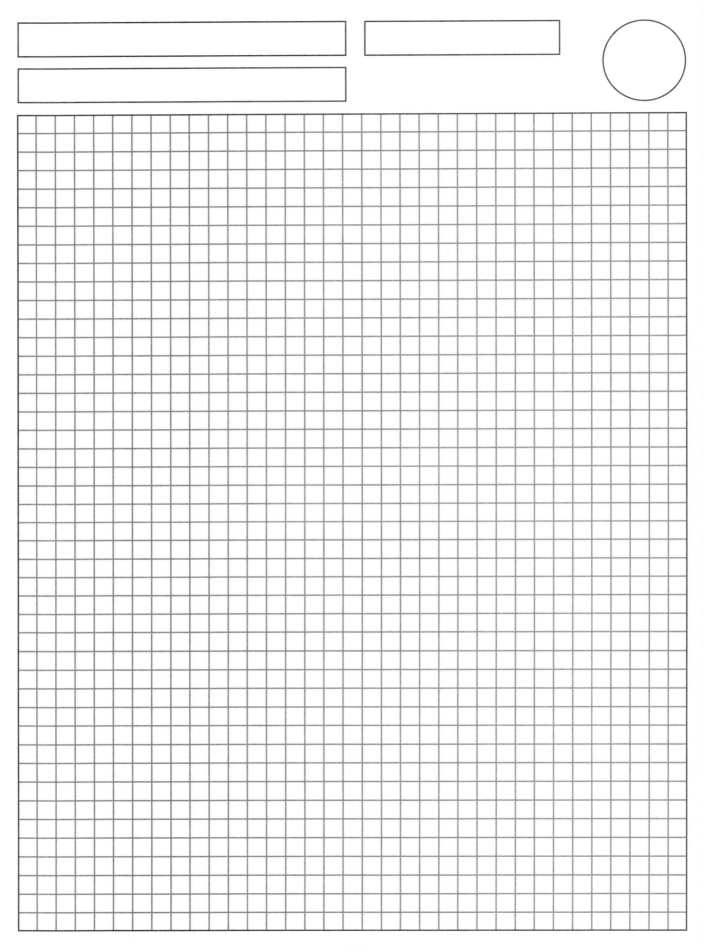

SECTOR 7

AVENUES OF APPROACH (AVP)

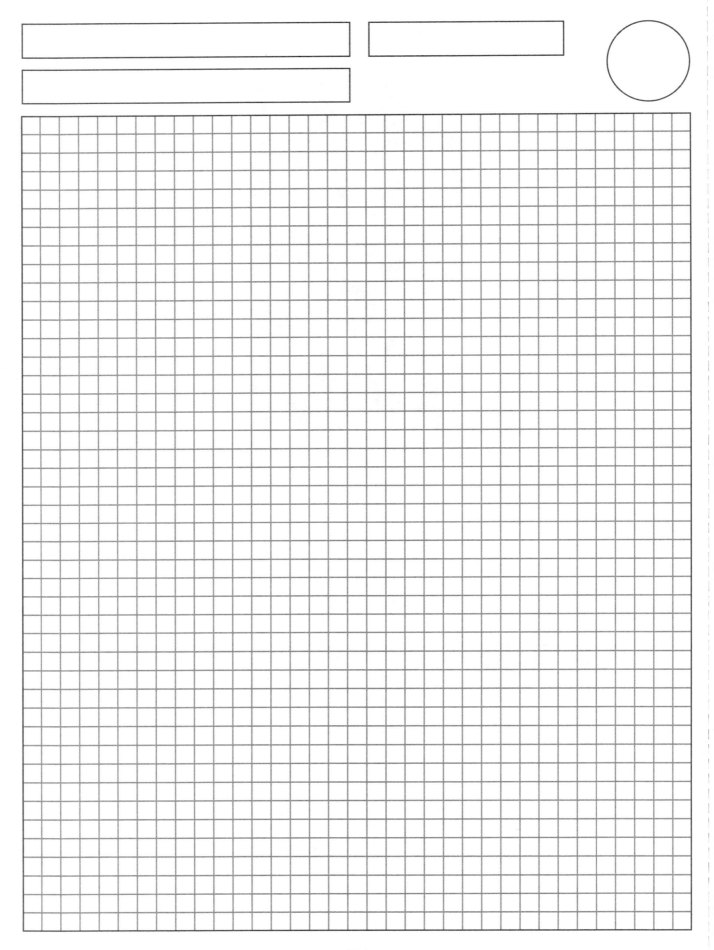

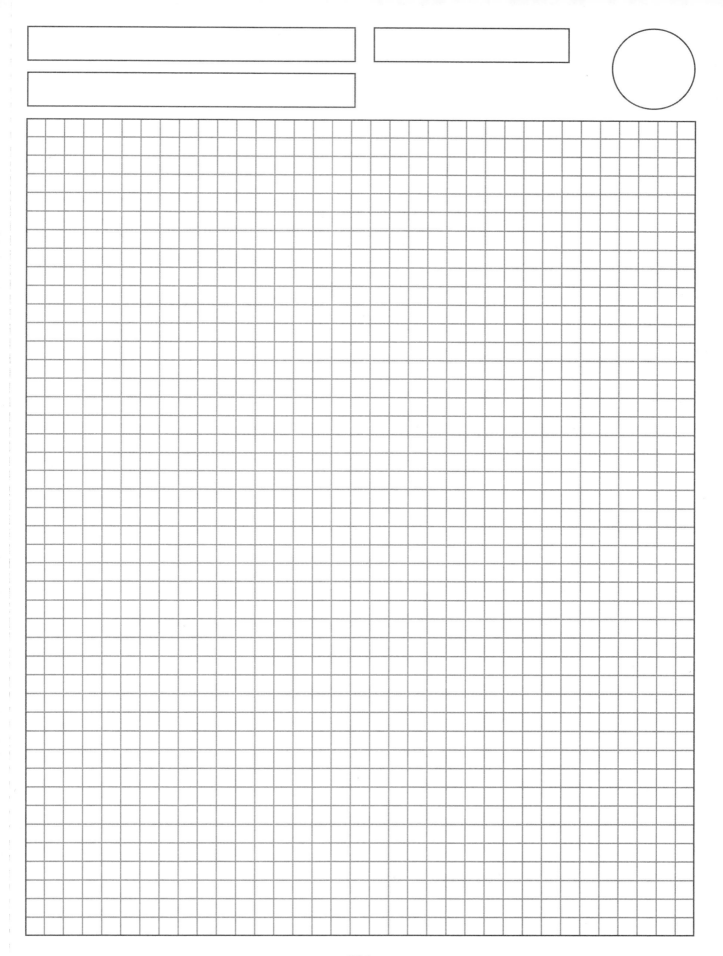

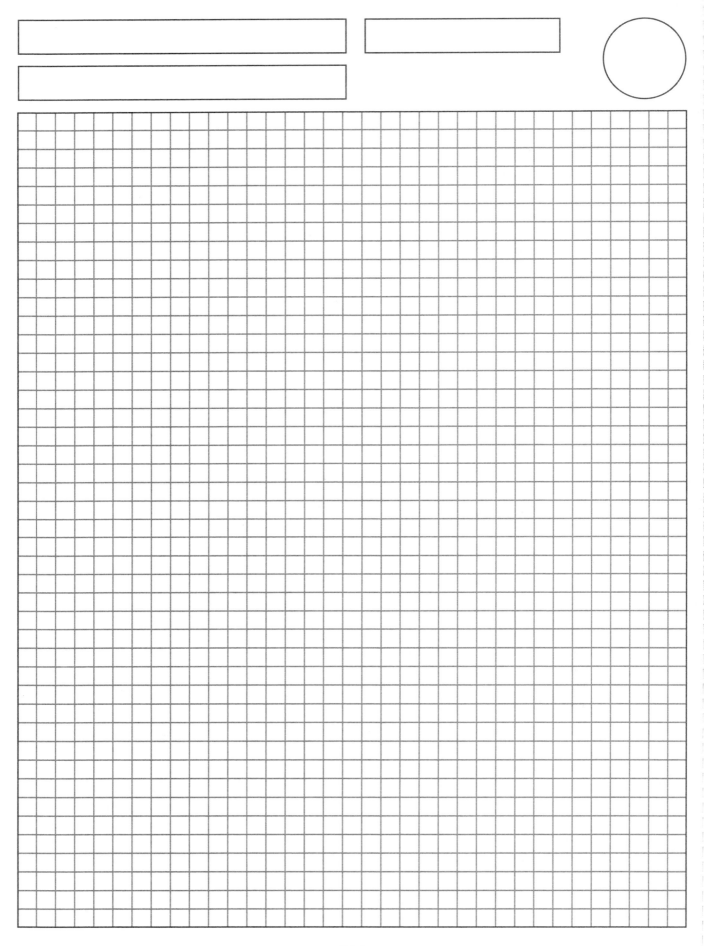

SECTOR 7

TARGET EQUATION

TARGET EQUATION WORKSHEET

Sector:

Date:

Type of attack:

Time of attack:

Avenues of Approach:

Vulnerabilities:

Type of attack:

Time of attack:

Avenues of Approach:

Vulnerabilities:

Type of attack:

Time of attack:

Avenues of Approach:

Vulnerabilities:

TARGET EQUATION WORKSHEET

Sector:	Date:

Type of attack:	Time of attack:

Avenues of Approach:

Vulnerabilities:

Type of attack:	Time of attack:

Avenues of Approach:

Vulnerabilities:

Type of attack:	Time of attack:

Avenues of Approach:

Vulnerabilities:

TARGET EQUATION WORKSHEET

Sector:	Date:

Type of attack:	Time of attack:

Avenues of Approach:

Vulnerabilities:

Type of attack:	Time of attack:

Avenues of Approach:

Vulnerabilities:

Type of attack:	Time of attack:

Avenues of Approach:

Vulnerabilities:

TARGET EQUATION WORKSHEET

Sector:

Date:

Type of attack:

Time of attack:

Avenues of Approach:

Vulnerabilities:

Type of attack:

Time of attack:

Avenues of Approach:

Vulnerabilities:

Type of attack:

Time of attack:

Avenues of Approach:

Vulnerabilities:

TARGET EQUATION WORKSHEET

Sector:

Date:

Type of attack:

Time of attack:

Avenues of Approach:

Vulnerabilities:

Type of attack:

Time of attack:

Avenues of Approach:

Vulnerabilities:

Type of attack:

Time of attack:

Avenues of Approach:

Vulnerabilities:

S8

SECTOR 8

SECTOR 8

OVERVIEW

THREAT ASSESSMENT SECTOR OVERVIEW

Sector:

Date:

Prepared by:

Situation:

Sector Overview:

Note: Make sure you print out map and directions to pertinent police precincts.

Police Departments:

PD Contact Information:

PD Response Times:

Crime Level:

Possible Threat Level:

Known Terror Threats:

Known Criminal Threats:

Note: Make sure you print out map and directions to all trauma centers. Always make the effort to proceed to a level 1 trauma center if the injury is life threatening.

Trauma Centers:

Trauma Center Level (I, II, III):

Response Times:

Weather Conditions:

Spring   Summer   Fall   Winter

SECTOR 8

CRITICAL ASSETS (CA)

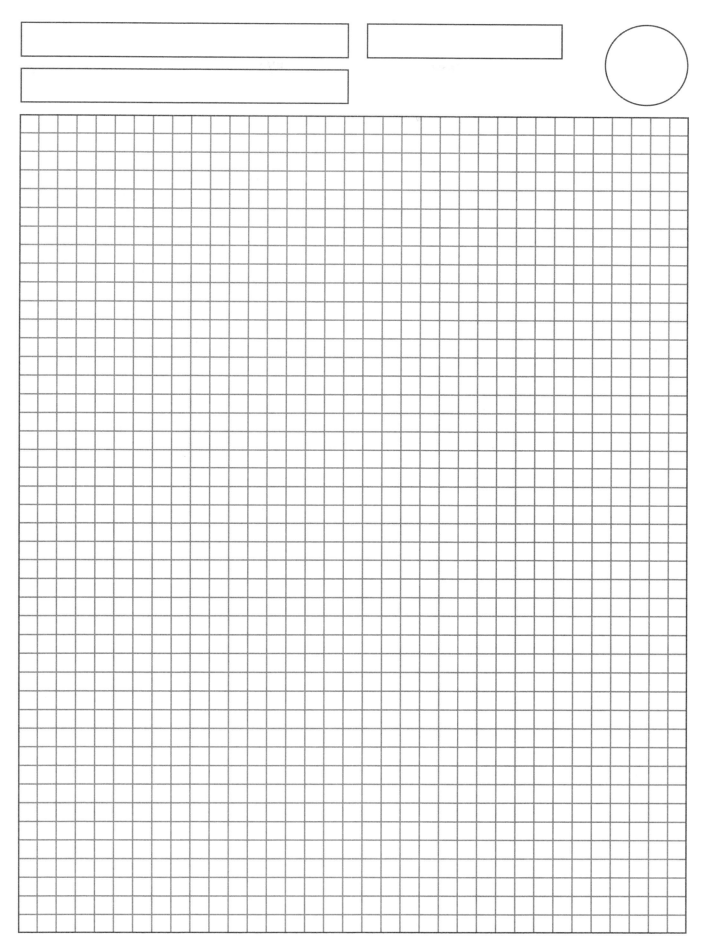

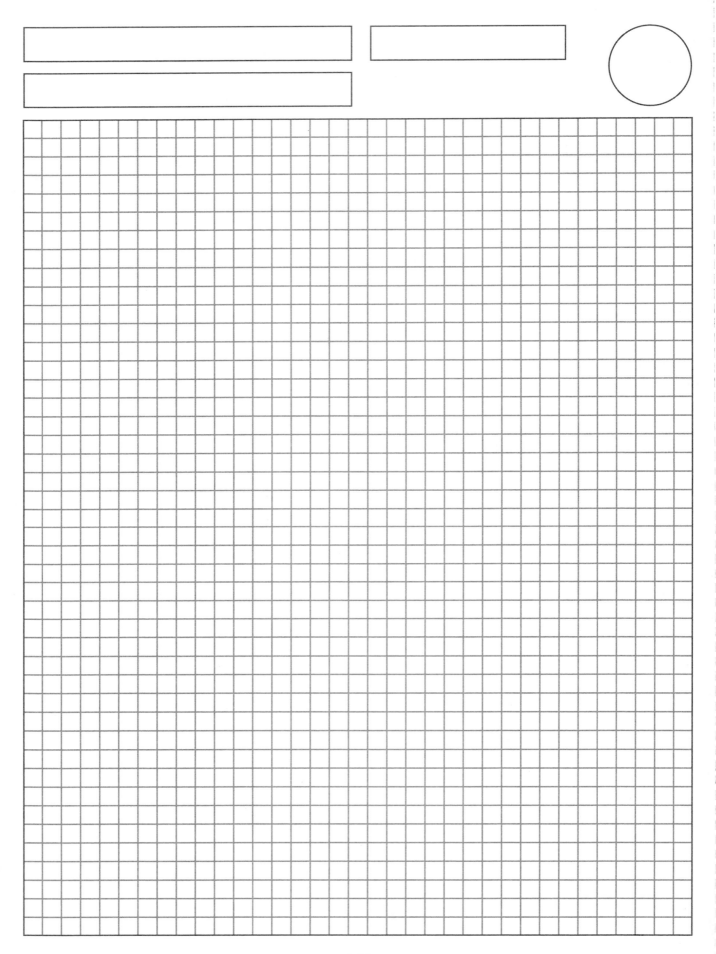

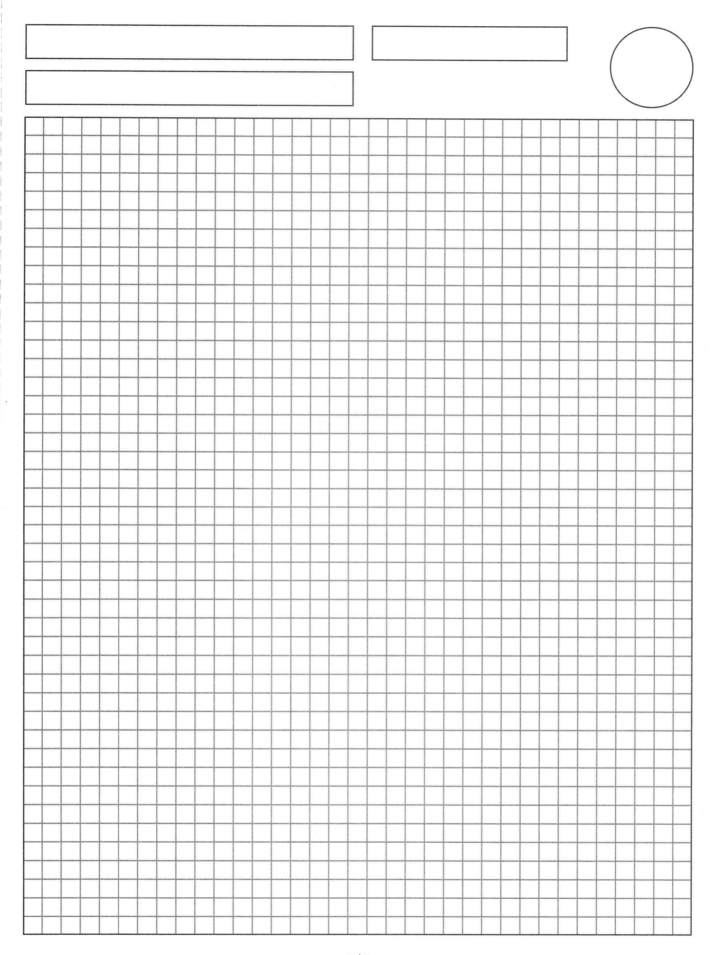

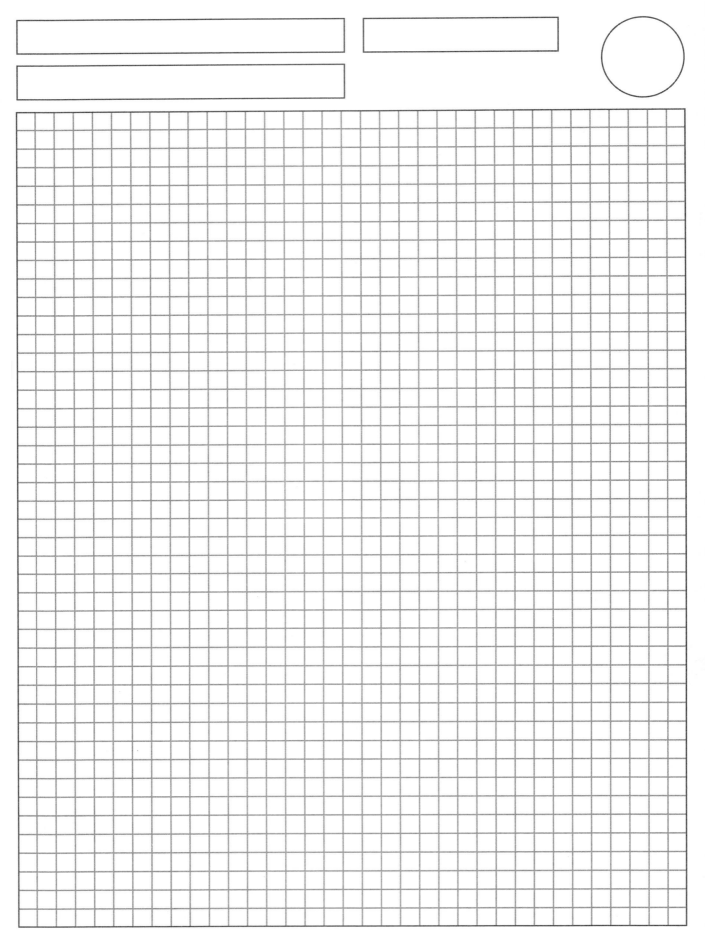

SECTOR 8

CRITICAL AREAS (CAR)

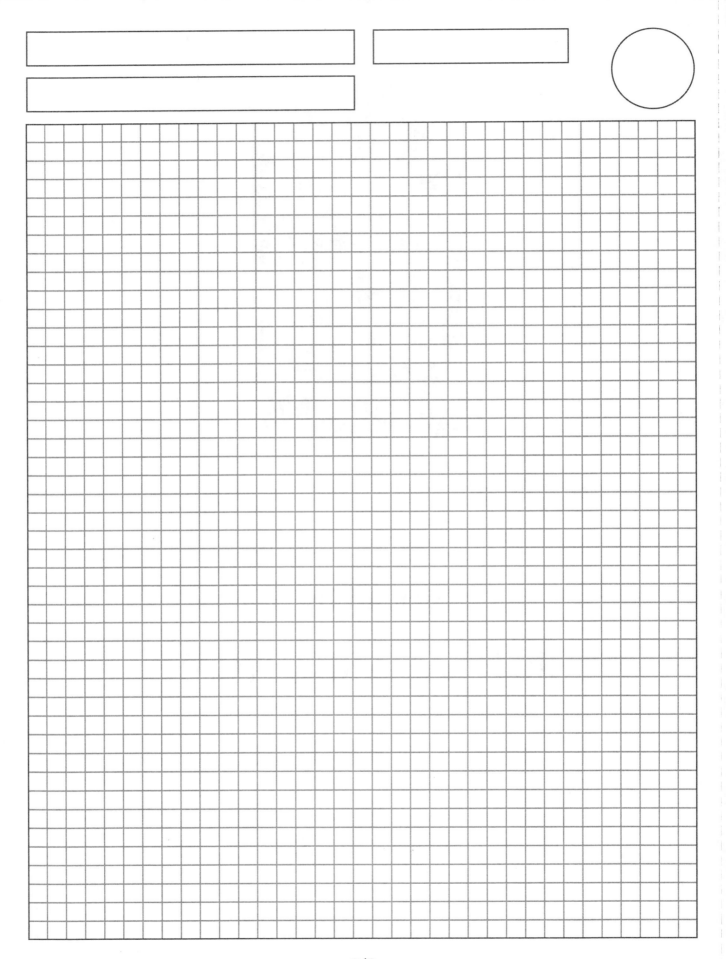

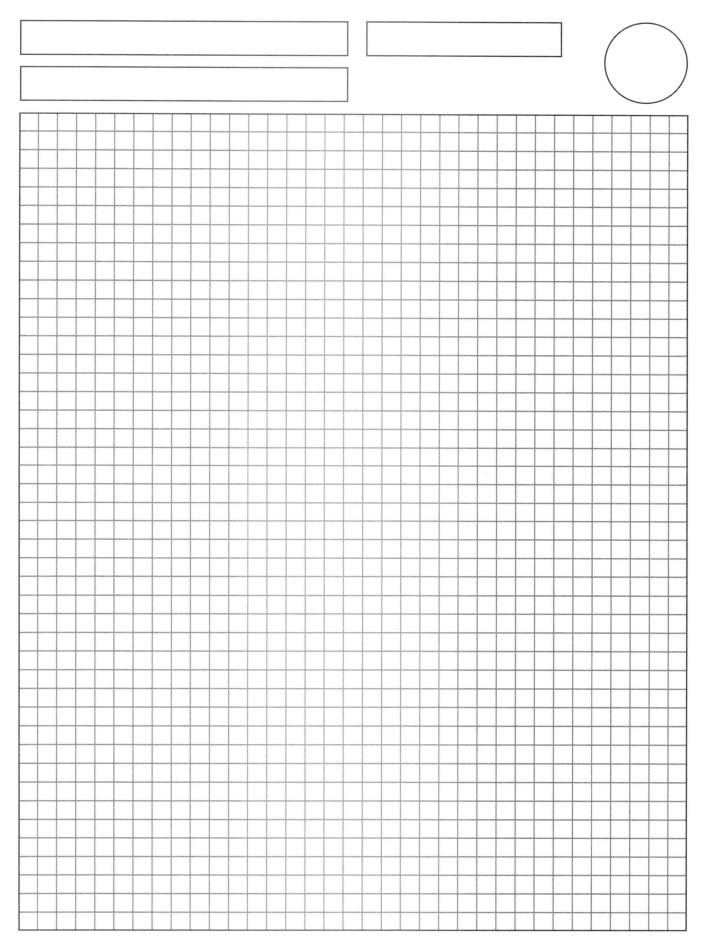

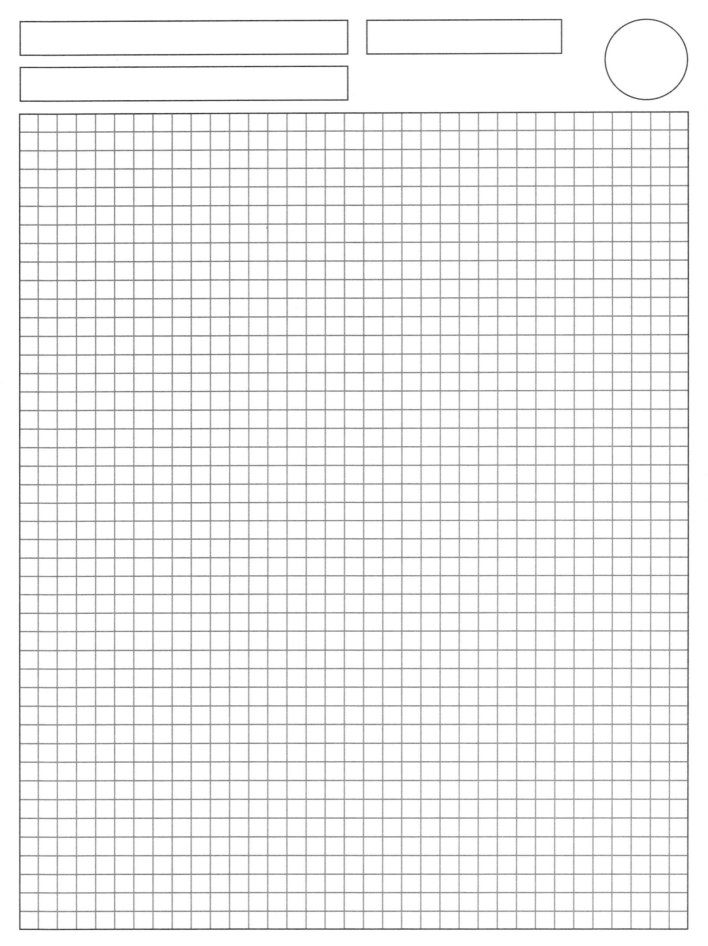

SECTOR 8

CRITICAL TIMES (CT)

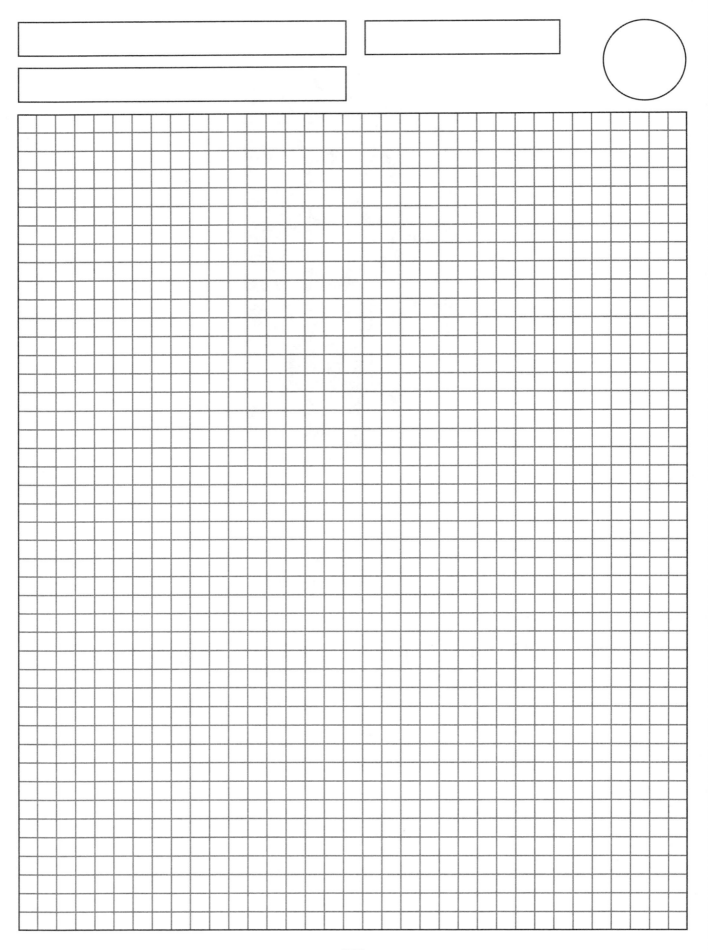

SECTOR 8

VULNERABILITIES

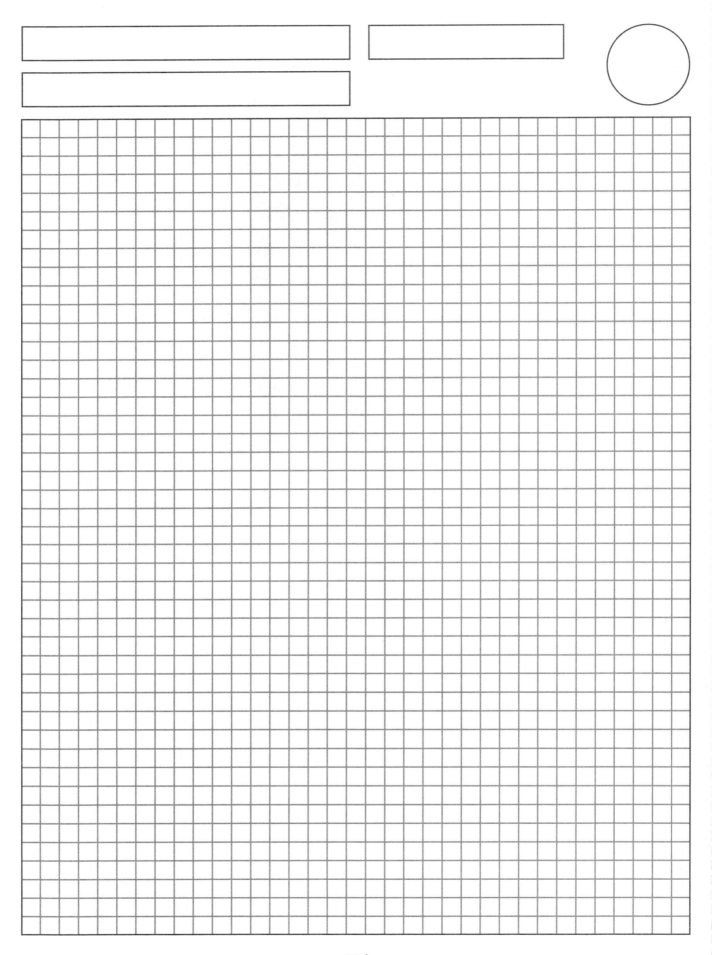

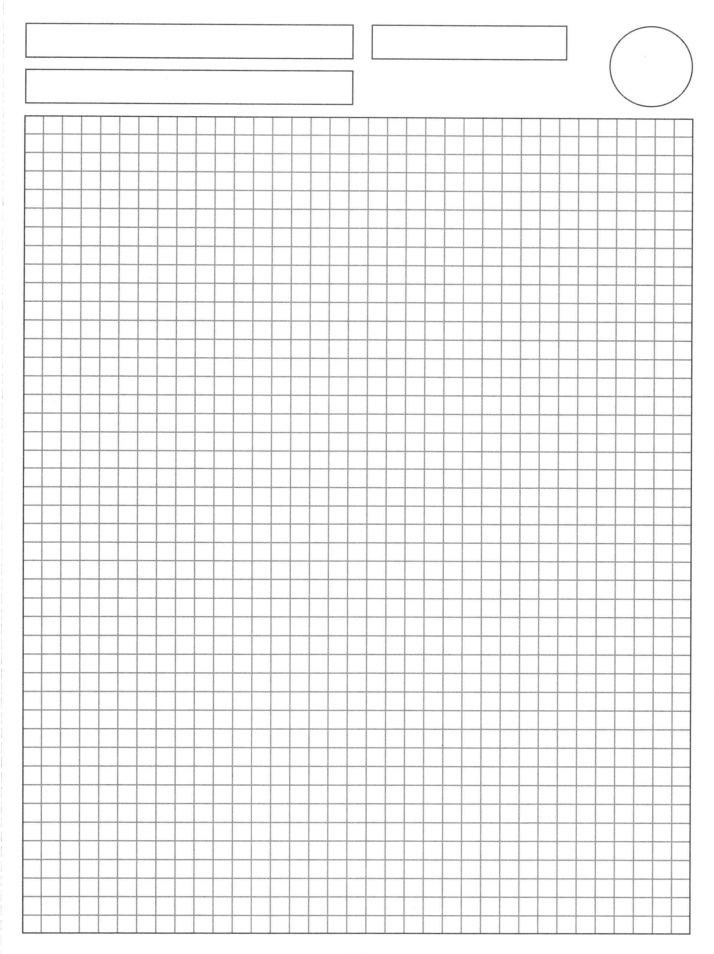

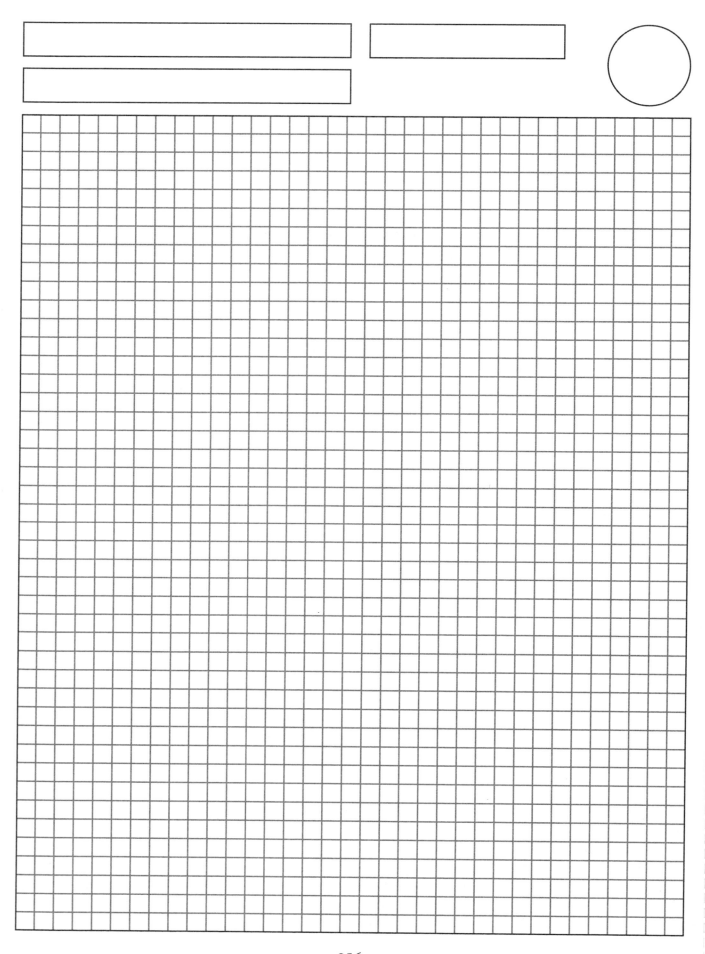

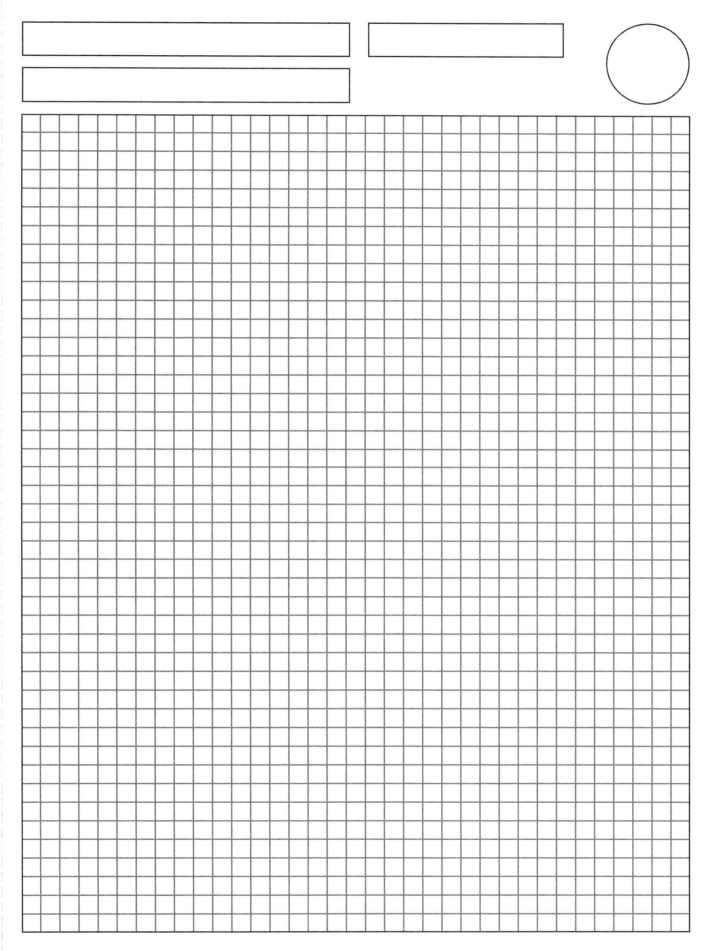

257

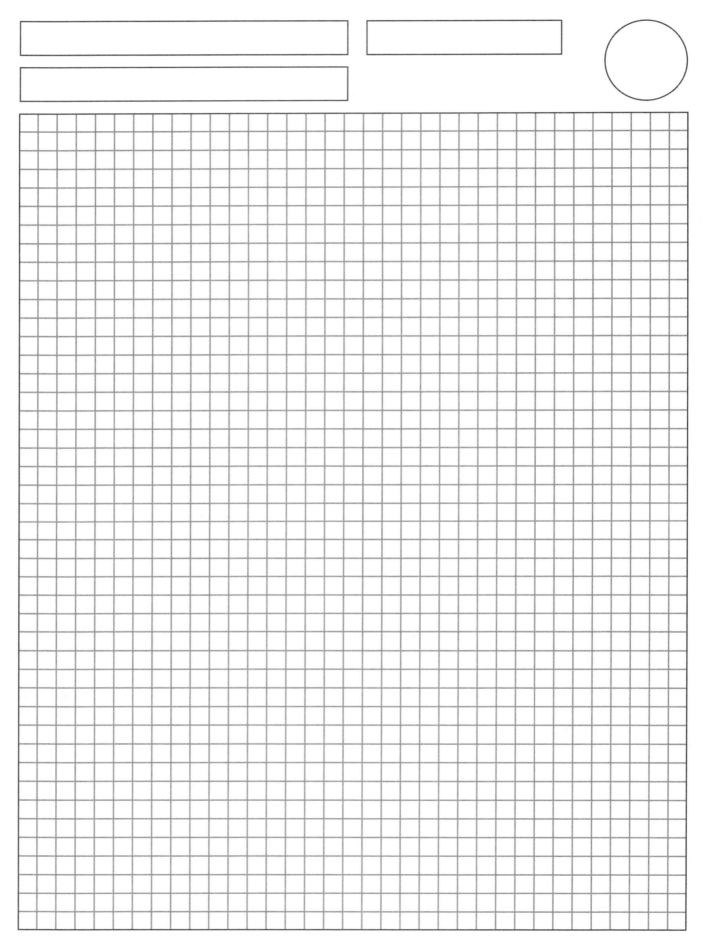

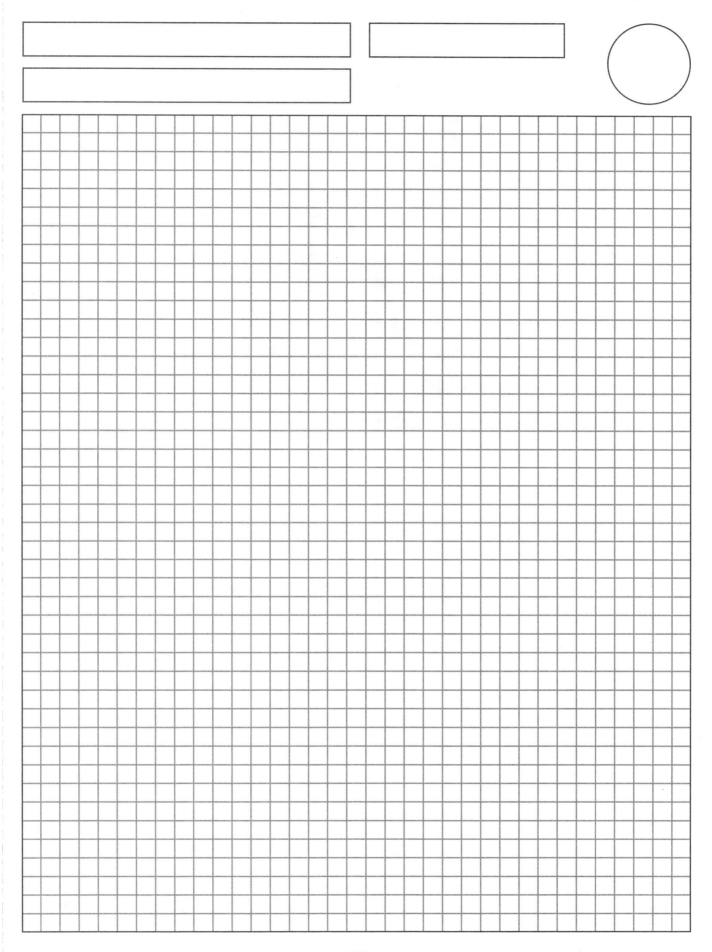

SECTOR 8

AVENUES OF APPROACH (AVP)

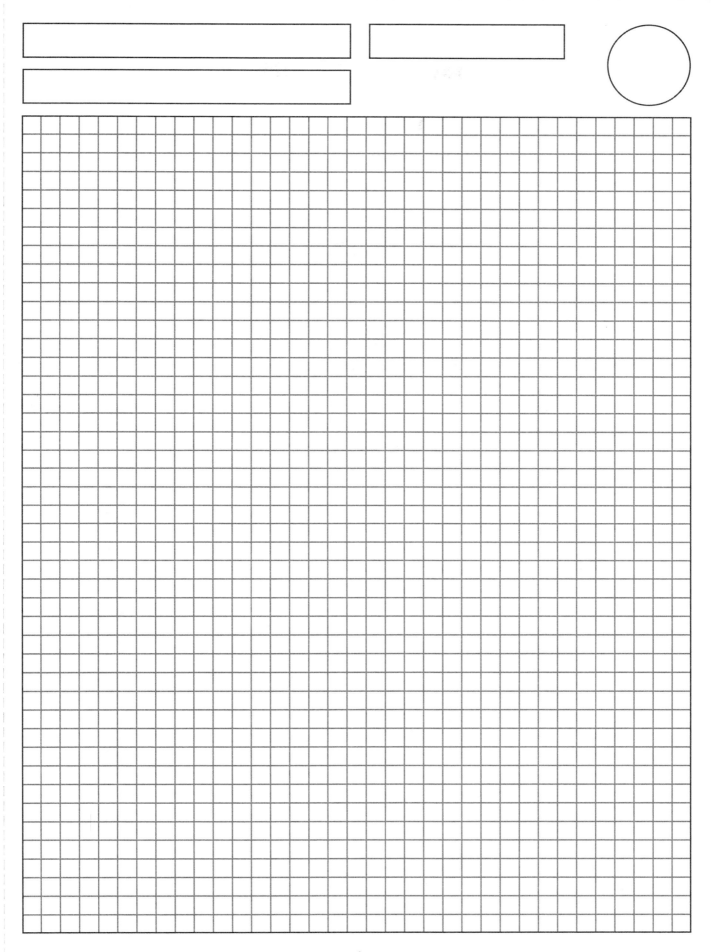

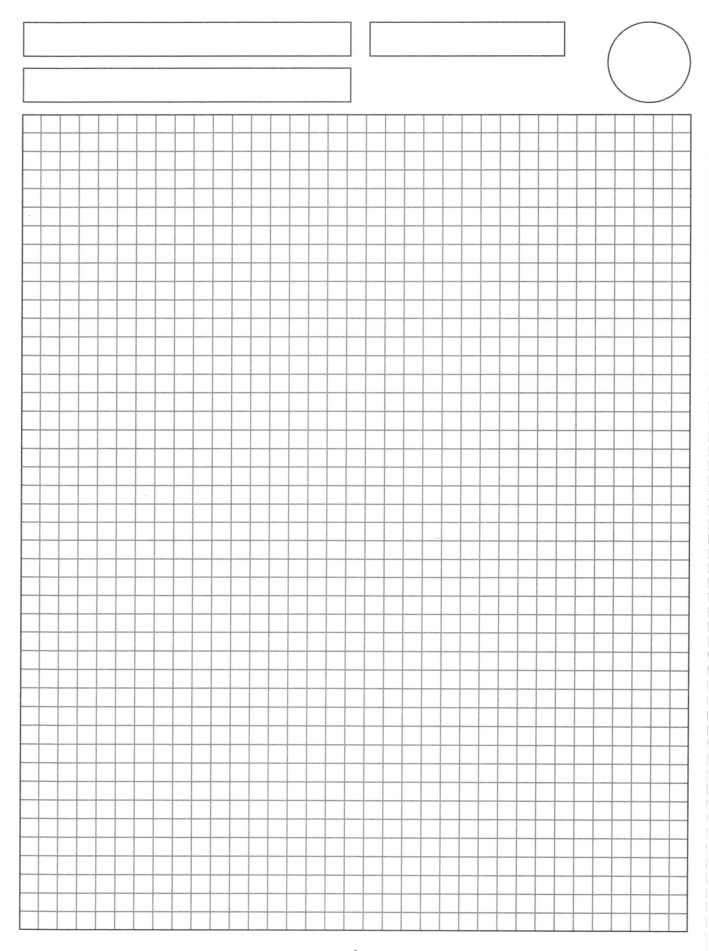

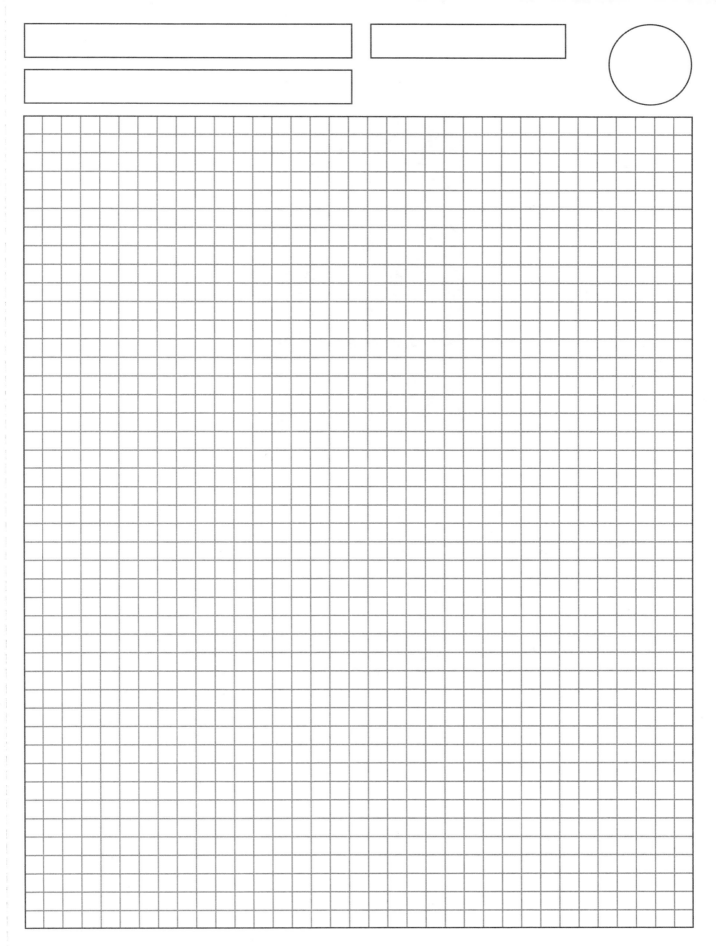

SECTOR 8

TARGET EQUATION

TARGET EQUATION WORKSHEET

Sector:

Date:

Type of attack:

Time of attack:

Avenues of Approach:

Vulnerabilities:

Type of attack:

Time of attack:

Avenues of Approach:

Vulnerabilities:

Type of attack:

Time of attack:

Avenues of Approach:

Vulnerabilities:

TARGET EQUATION WORKSHEET

Sector:

Date:

Type of attack:

Time of attack:

Avenues of Approach:

Vulnerabilities:

Type of attack:

Time of attack:

Avenues of Approach:

Vulnerabilities:

Type of attack:

Time of attack:

Avenues of Approach:

Vulnerabilities:

TARGET EQUATION WORKSHEET

Sector:

Date:

Type of attack:

Time of attack:

Avenues of Approach:

Vulnerabilities:

Type of attack:

Time of attack:

Avenues of Approach:

Vulnerabilities:

Type of attack:

Time of attack:

Avenues of Approach:

Vulnerabilities:

TARGET EQUATION WORKSHEET

Sector:

Date:

Type of attack:

Time of attack:

Avenues of Approach:

Vulnerabilities:

Type of attack:

Time of attack:

Avenues of Approach:

Vulnerabilities:

Type of attack:

Time of attack:

Avenues of Approach:

Vulnerabilities:

TARGET EQUATION WORKSHEET

Sector:

Date:

Type of attack:

Time of attack:

Avenues of Approach:

Vulnerabilities:

Type of attack:

Time of attack:

Avenues of Approach:

Vulnerabilities:

Type of attack:

Time of attack:

Avenues of Approach:

Vulnerabilities:

S9

SECTOR 9

SECTOR 9

OVERVIEW

THREAT ASSESSMENT SECTOR OVERVIEW

Sector:

Date:

Prepared by:

Situation:

Sector Overview:

Note: Make sure you print out map and directions to pertinent police precincts.

Police Departments:

PD Contact Information:

PD Response Times:

Crime Level:

Possible Threat Level:

Known Terror Threats:

Known Criminal Threats:

Note: Make sure you print out map and directions to all trauma centers. Always make the effort to proceed to a level 1 trauma center if the injury is life threatening.

Trauma Centers:

Trauma Center Level (I, II, III):

Response Times:

Weather Conditions:

Spring   Summer   Fall   Winter

SECTOR 9
CRITICAL ASSETS (CA)

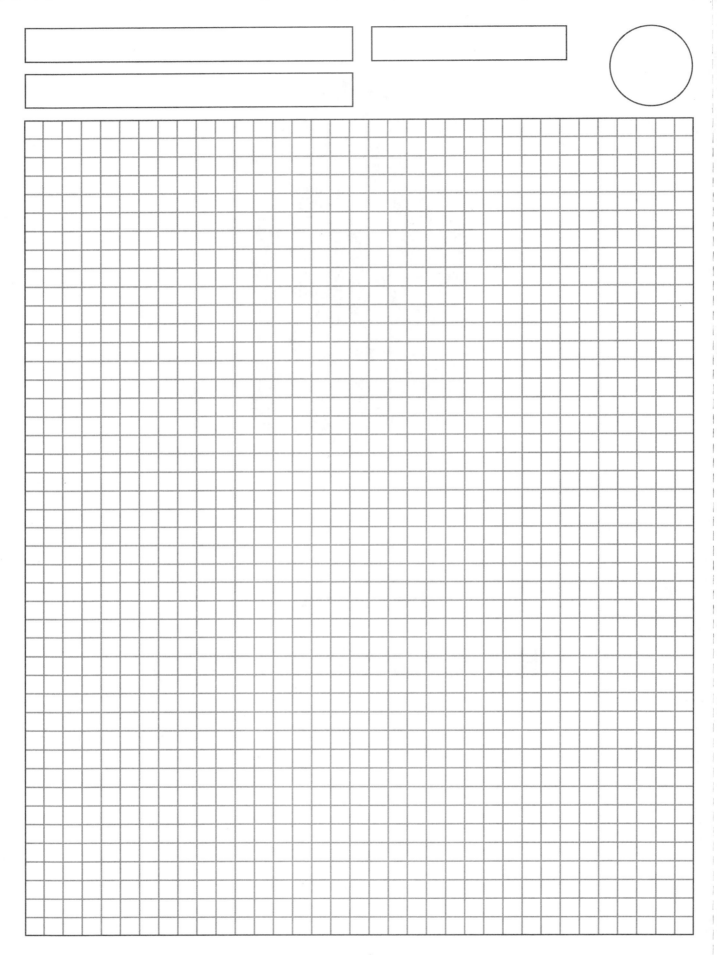

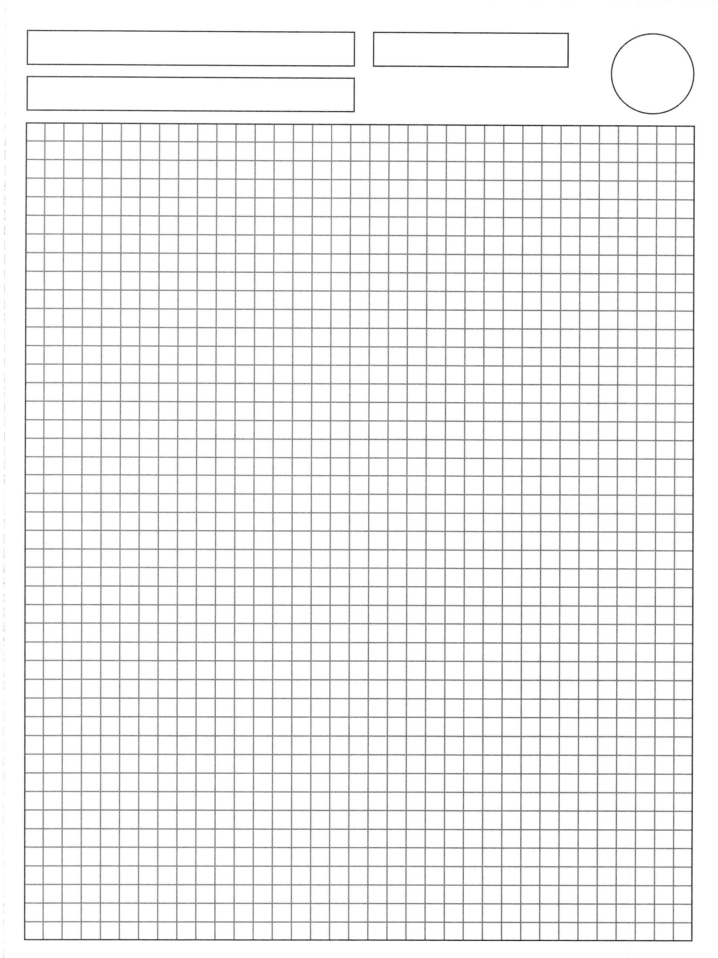

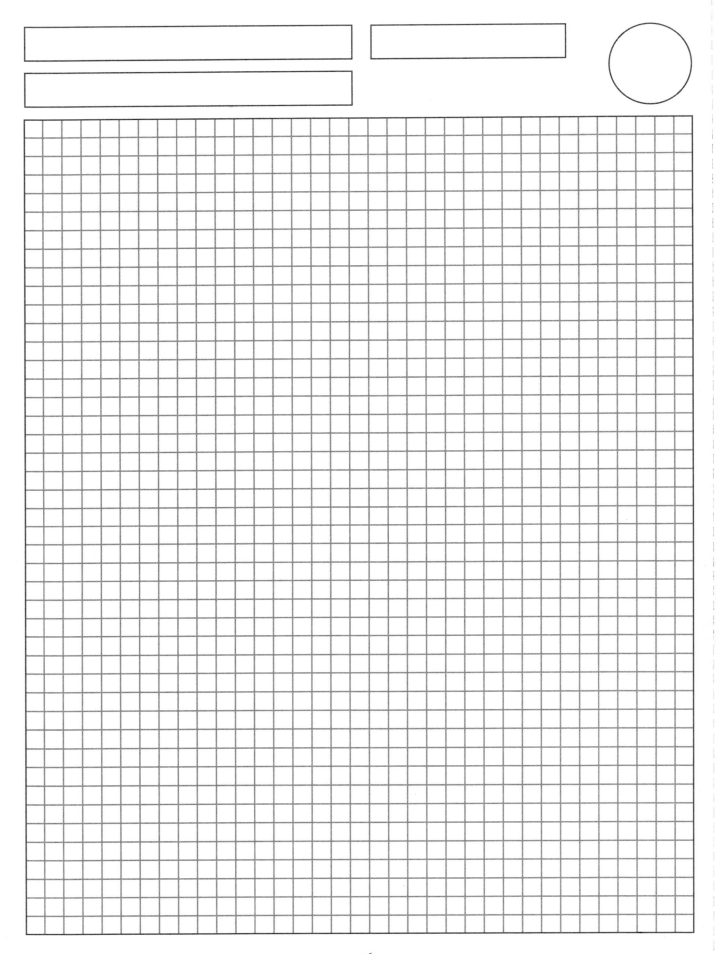

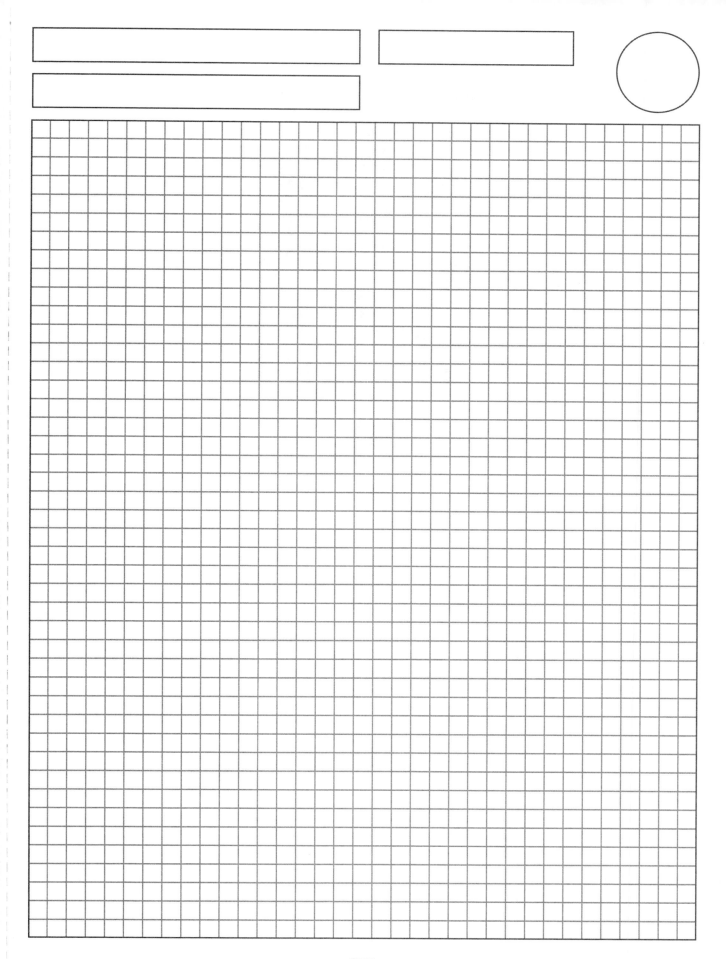

SECTOR 9

CRITICAL AREAS (CAR)

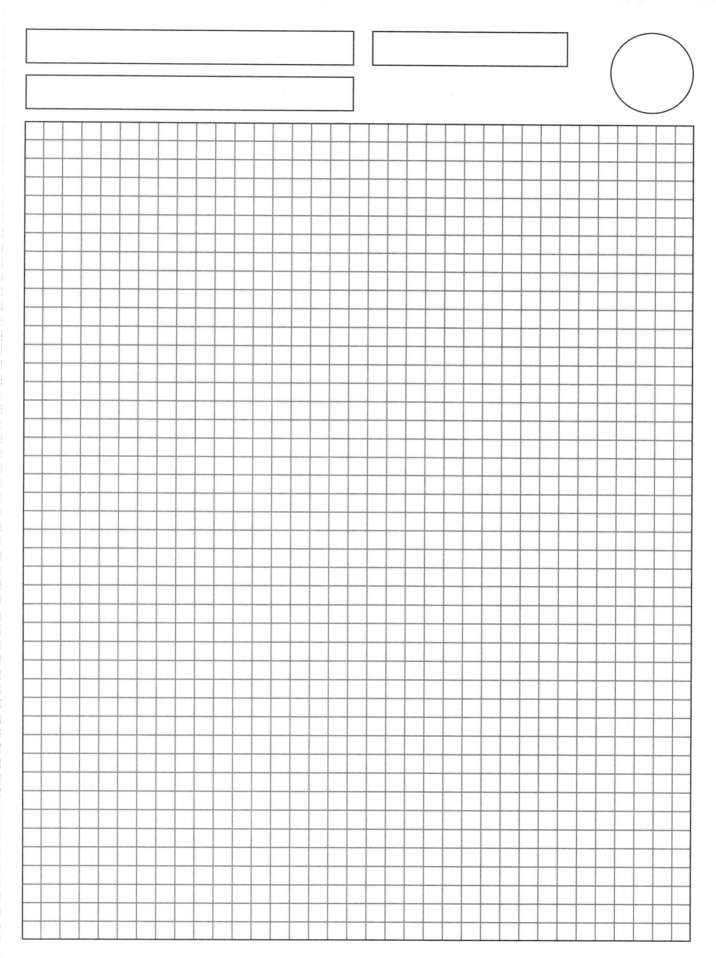

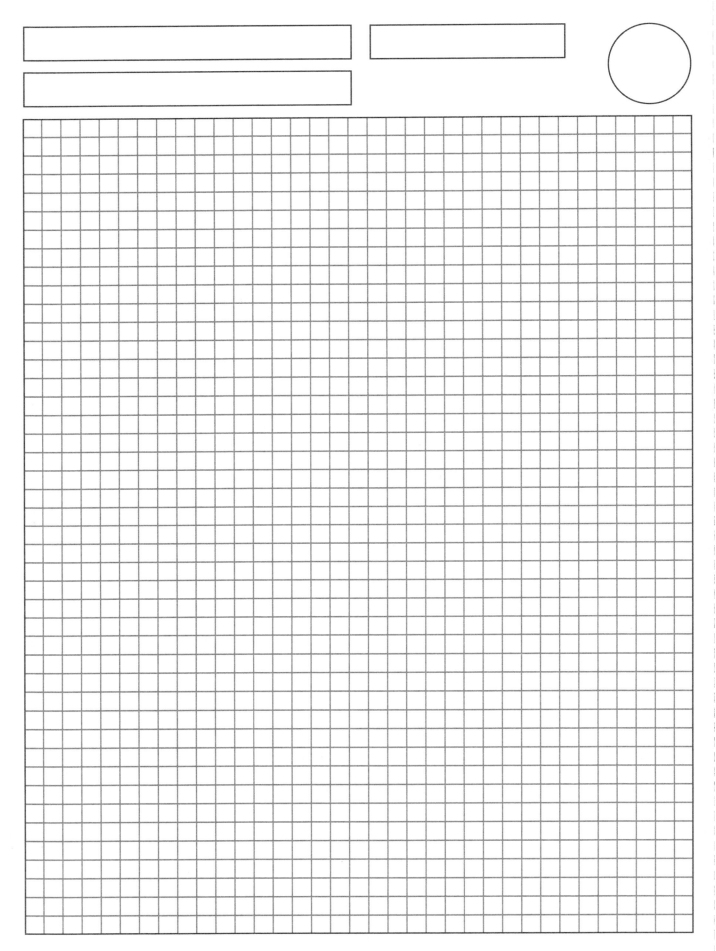

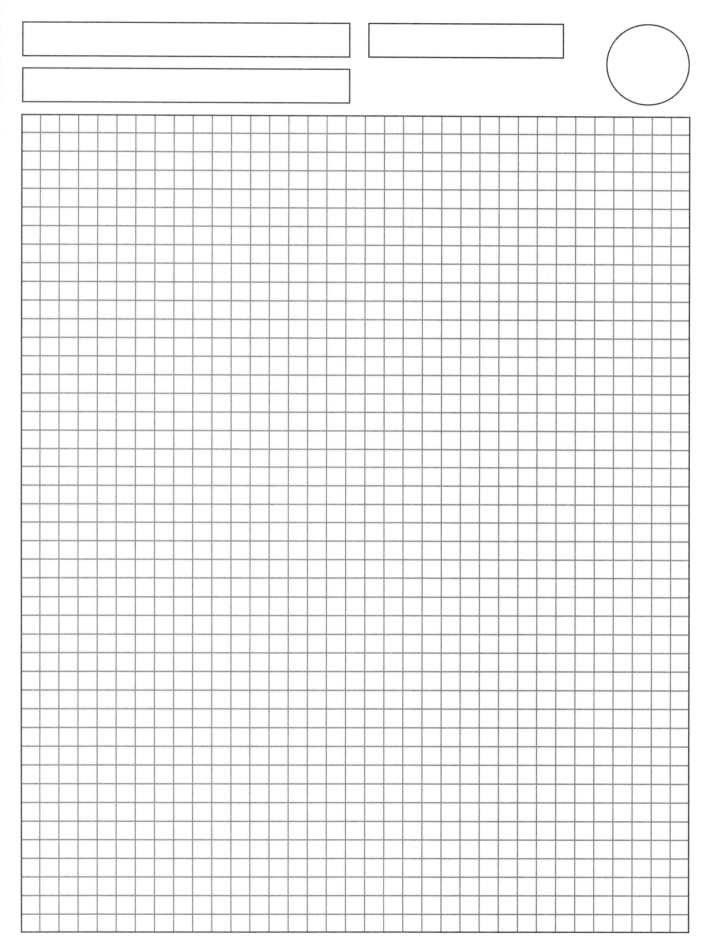

SECTOR 9

CRITICAL TIMES (CT)

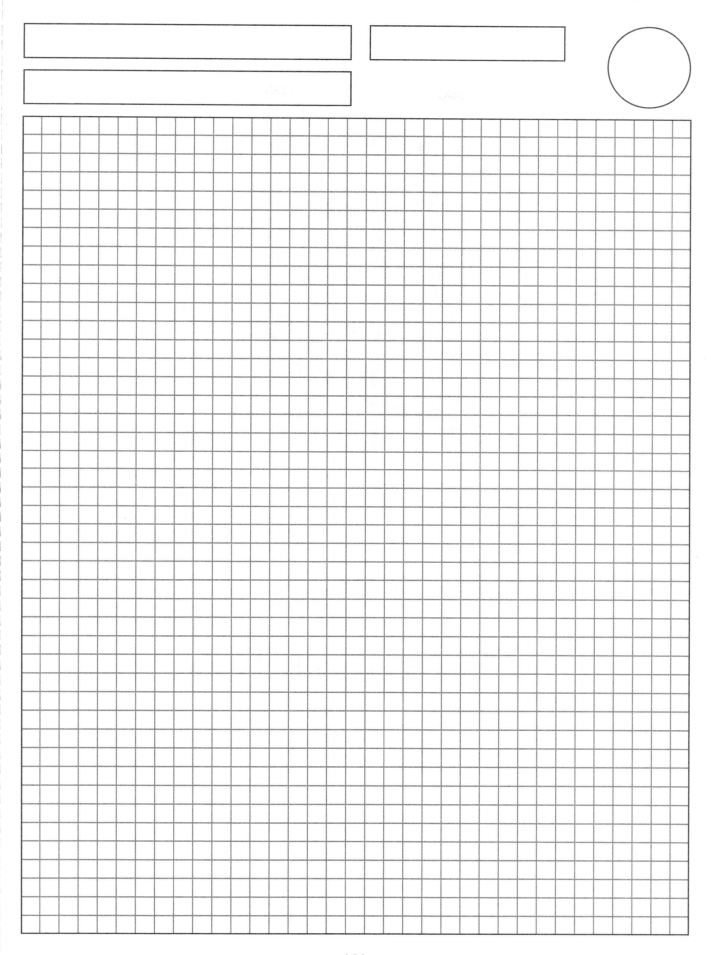

SECTOR 9

VULNERABILITIES

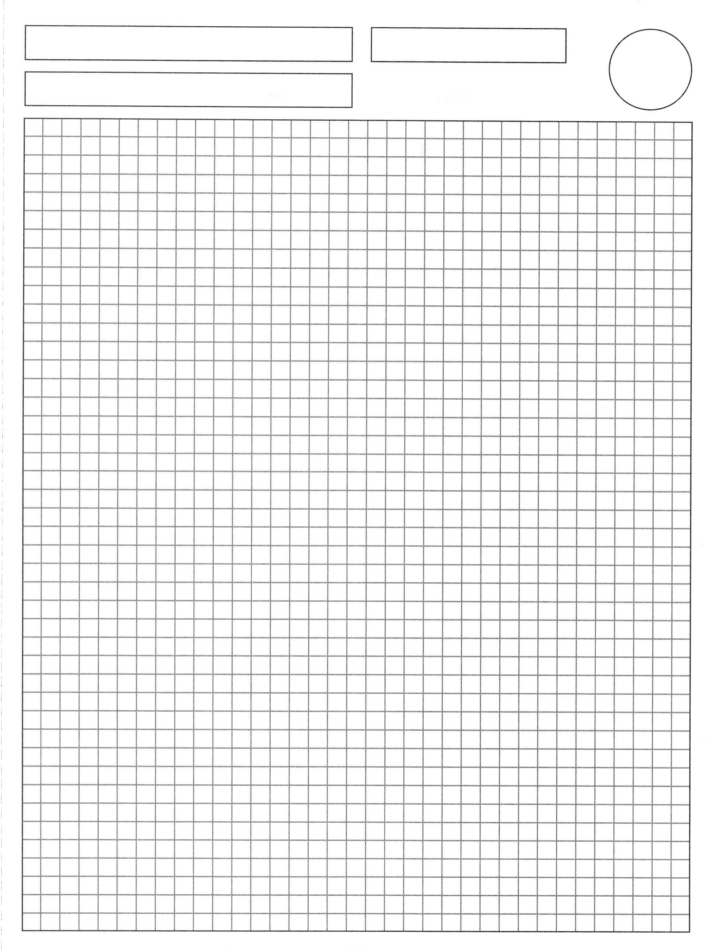

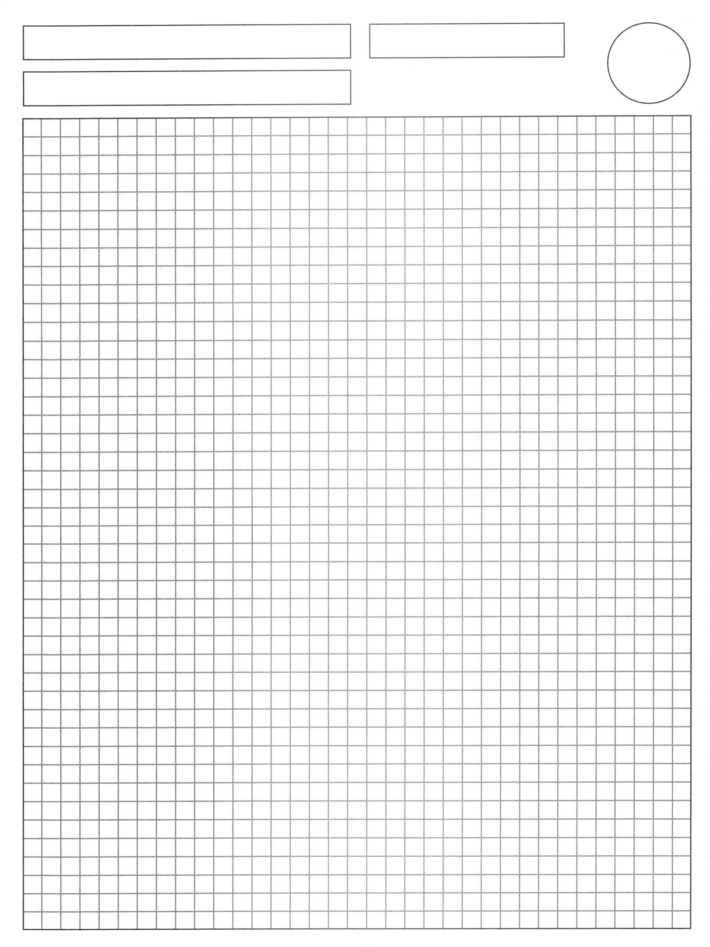

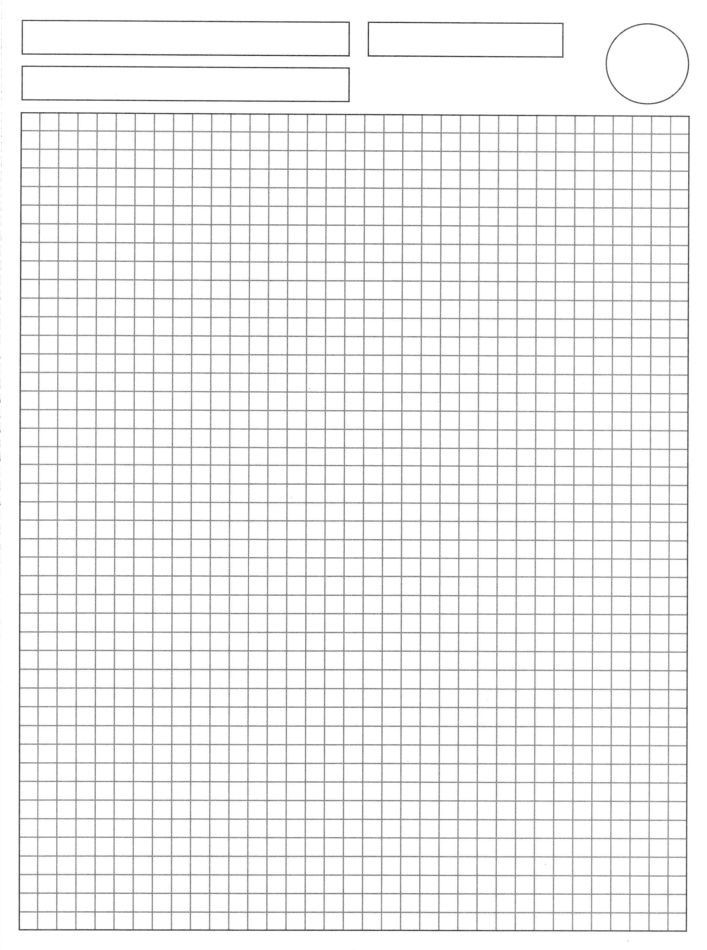

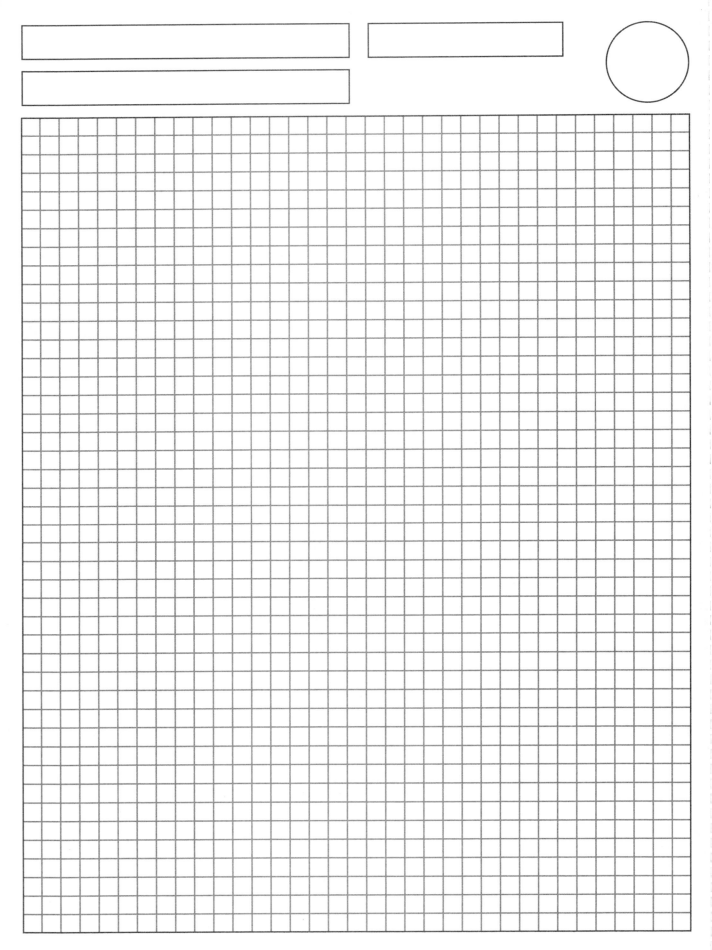

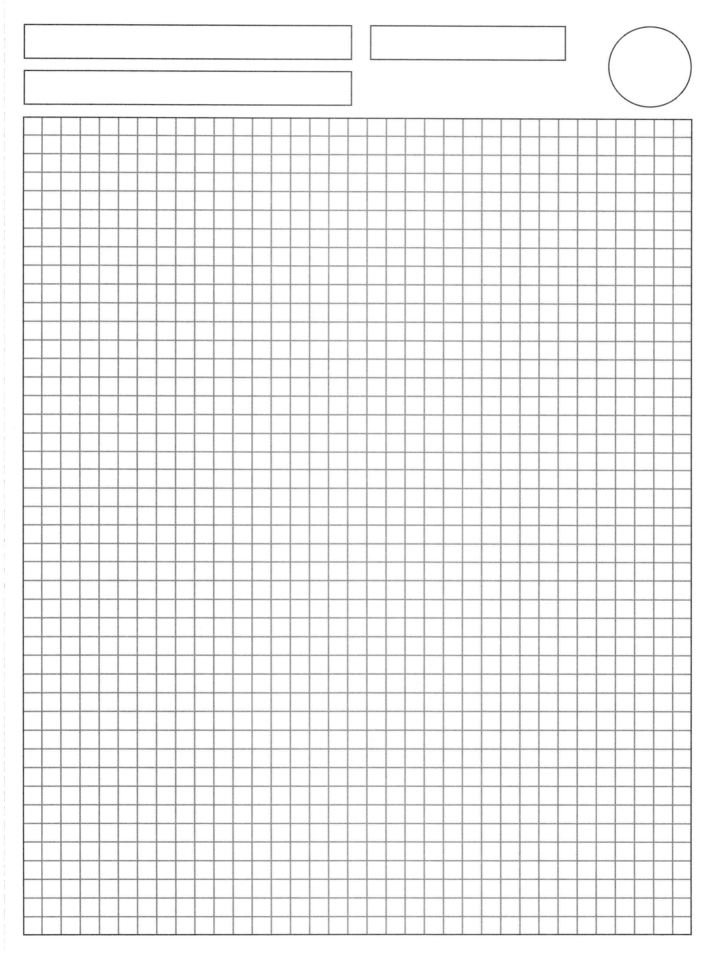

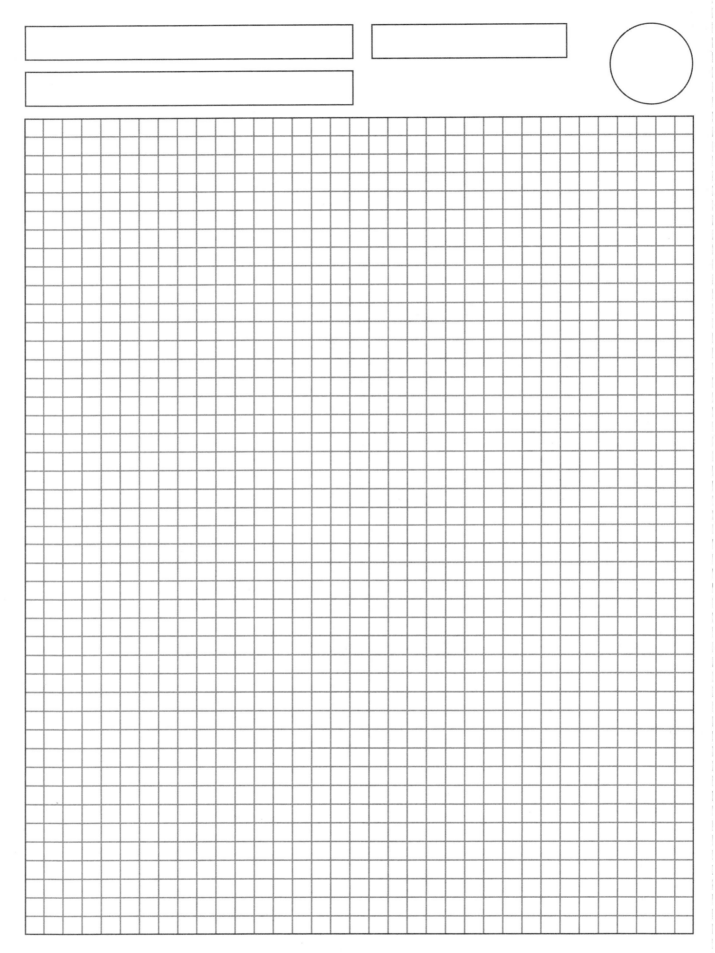

SECTOR 9

AVENUES OF APPROACH (AVP)

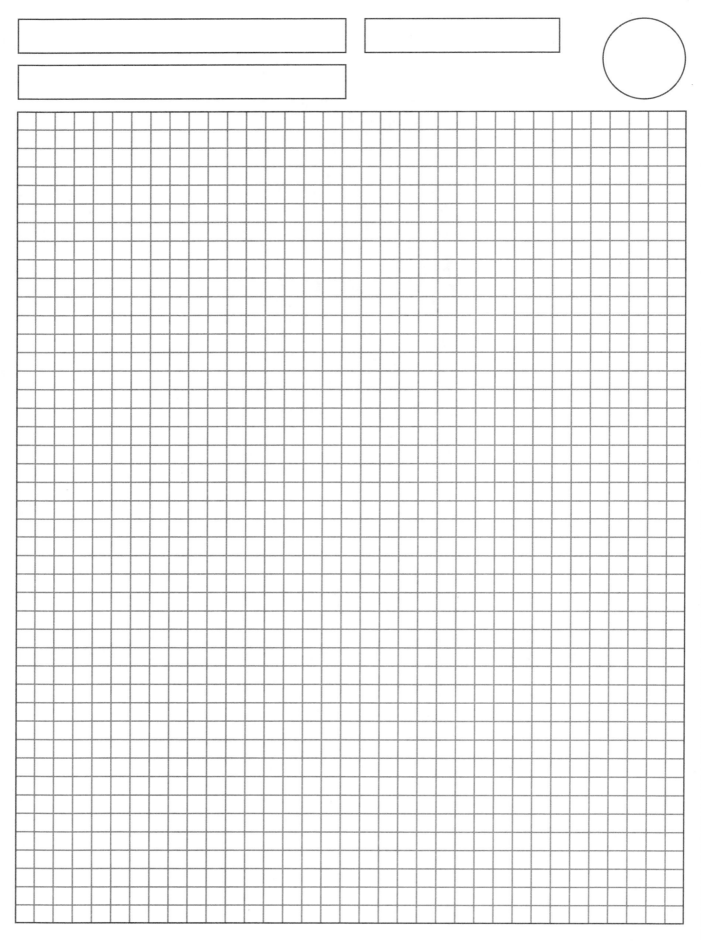

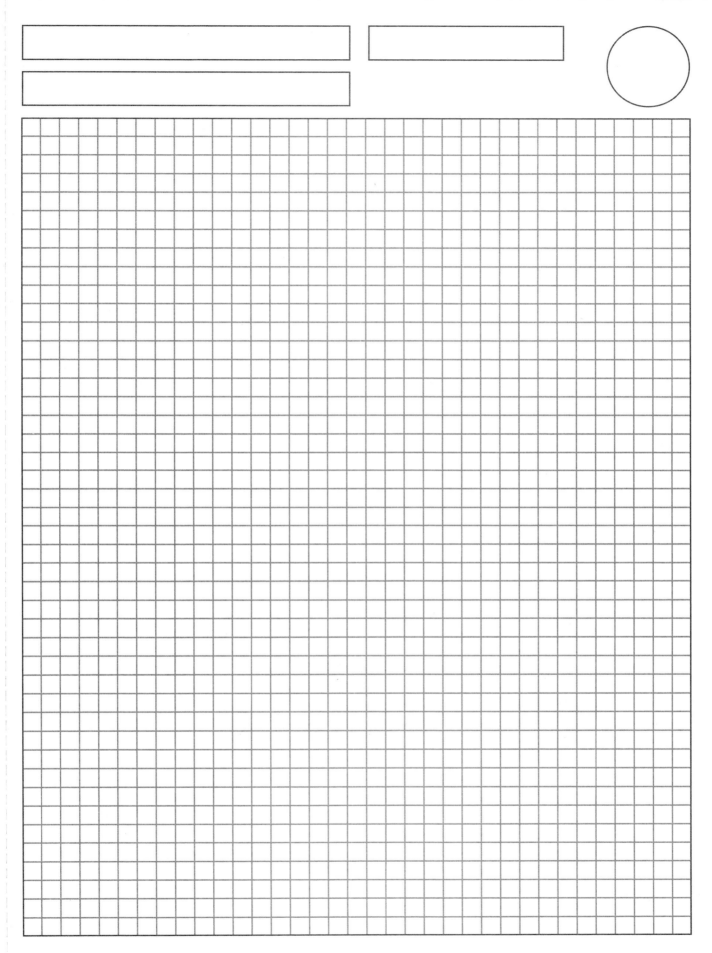

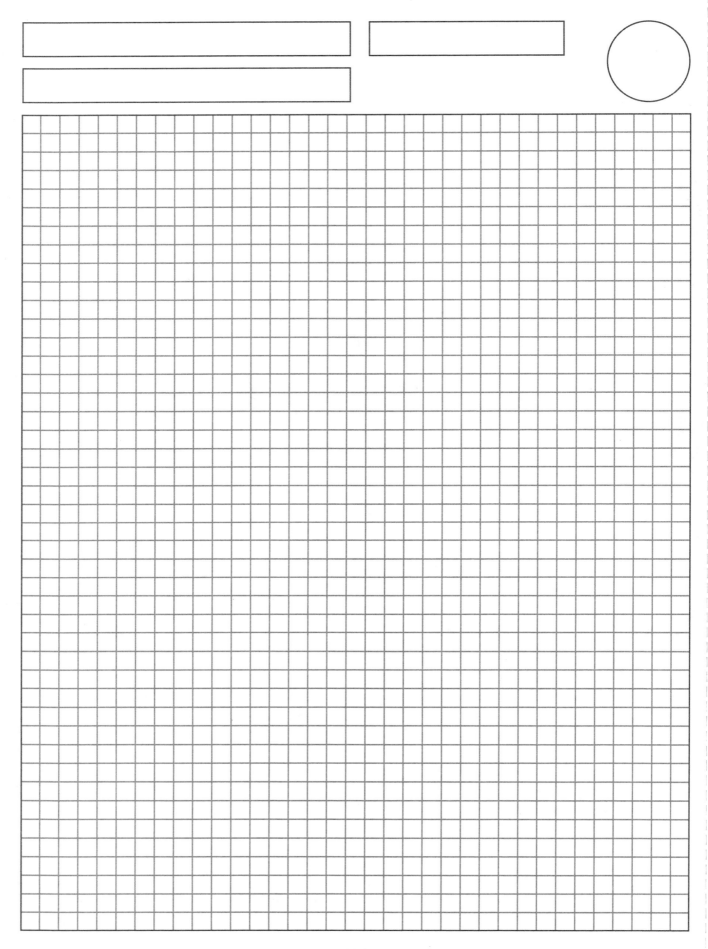

SECTOR 9

TARGET EQUATION

TARGET EQUATION WORKSHEET

Sector:	Date:

Type of attack:	Time of attack:

Avenues of Approach:

Vulnerabilities:

Type of attack:	Time of attack:

Avenues of Approach:

Vulnerabilities:

Type of attack:	Time of attack:

Avenues of Approach:

Vulnerabilities:

TARGET EQUATION WORKSHEET

Sector:

Date:

Type of attack:

Time of attack:

Avenues of Approach:

Vulnerabilities:

Type of attack:

Time of attack:

Avenues of Approach:

Vulnerabilities:

Type of attack:

Time of attack:

Avenues of Approach:

Vulnerabilities:

TARGET EQUATION WORKSHEET

Sector:

Date:

Type of attack:

Time of attack:

Avenues of Approach:

Vulnerabilities:

Type of attack:

Time of attack:

Avenues of Approach:

Vulnerabilities:

Type of attack:

Time of attack:

Avenues of Approach:

Vulnerabilities:

TARGET EQUATION WORKSHEET

Sector:

Date:

Type of attack:

Time of attack:

Avenues of Approach:

Vulnerabilities:

Type of attack:

Time of attack:

Avenues of Approach:

Vulnerabilities:

Type of attack:

Time of attack:

Avenues of Approach:

Vulnerabilities:

TARGET EQUATION WORKSHEET

Sector:	Date:

Type of attack:	Time of attack:

Avenues of Approach:

Vulnerabilities:

Type of attack:	Time of attack:

Avenues of Approach:

Vulnerabilities:

Type of attack:	Time of attack:

Avenues of Approach:

Vulnerabilities:

S10

SECTOR 10

SECTOR 10

OVERVIEW

THREAT ASSESSMENT SECTOR OVERVIEW

Sector:

Date:

Prepared by:

Situation:

Sector Overview:

Note: Make sure you print out map and directions to pertinent police precincts.

Police Departments:

PD Contact Information:

PD Response Times:

Crime Level:

Possible Threat Level:

Known Terror Threats:

Known Criminal Threats:

Note: Make sure you print out map and directions to all trauma centers. Always make the effort to proceed to a level 1 trauma center if the injury is life threatening.

Trauma Centers:

Trauma Center Level (I, II, III):

Response Times:

Weather Conditions:

Spring   Summer   Fall   Winter

SECTOR 10

CRITICAL ASSETS (CA)

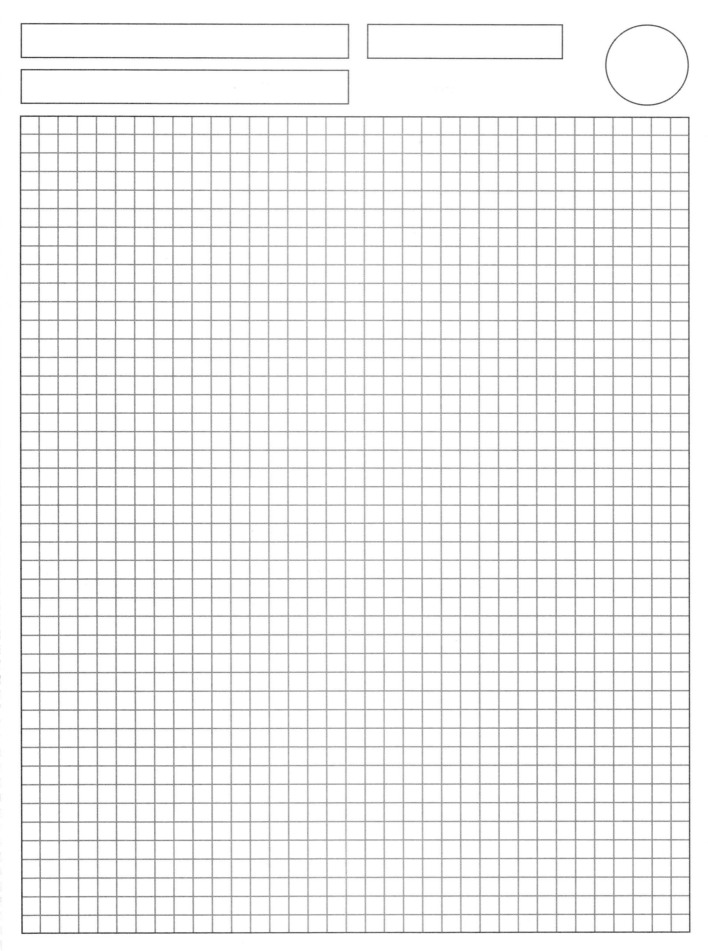

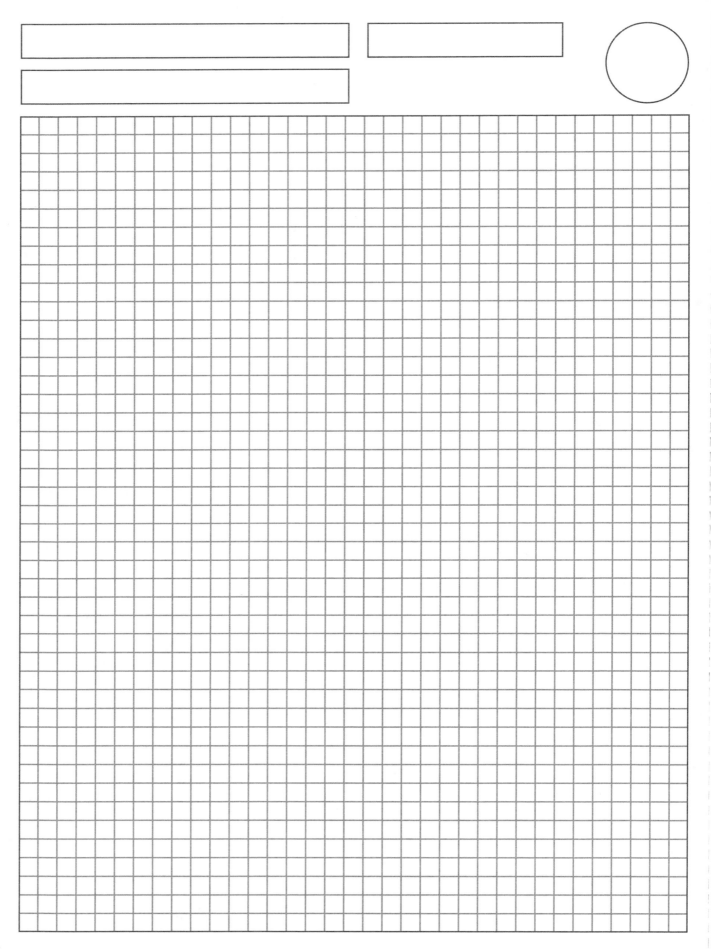

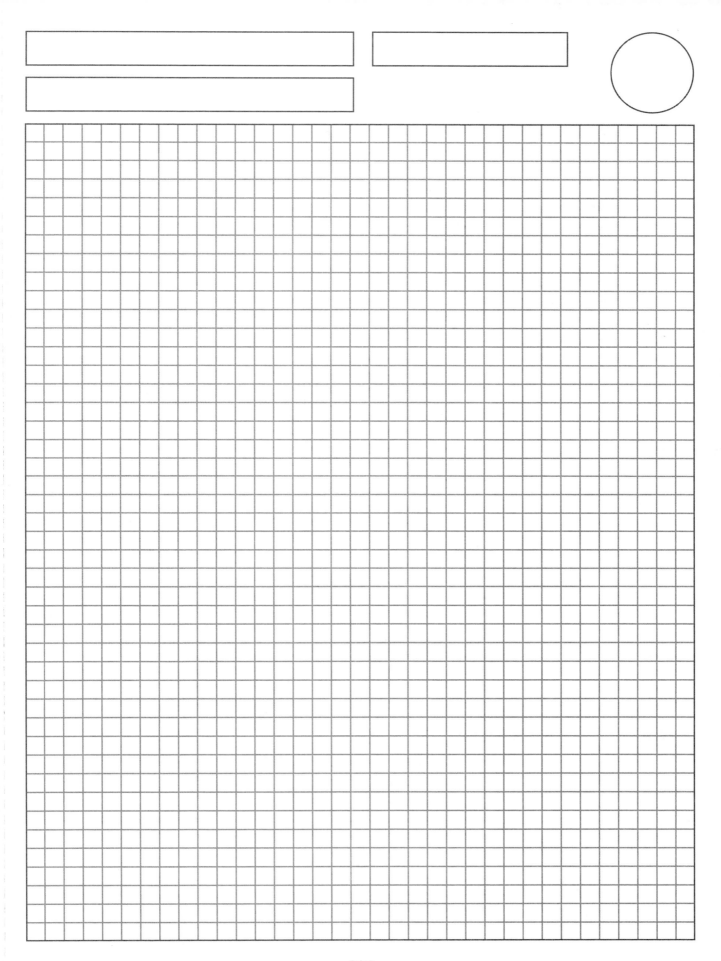

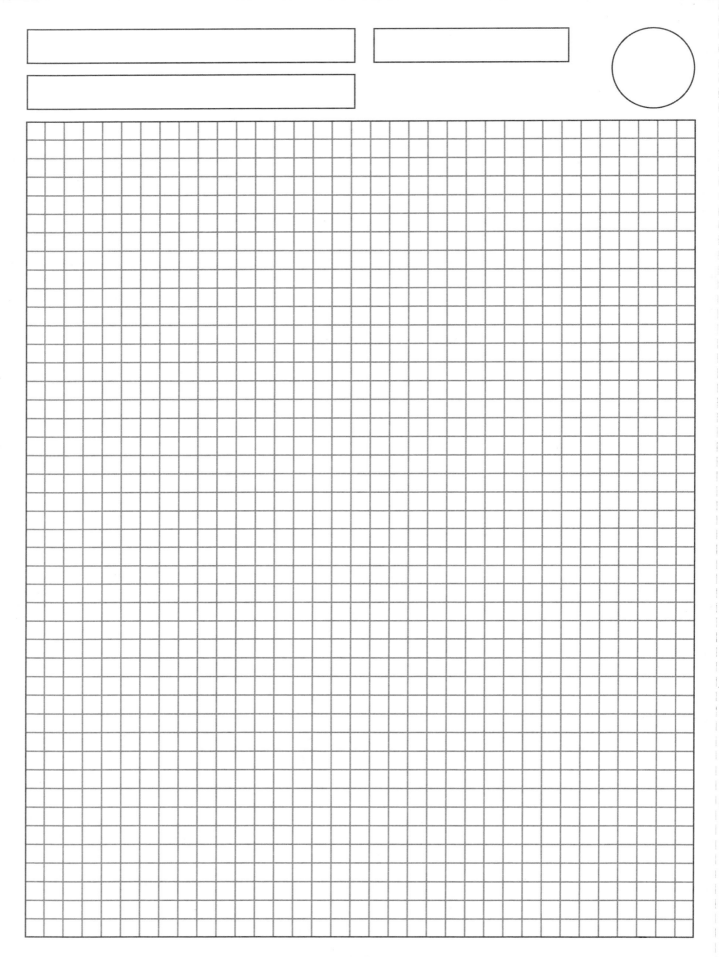

SECTOR 10

CRITICAL AREAS (CAR)

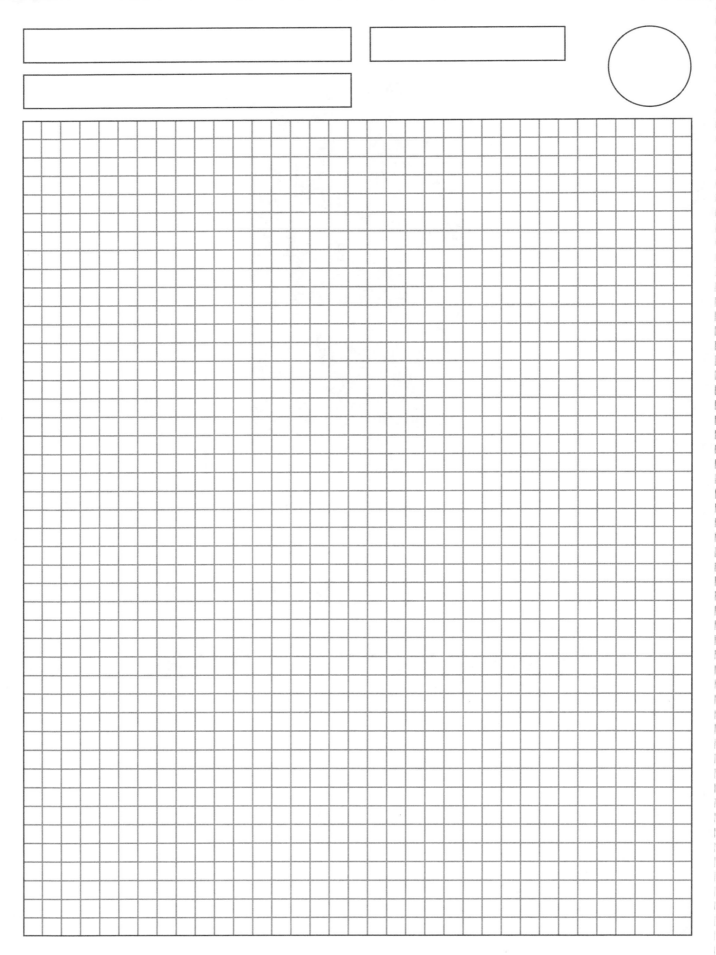

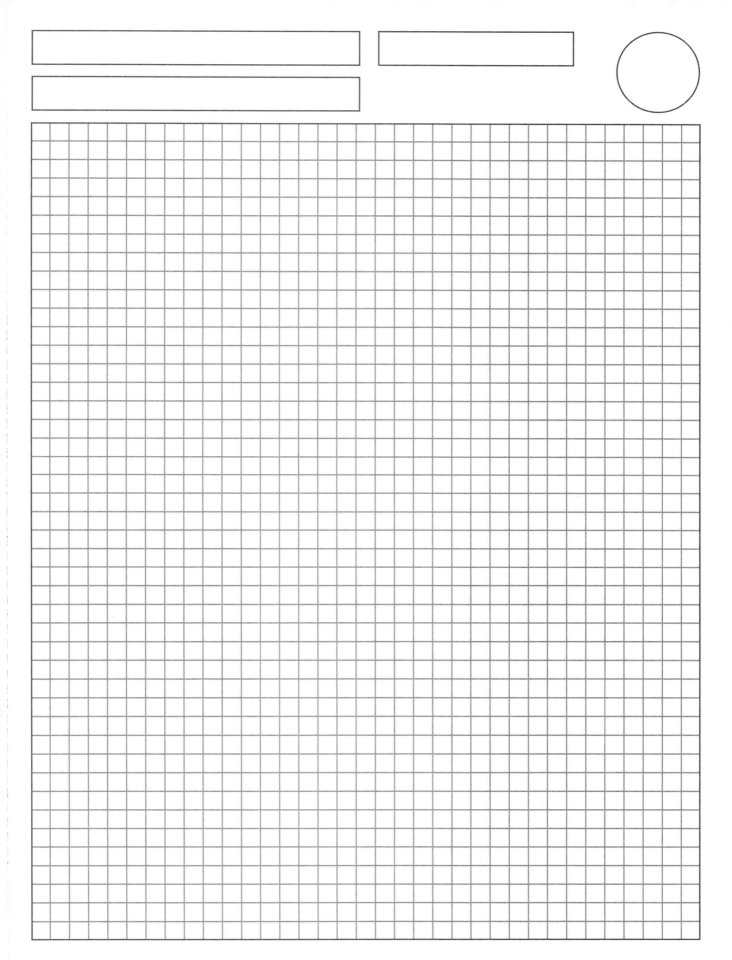

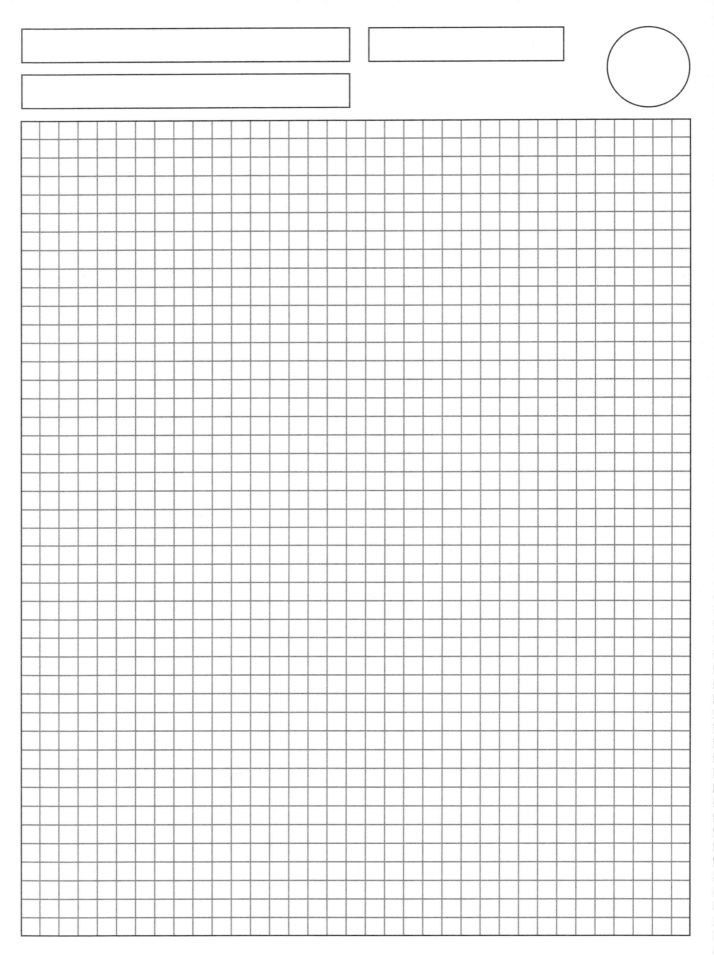

SECTOR 10
CRITICAL TIMES (CT)

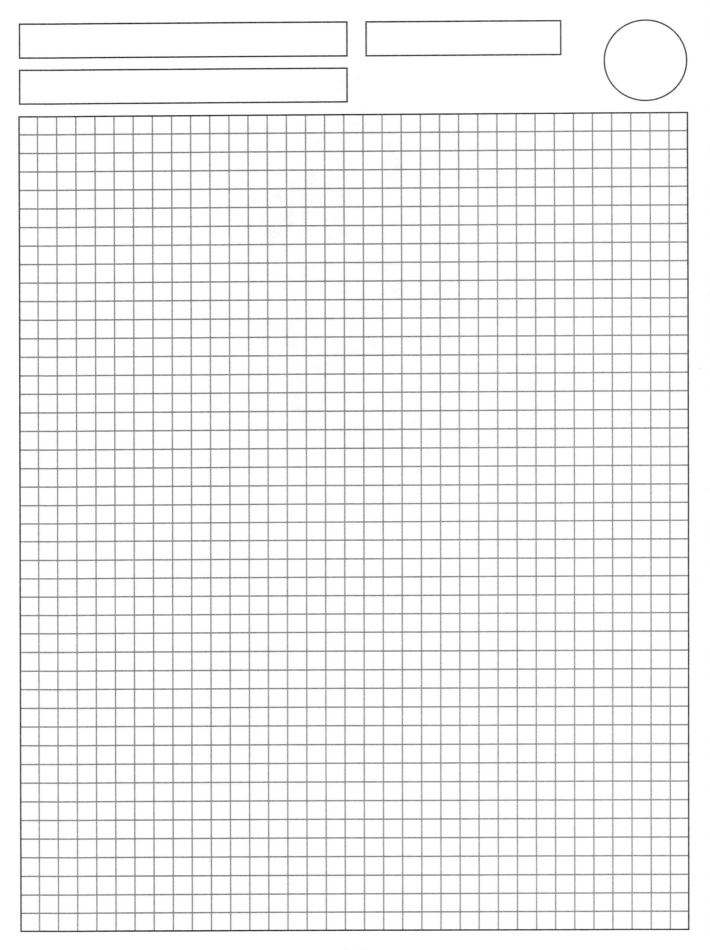

SECTOR 10

VULNERABILITIES

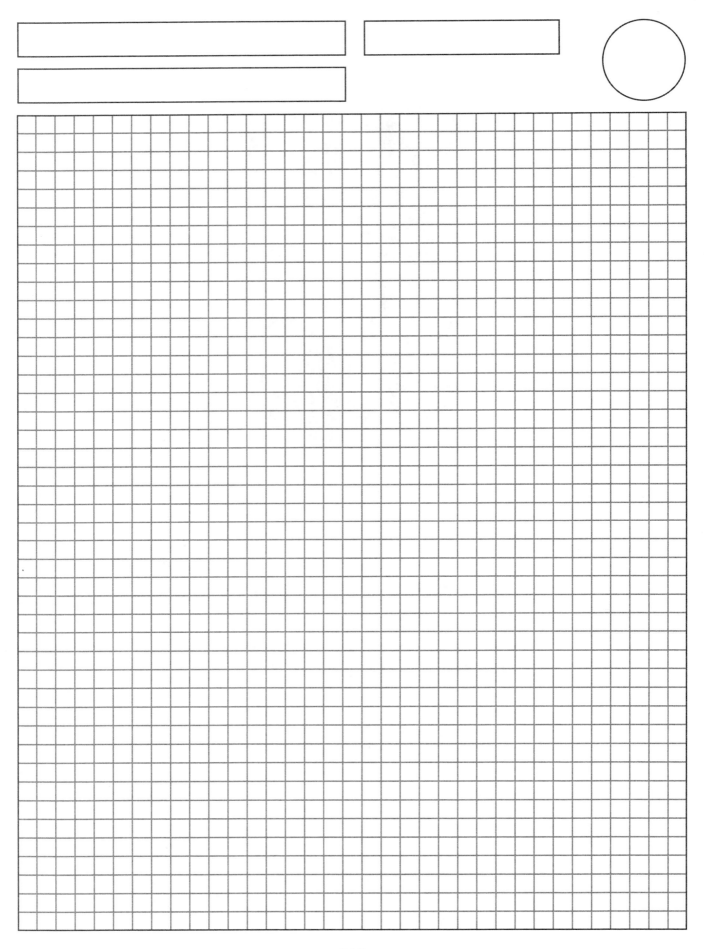

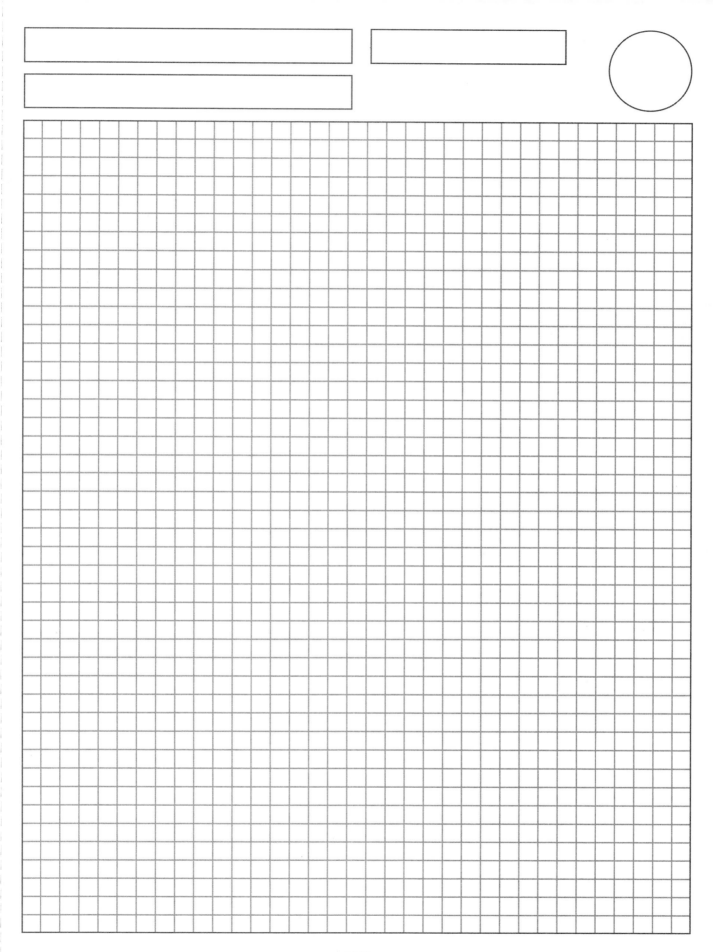

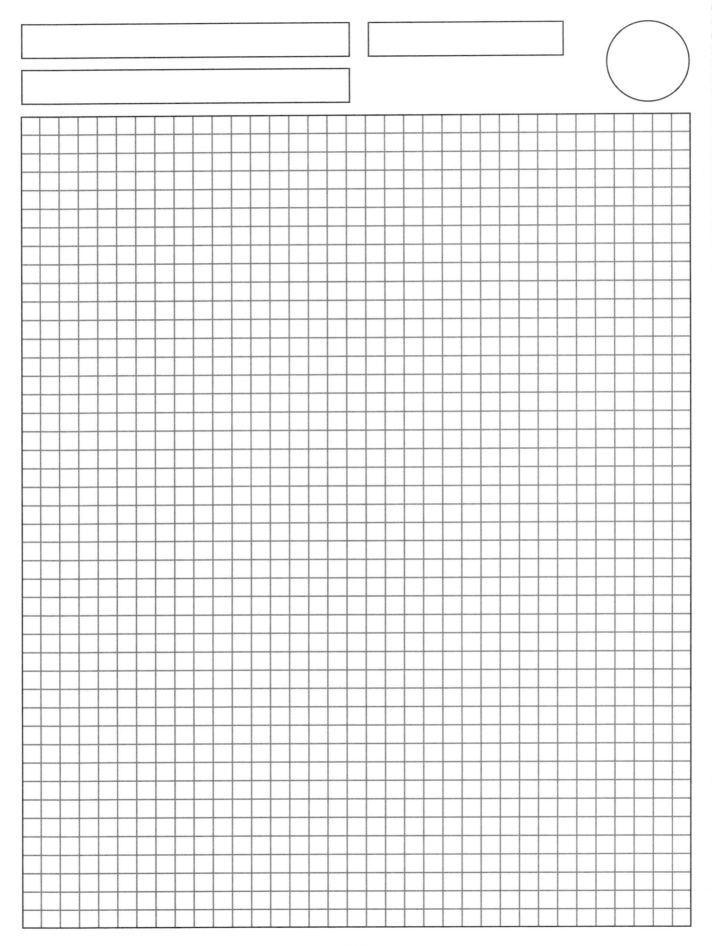

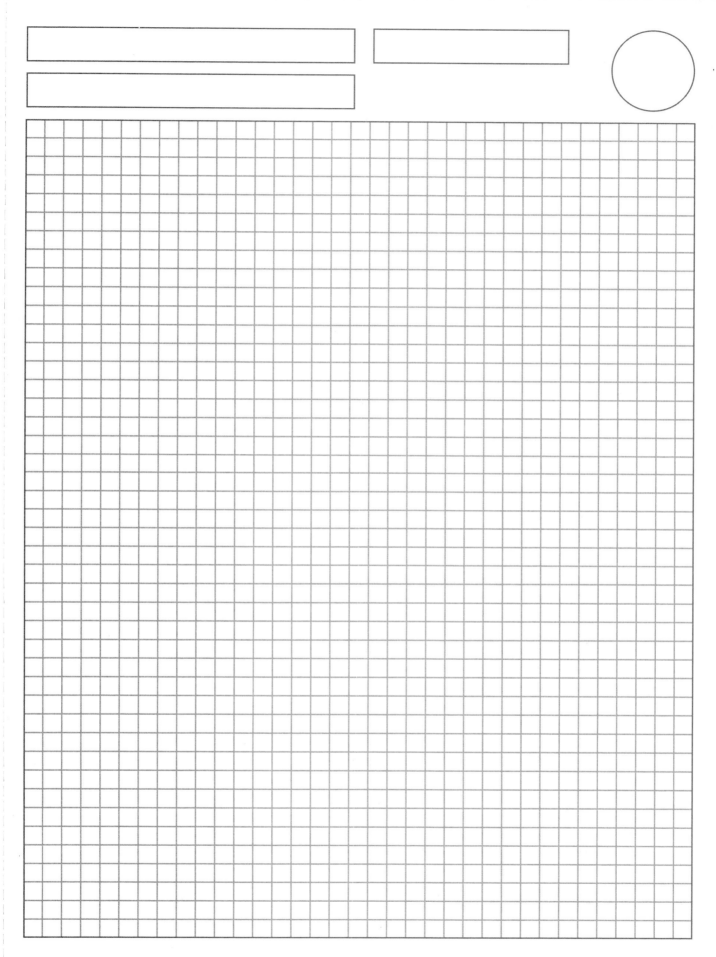

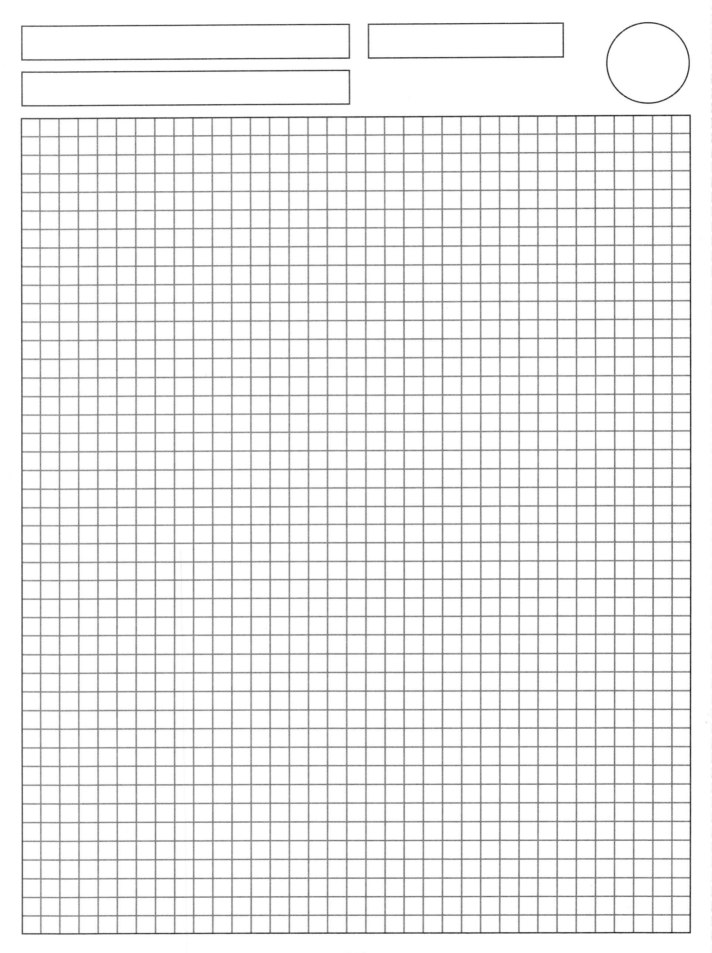

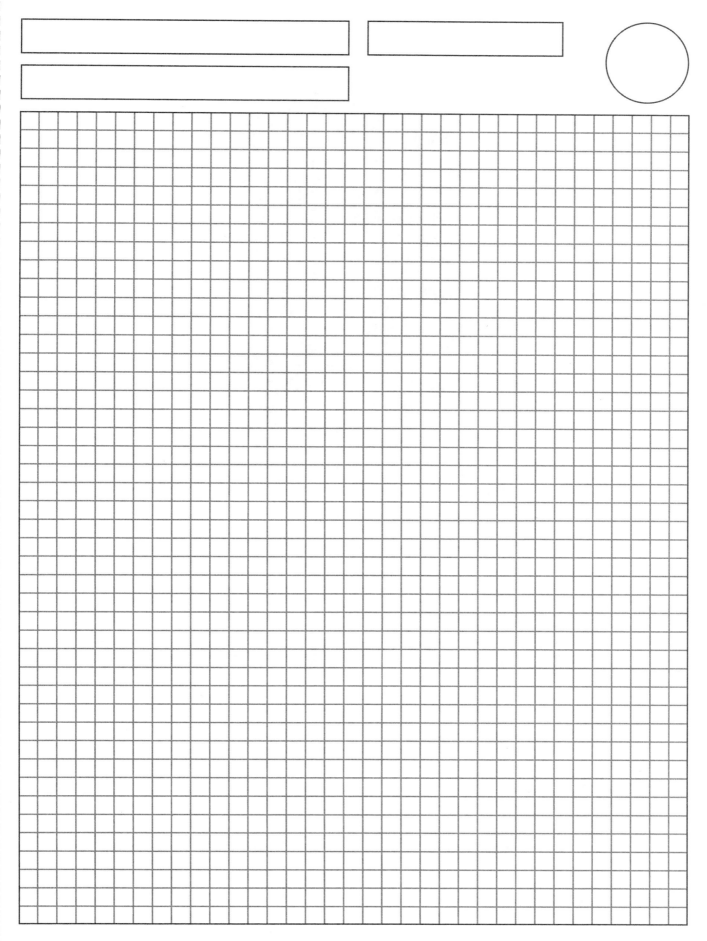

SECTOR 10

AVENUES OF APPROACH (AVP)

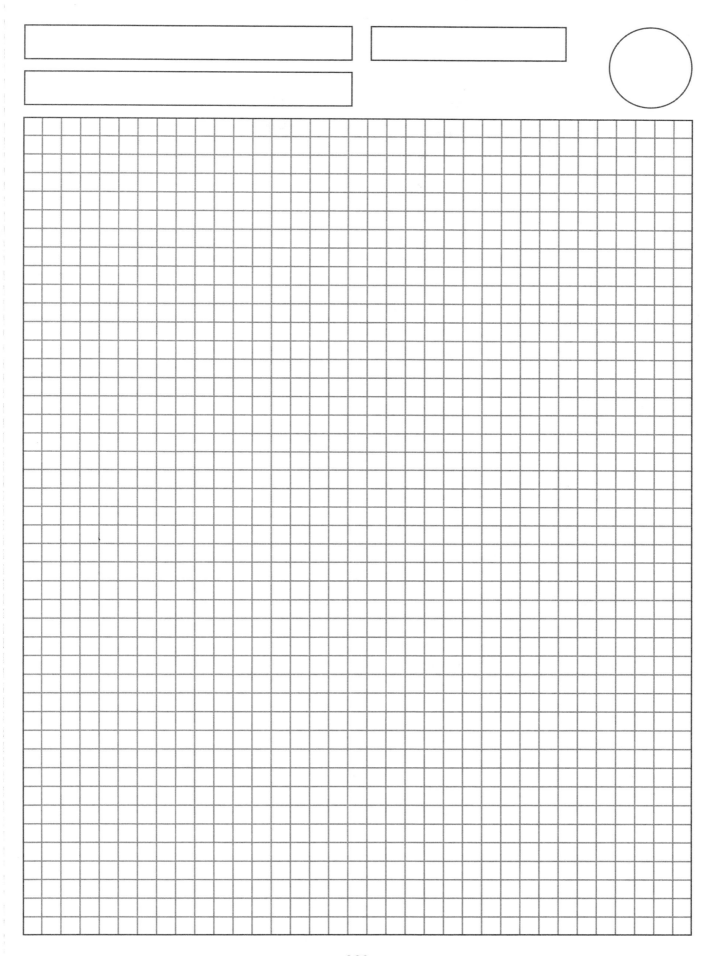

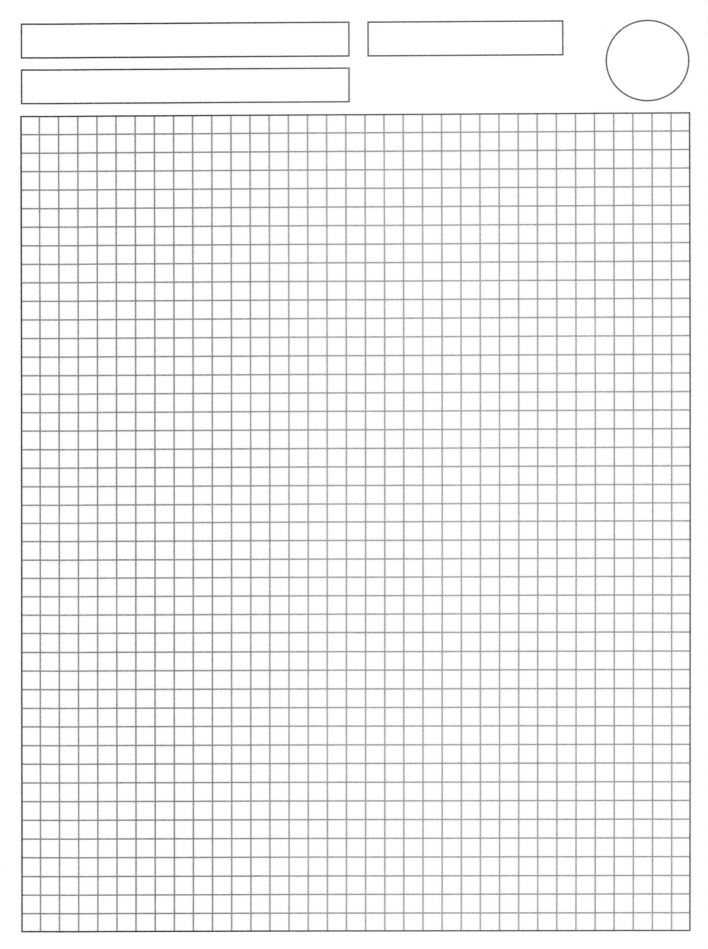

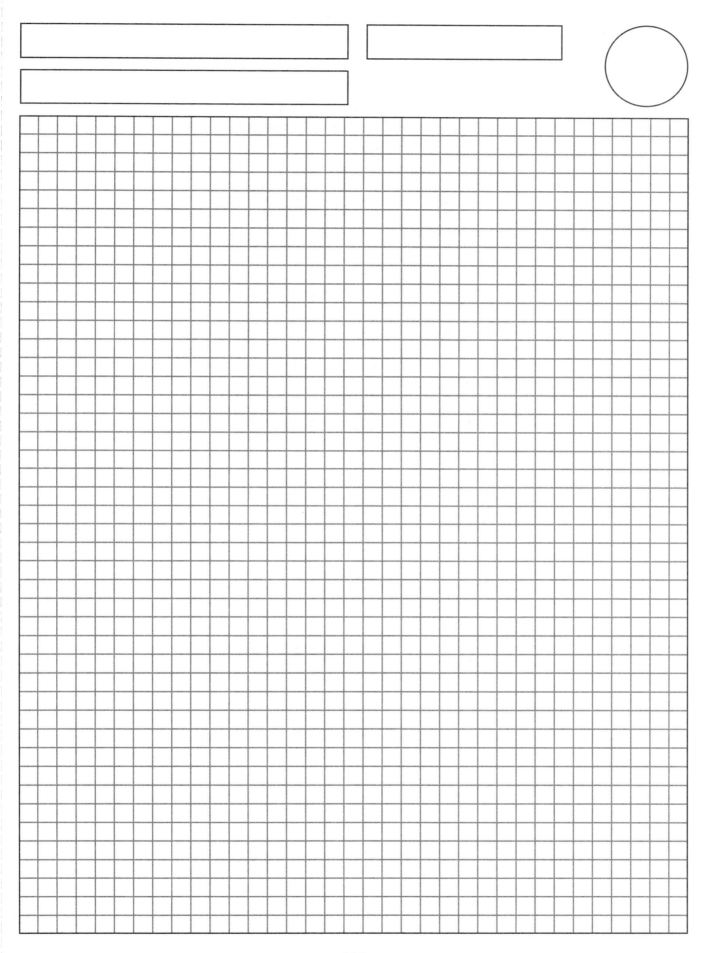

SECTOR 10

TARGET EQUATION

TARGET EQUATION WORKSHEET

Sector:	Date:

Type of attack:	Time of attack:

Avenues of Approach:

Vulnerabilities:

Type of attack:	Time of attack:

Avenues of Approach:

Vulnerabilities:

Type of attack:	Time of attack:

Avenues of Approach:

Vulnerabilities:

TARGET EQUATION WORKSHEET

Sector:

Date:

Type of attack:

Time of attack:

Avenues of Approach:

Vulnerabilities:

Type of attack:

Time of attack:

Avenues of Approach:

Vulnerabilities:

Type of attack:

Time of attack:

Avenues of Approach:

Vulnerabilities:

TARGET EQUATION WORKSHEET

Sector:

Date:

Type of attack:

Time of attack:

Avenues of Approach:

Vulnerabilities:

Type of attack:

Time of attack:

Avenues of Approach:

Vulnerabilities:

Type of attack:

Time of attack:

Avenues of Approach:

Vulnerabilities:

TARGET EQUATION WORKSHEET

Sector:

Date:

Type of attack:

Time of attack:

Avenues of Approach:

Vulnerabilities:

Type of attack:

Time of attack:

Avenues of Approach:

Vulnerabilities:

Type of attack:

Time of attack:

Avenues of Approach:

Vulnerabilities:

TARGET EQUATION WORKSHEET

Sector:

Date:

Type of attack:

Time of attack:

Avenues of Approach:

Vulnerabilities:

Type of attack:

Time of attack:

Avenues of Approach:

Vulnerabilities:

Type of attack:

Time of attack:

Avenues of Approach:

Vulnerabilities:

NEVER STOP ASSESSING YOUR ASSESSMENT

The key to staying safe lies in staying aware. Never assume you figured it all out, because as soon as you stop assessing, all the bad guys have to do is pick up their targeting where you stopped. Regardless of what society may tell you, safety is a personal endeavor that requires your involvement. Resting on the hopes that others will protect you, your family, your businesses or even your community is simply exercising learned helplessness.

Refuse to be helpless!

Now that you have completed this assessment, sit back and reward yourself and those around you with the greatest defensive tool a person can have, awareness!

Next step, The Defensive Standard Operating Procedures Workbook

Jonathan T Gilliam

"Be strong and of good courage. Do not be afraid nor be dismayed for the Lord your God is with you wherever you go." — God

TO LEARN MORE GO TO
www.jonathanTGilliam.com

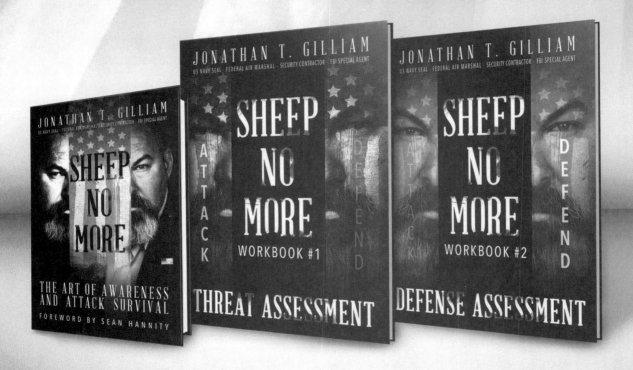

EXTRA WORKSHEETS

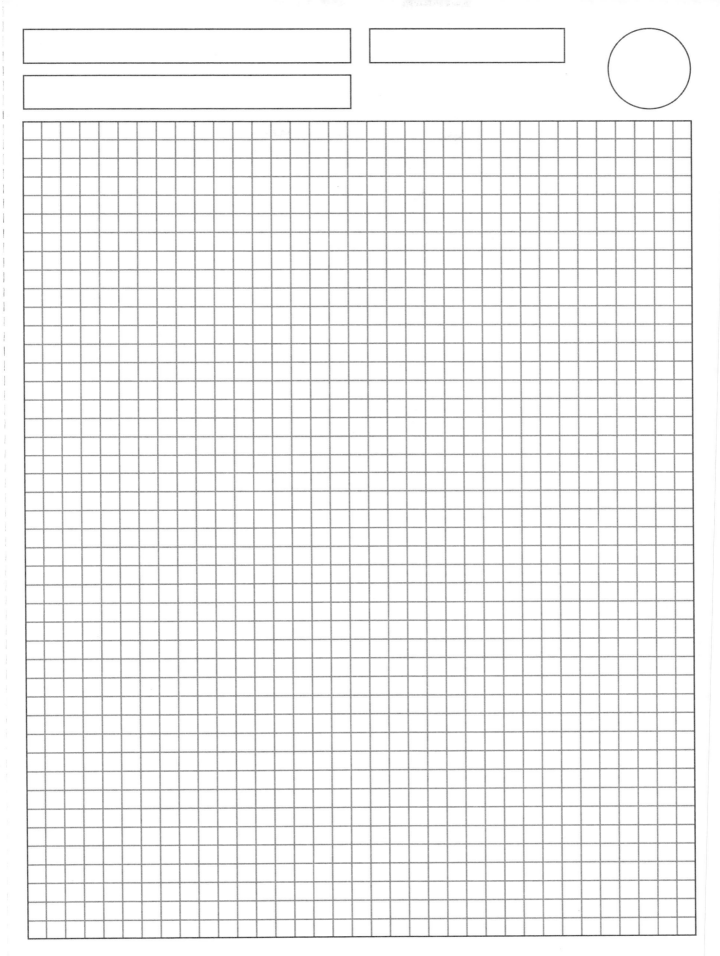

335

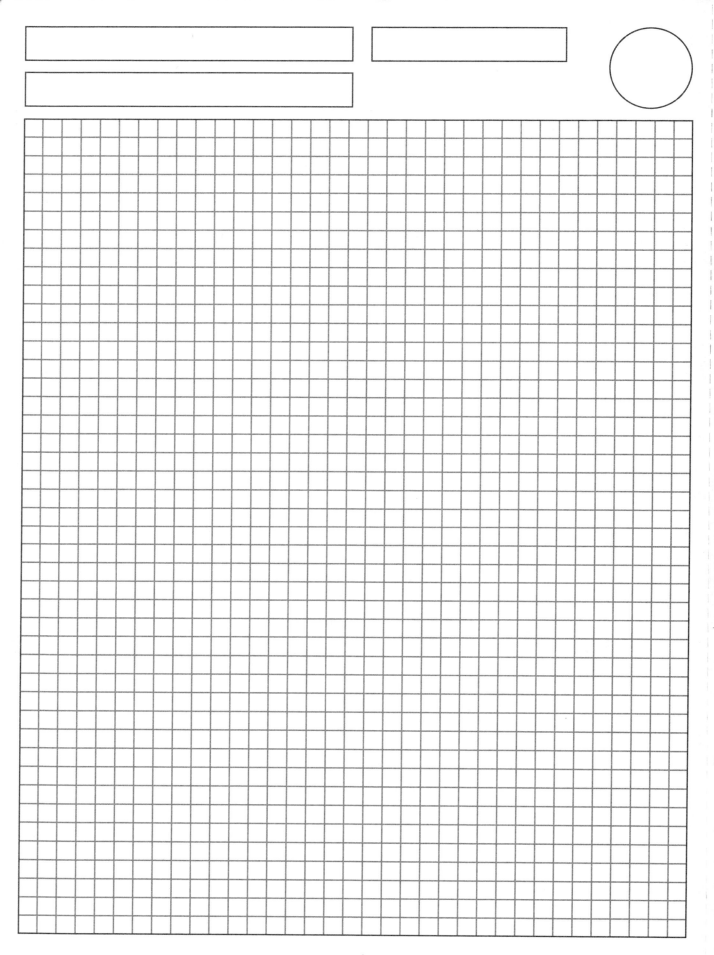

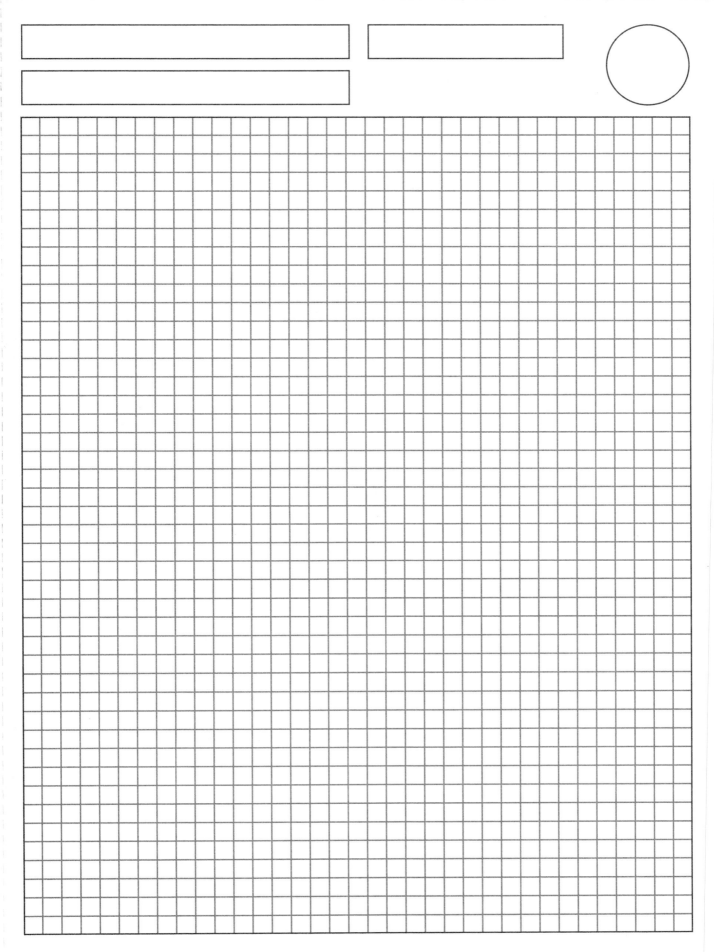

337

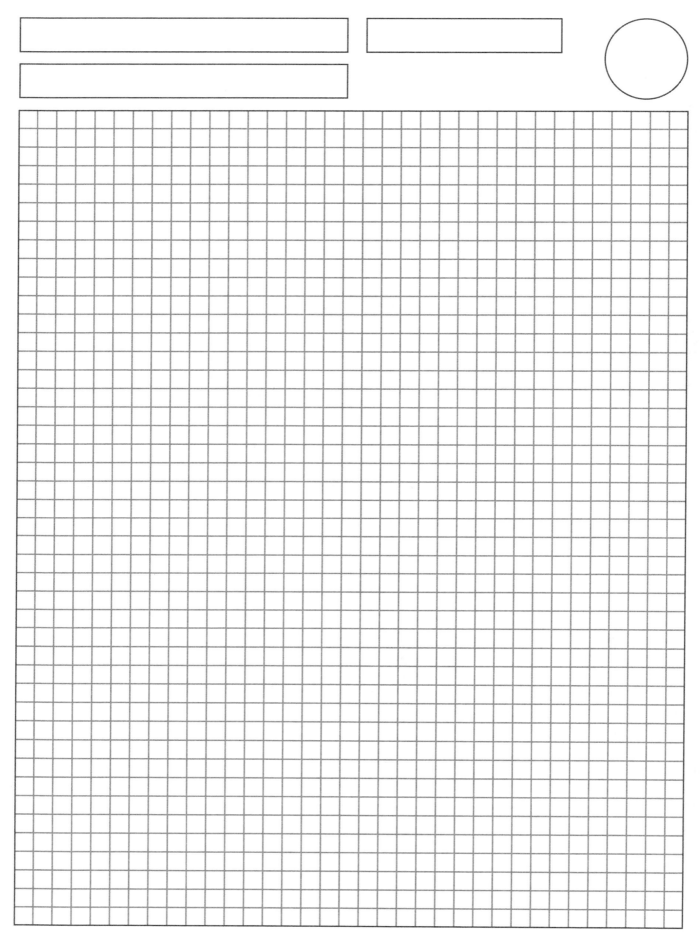

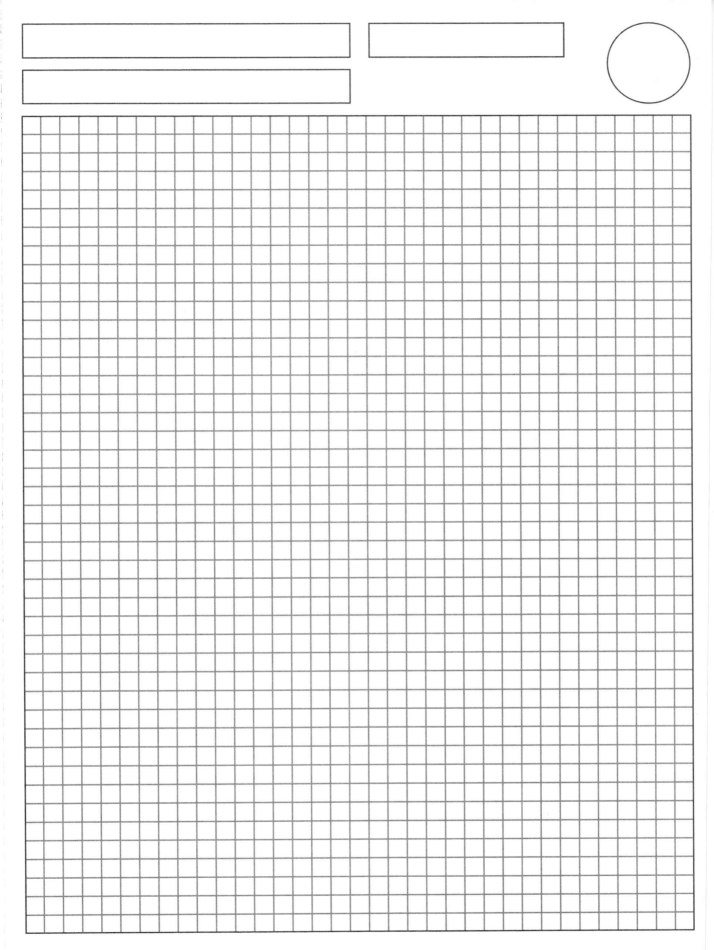

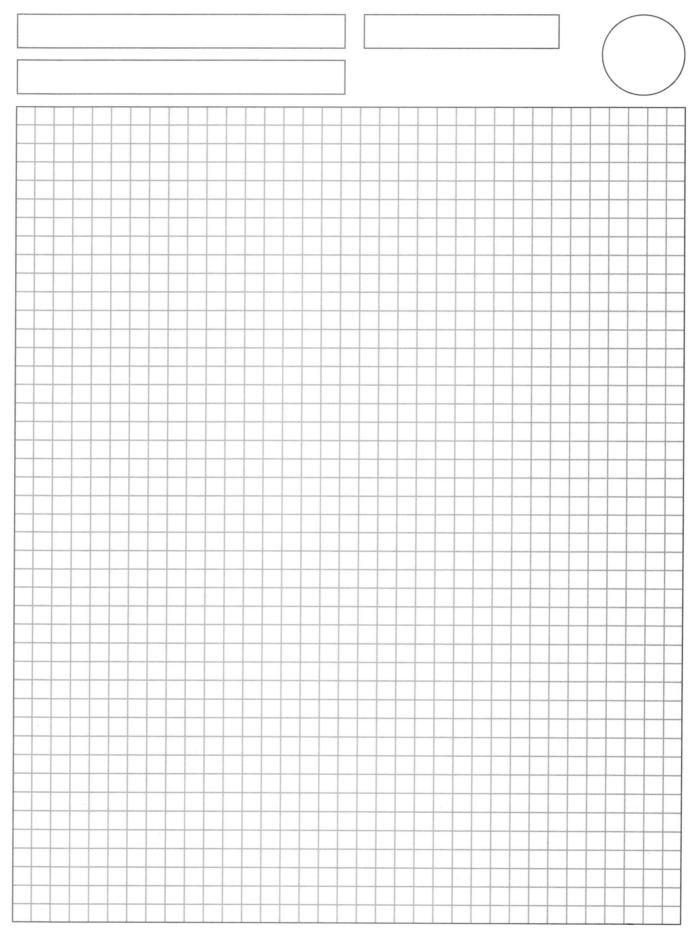

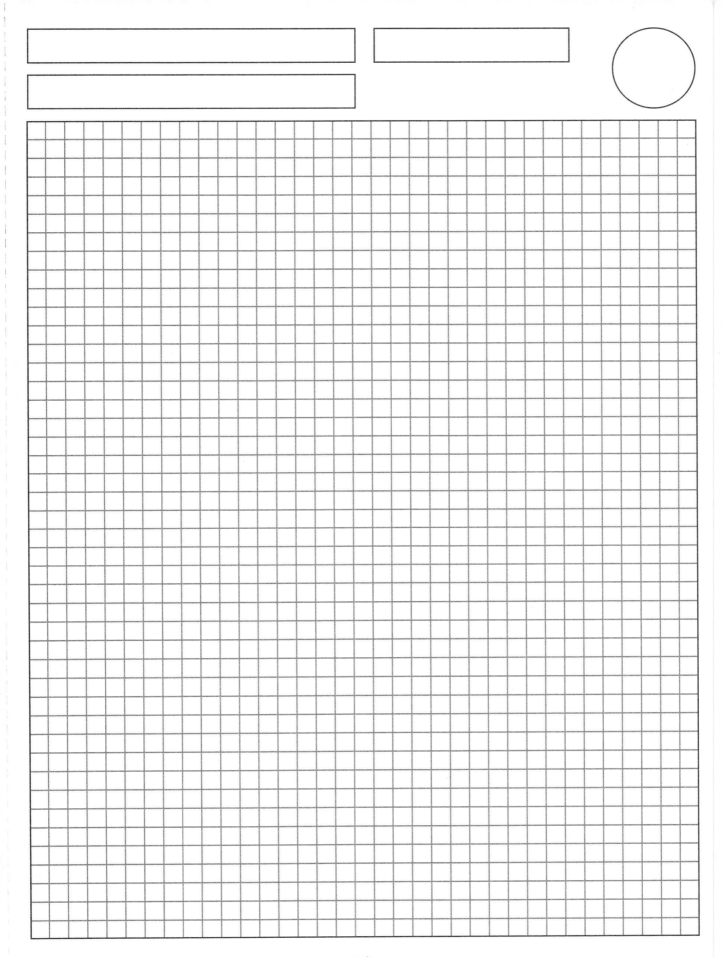

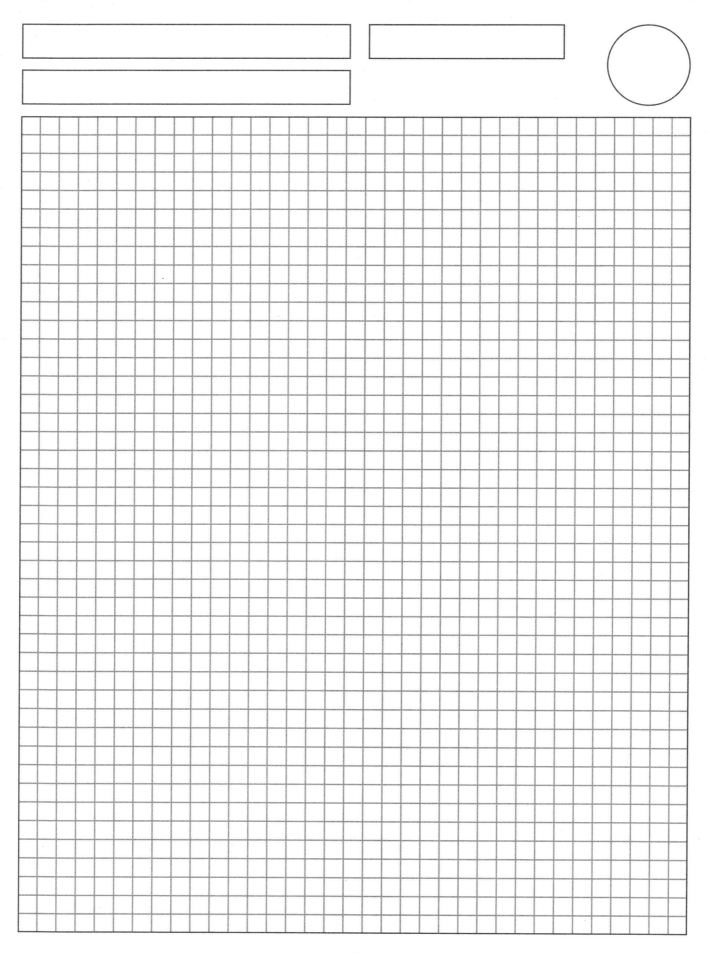